Sable
&
Rosenfeld

the Sable & Rosenfeld Cookbook

Myra Sable and Colleen Mathieu

FIREFLY BOOKS

A FIREFLY BOOK

Published by

Firefly Books (U.S.) Inc.
P.O. Box 1325
Ellicott Stn.,
Buffalo, NY 14205

CATALOGUING IN PUBLICATION DATA

Sable, Myra
Sable and Rosenfeld Cookbook

Includes Index.
ISBN 0-895565-73-1

1. Cookery.   1. Mathieu, Colleen, 1942-   11. Title.

TX714.53 1995   641.5   C95-931074-6

 PRINTED IN CANADA

Table of Contents

Introduction

I had no intention of writing a cookbook—ever. Yet here I am publishing cookbook No. 2, and for much the same reasons I got roped into writing my first, *Elegant Entertaining Cookbook*, in 1986. Demand, demand, and more blessed demand.

It all started in 1971 when my friend and former partner, Carol Rosenfeld, and I opened a specialty food boutique in Toronto. We sold our own special sauces, condiments and preserves, from Carol's Sweet Russian Mustard, handed down to her from her grandmother, to my crunchy antipasto, which I use for everything from a taco dip to pasta sauce to a tangy soup base.

Our customers always had questions or comments, and it was fun to discuss menus, serving tips and recipes with them. Pretty soon, I was constructing an entire dinner menu for someone who had bought Poached Pears in Cointreau and needed an appetizer, main course, and vegetable to serve around it.

Out of all those conversations and customer requests was born that first cookbook. It was a fabulous experience—rewarding, exhilarating, wildly successful—and one I swore I'd never repeat.

As time went on, however, and the *Elegant Entertaining Cookbook* became harder and harder for people to find, I found myself in the pleasant position of being very much in demand the world over. At food shows in New York and California, people from Singapore to Australia were asking me how they could get copies of *Elegant Entertaining*. In Houston, on a food tour, a customer called out from the back of a bus, "Myra! When are you going to do another cookbook?" A few ardent fans have even accused me of being some kind of cult figure, with a cookbook that everybody wants but which nobody can actually find. Year-round, I receive at least three phone calls a week asking for a Sable & Rosenfeld cookbook.

A second reason to publish another cookbook was the change taking place within my company, Sable & Rosenfeld. Over the last year, I've gone through every one of my 50 plus products and updated them. At the end of this century and beginning of the next, people (including me) want clean, pure, direct products and communication. In response to customers' interest, and requests, and with a little experimentation, I've found that some changes have improved my products—Cranberries in Chambord, for example, is just as delicious without the liquor. The direction of my company made it appropriate to publish another cookbook, one more in tune with the '90s.

With all these considerations in mind, I didn't want to simply reissue *Elegant Entertaining*. Nor did I want to tackle another book all on my own. In a fit of sanity, my partner Carol had retired from the food business, so I had to talk a dear friend, Colleen Mathieu, into doing it with me. And this is the part where I have to say I couldn't have done this book without her. We've been friends for 30 years (we met when we both had small children and felt we were the only two feminists in Toronto). I don't know *anybody* who documents recipes the way Colleen does—she has an index card for every recipe she's ever tried, noting the changes she's made, and what variations have worked or not. My grown children still talk about Colleen's customized birthday cakes with a shiny penny in every slice, her homebaked cookies for special occasions and her Christmas tree-decorating parties open to every child she could round up.

I wanted a perfect cookbook and I knew Colleen would feel the same commitment. She has a natural finesse that comes out in everything she does, and there's nothing she wouldn't do to make a recipe perfect. At two in the morning, she's still ready for an enthusiastic discussion on the size of nuts as a garnish in a mushroom soup recipe. Should they be coarsely chopped instead of thinly sliced? Or crushed?

Together we looked at every single recipe in *Elegant Entertaining*. It was agonizing, but somehow we managed to discard about half the recipes in the old book, and then sift through oodles of our own new discoveries and decide on over 150 new recipes to put in.

We also went over the old favorites and took out a lot of the cognac and brandy, substituting a lot of sautéed pears and apples. But I have to admit that I've never sacrificed taste in either my products or my cookbook. If fats are required to make a recipe work, I call for oil or sweet butter with no apologies. On the other hand, where heavy cream is called for but truly won't be missed, we've substituted milk or even yogurt. And with something like Mushrooms Caps Stuffed with Pecans, we discovered they taste just as splendid with only half the cream.

A few of the recipes have remained untouched; Cabbage Rolls, Sesame Baked Chicken and Filet of Sole East Indian, for example, are excellent old recipes that needed no improving.

About the only thing Colleen and I did disagree on was the length of each recipe. Colleen loves to lose herself in three pages of ingredients and preparations.

I tend to flip past long recipes and go for the short and simple. But we both adore entertaining, and our biggest strength is organization—without sacrificing taste and presentation. Let me put it this way: I set out hors d'oeuvres, but I refuse to pass them around in case it interrupts conversation. And I refuse to hustle my guests to the table when they're just starting to unwind in case the roast burns. With one or two fun exceptions, such as a Chinese wok dinner when guests are invited into the kitchen, everything in this book can be prepared ahead and served at room temperature if desired.

I am also indebted to Sable & Rosenfeld's Export Marketing Director and resident wine expert for his valuable advice and thoughtful recommendation for the best pairings of wine and food in this cookbook. Thanks should also go to Liam McKenna, a brewmaster and consultant to the microbrewing industry, for his recommendations on beer.

None of the recipes in this book depends on Sable & Rosenfeld products, but my love of condiments is definitely reflected in my approach to food. Relishes, chutneys, mustards and other accompaniments can dress up an otherwise ordinary meal. Plain roast chicken is suddenly festive when you serve it with sweet plum chutney, hot curried fruits, gingered pears, and a Dijon mustard—especially if all is arranged in sparkling silver jam pots adorned with a sprig of spring lilac or pine cones and winter berries. A simple rare roast beef sandwich becomes elegant when the beef is topped with chili sauce and garnished with crunchy mustard beans. And for the diet conscious, condiments and accompaniments deliver diversity and taste without extra calories.

Our goal was to present a wide variety of dishes that are easy to prepare, simple to serve, in tune with current trends and—most important of all—absolutely, uncompromisingly delicious. One thing's for sure, I know we'll hear about it from all our friends and customers as to whether we've succeeded or not!

We hope you enjoy whipping up these old favorites and exploring the new dishes as much as we did.

Myra Sable

Hors d'oeuvres & Starters

Hors D'oeuvres and Starters

Whatever kind of entertainment you want to create—small and intimate like a little revue, a formal sitdown meal with several courses and a caterer, a picnic, a wedding, a themed evening to celebrate an event, or a holiday party with all the traditional trappings—the most important part is the preproduction. Survey your resources and see what will work best in your urban apartment or suburban villa. Is your freezer full of ready-to-heat-and-serve goodies or will you start from scratch? What's plentiful in the supermarket and how much time can you devote to getting it ready? Plan, plan, plan! Make notes and consult them and adjust them as you go along. Write them down or hold them in your head if you can.

Cheese

Lemon Pepper Boursin Pâté
Cheddar Crisps
Liptauer Cheese
Pesto Cheese with Sundried Tomatoes
Marinated Chêvre with Roasted Garlic
Mozzarella in Carrozza
Smoked Salmon Cheesecake

Oriental

California Rolls
Sashimi
Vegetable Thai Bundles
Shrimp Toasts
Imperial Rolls with Hot Chinese Mustard
Deep Fried Wontons with Sweet and Tangy Dipping Sauce
Pungent Peking Chicken Bites
Chun King Chinese Pork Slices
Roast Duck with Hoisin Sauce in Chinese Pancakes
Rainbow Chopped in Crystal Fold

Dips and Crocks

Beet Dip
Brandade de Morue
Tapenade d'Antibes
Tapenade de Marsailles
Hot Crabmeat Dip
Dipsidoodle Crab Dip
Baba Ganouj with Cayenne Pita Toasts
Tzatziki
Indian Dip with Crisp Curried Crackers
Quick Pâté
Peppercorn Pâté with Madeira
Diet Chopped Liver

Other

Artichoke Bottoms with Parmesan Cheese
Swedish Meatballs
Scampi Allegro (Garlic Shrimp)
Beef Empanadas
Tuna Empanada Squares
Mushroom Caps Stuffed with Pecans

Lemon Pepper "Boursin" Pâté

Creamy, peppery spread. Serve on warm crackers or place it on a big lettuce leaf surrounded by homemade melba toast. Or dot each individual serving with a small square of smoked salmon.

1	pkg (8 oz/250 g) cream cheese	1
1	clove garlic, minced	1
1 tsp	chopped fresh chives	5 ml
1 tsp	chopped fresh basil	5 ml
1 tsp	caraway seed	5 ml
1 tsp	dill weed	5 ml
	lemon pepper	

1. In a small bowl, beat cheese. Add garlic, chives, basil, caraway seed and dill. Stir well to blend.
2. Spoon into a small dish or crock. Cover and chill. Serve with crackers or toast.

Makes 1 cup (250 ml).

At cocktail parties, smaller flower arrangements are lost in the crowd. Go for large-scale impact on a hall table or dining room sideboard.

Cheddar Crisps

Thin, crispy, nippy cheese bites that are great for a nibble or to serve with an asparagus salad for a first course.

2 cups	sharp Cheddar cheese, grated	500 ml
¼ cup	soft sweet butter	50 ml
½ cup	all-purpose flour	125 ml
1½ tsp	Worcestershire sauce	7 ml
1 tsp	salt	5 ml
¼ tsp	cayenne pepper	1 ml

1. In a bowl, combine cheese and butter; blend well. Stir in flour, Worcestershire sauce, salt and cayenne pepper.
2. Shape into a long roll, 1-inch (2.5-cm) round. Chill well for at least 3 hours, until firm.
3. Preheat oven to 450°F (230°C).
4. Cut roll into thin slices and arrange on ungreased baking sheets.
5. Bake for 5 minutes, until lightly browned.

Makes 4 dozen wafers.

The Champagne Waltz — With champagne I can never imagine doing any dance except a waltz, but there are lots of other things to do with it and all as easy as one-two-slide, one-two-slide. I like to make my own version of Kir. That is lacing the bubbly with a teaspoon or two of exotic eau de vie or liqueurs. Try Framboise (raspberry), Mirabelle (small yellow plums), Poire William (pear liqueur). The eaux de vie were invented by a convent of quiet little French nuns, but they pack a punch that would rock a pontiff. Be careful! Just enough to make guests wonder what kind of champagne you've discovered.

Liptauer Cheese

A delicious classic Austrian spread with plenty of taste to carry your guests away on wings of praise. Use on sandwiches in place of butter or mayonnaise.

1	pkg (8 oz/250 g) cream cheese	1
1 cup	salted butter	250 ml
1 tbsp	chopped onions	15 ml
1 tbsp	drained capers	15 ml
1	can (1.75 oz/50g) anchovy fillets, drained and chopped	1
1 tsp	white pepper	5 ml
1 tsp	prepared mustard	5 ml
1 tsp	caraway seed	5 ml
	pumpernickel bread	

1. In a blender or food processor, combine cream cheese and butter. Process 1 to 2 minutes, until smooth. Add onions, capers and anchovies; process 10 seconds.
2. Transfer to a small bowl. Stir in white pepper, mustard and caraway seed.
3. Press into a crock, cover, and store in refrigerator until serving time.
4. Serve with pumpernickel bread.

Makes 16 to 20 appetizer servings.

Hint: *Never scrape burnt toast with a knife. Simply rub two pieces together and the burnt bits will hardly be noticeable.*

Pesto Cheese with Sundried Tomatoes

The great colors in this cheese spread set the stage for a successful party. Light cream cheese works perfectly well if you're trying to cut calories.

8 oz	cream cheese	250 g
4 oz	goat cheese	125 g
4 oz	soft sweet butter	125 g
1 cup	pesto	250 ml
¾ cup	sundried tomatoes, rehydrated and chopped	375 ml
½ cup	pine nuts, toasted	125 ml

1. In a blender or food processor, combine cream cheese, goat cheese, butter, pesto and sundried tomatoes until smooth.
2. Pack into a crock and chill for at least 2 hours. Garnish with pine nuts and serve with toast.

Makes 8 to 10 servings.

Purposeful Leftovers – Transform dips into sandwich spreads by adding herbs, hot sauce or pepper.

Marinated Chêvre with Roasted Garlic

The first time I tasted marinated chêvré was at a tiny bistro in Paris when I used to import incredible food products from Fauchon. Last year, in the Napa Valley, I tried this combination and thought I'd gone to heaven. As an hors d'oeuvre, it looks delectable in leaves of radicchio on a large glass platter strewn with purple cosmos. As a starter to an important dinner, heat the chêvre and garnish it with red and yellow tomatoes on individual plates. Make sure to use large heads of garlic so that you can halve them horizontally.

½ lb	goat cheese, cylinder shaped	250 g
½ cup	olive oil	125 ml
1 tsp	dried parsley	5 ml
1 tsp	dried thyme	5 ml
1 tsp	savory	5 ml
1 tsp	dried oregano	5 ml
2	large heads of garlic, halved horizontally	2
2 tsp	rosemary	10 ml
2 tsp	savory	10 ml
1	head radicchio	1

1. Cut goat cheese into four rounds and place in a shallow dish. Sprinkle with parsley, thyme, savory, oregano and ¼ cup (50 ml) of the olive oil. Refrigerate 3 hours or overnight.

2. Preheat oven to 400°F (200°C).

3. Brush cut side of garlic with olive oil. Place garlic in baking dish, cut side up, lightly cover with foil and bake 30 minutes until golden and soft to the touch.

4. Cool 5 minutes, then marinate with ¼ cup (50 ml) of the remaining olive oil, rosemary and savory.

5. Remove cheese from marinade and reserve oil.

6. Place one slice of cheese on a radicchio leaf and garnish with garlic half; drizzle with reserved herbed oil. Repeat for each serving.

Makes 4 servings.

Mozzarella in Carrozza

It is thanks to the Bar Italia restaurant in Toronto that I discovered this scrumptious Southern Italian dish. It's the comfort food equivalent of English bangers and mash or American grilled cheese and ham—but much better tasting. It's also easy to prepare ahead and not as fiddly as it sounds. The original recipe calls for deep-frying but you can make it just as crispy, melted and delicious through baking. I serve this with glazed onions and a green salad when friends drop over for a movie night.

⅓ cup	soft sweet butter	75 ml
2	anchovy fillets, finely chopped	2
1 tsp	lemon juice	5 ml
⅛ tsp	freshly ground black pepper	.5 ml
1	loaf round crusty Italian bread (10-inch/25-cm)	1
4	slices Provolone cheese	4
4	slices Bel Paese or Fontina cheese	4
4	slices Mozzarella cheese	
	freshly ground black pepper	
2 tbsp	melted butter	25 ml

Egg Wash

2	eggs, beaten	2
2 tbsp	milk	25 ml

1. In a small bowl, combine butter, anchovies, lemon juice and pepper until well mixed. Roll into a log 3½x1-inch (9x2.5-cm). Wrap in wax paper and refrigerate until firm, about 30 minutes.
2. Preheat oven to 400°F (200°C).
3. Cut butter mixture into eight slices and set aside.
4. Trim crusts from top and sides of bread and cut into four wedges.
5. Cut each wedge in half horizontally without cutting through the back.

6. Open up bread wedge and scoop out bread on bottom half leaving a ½-inch (1-cm) rim all the way around (making a hollow for the butter).
7. Place one slice anchovy butter in hollow, one slice Provolone, one slice Bel Paese, one slice Mozzarella, black pepper and another slice anchovy butter.
8. Close the bread to form a sandwich, flatten with your hand and secure with a toothpick.
9. Brush tops with melted butter. Brush egg wash over entire surface of sandwich.
10. Repeat with remaining three wedges of bread.
11. Place sandwiches on ungreased cookie sheet. Bake 15 to 20 minutes, or until golden.

Makes 4 large servings or 8 appetizers.

Hint – when using a caterer, never surrender your individuality. State clearly what you want, otherwise what you will end up with is a smoothly running, fashionable party that is the caterer's statement and not your own. For cocktail parties, be specific and hold yourself to the times given, 6 to 8 p.m. or 7 to 9 p.m. Encourage people to be on time, as it is unfair for the kitchen to have to come up with 10 rounds of hors d'oeuvres for late arrivals when they were only scheduled to produce them for 2 hours. Although most caterers always bring extra, don't strain them by deciding to invite the neighbors at the last minute.

Smoked Salmon Cheesecake

My youngest daughter Kelly requests this for her birthday supper every year. I serve it in individual ramekins turned out on a bed of watercress. Her favorite dish of rare fillet roast and pommes frites is next, followed by fudge brownies smothered in mocha buttercream frosting.

14 oz	cream cheese, softened	425 g
2	eggs	2
3 tbsp	heavy whipping cream	50 ml
2 tbsp	Parmesan cheese, freshly grated	25 ml
¼ cup	Gruyere cheese, grated	50 ml
¼ tsp	salt	1 ml
¼ tsp	freshly ground black pepper	1 ml
2 tbsp	sweet butter	25 ml
1	leek, white only, chopped	1
¼ lb	smoked salmon, sliced	250 g
¼ lb	smoked salmon, cut in 1½-inch (3.5-cm) strips	250 g

1. Preheat oven to 300°F (150°C).
2. Generously butter four 3-inch (8-cm) ramekins.*
3. In a food processor, beat together the cream cheese, eggs, cream, Parmesan, Gruyere, salt and pepper until smooth.
4. Pour enough of the cheese mixture into the ramekins to cover the bottom. Spread on leeks, pour on a layer of cheese mixture, followed with a layer of sliced smoked salmon and finishing with a layer of cheese mixture to make five layers.
6. Place the ramekins in a baking pan and add water to the pan until it comes halfway up the sides of the ramekins. Bake 40 minutes until tester comes out clean. Turn off the oven and let sit for another 40 minutes. Let the ramekins sit for an additional 30 minutes out of the oven before unmolding.
7. Cover the cheesecakes with the remaining smoked salmon. Serve with pumpernickel toast.

Makes 4 servings.

* Can be made in a 13x4-inch (32x10-cm) loaf pan.

California Rolls

I always use short-grained Japanese rice in this recipe, partly because it's a good excuse to visit the oriental markets. Don't be intimidated by the length of the recipe—I promise it takes only moments to prepare, especially if you prepare the rice the night before you assemble the sushi. Once you see how easy it is, you'll want to make these tasty rolls often. Experiment with substitutions: raw tuna, shrimp, julienned carrots, slivered green onions—use your imagination. If you're lucky enough to have any rolls left over, just wrap them up for a delicious treat the next day. The sushi rice is also a great side dish to BBQ ribs.

Sushi Rice

1½ cups	short-grained white rice	375 ml
1¾ cups	cold water	425 ml
¼ cup	rice wine vinegar	50 ml
2 tbsp	sugar	25 ml
1½ tsp	salt	7 ml
1 tbsp	mirin or dry sherry	15 ml
2 tsp	wasabi powder	10 ml
1 tbsp	water	15 ml
1	medium avocado, cut into ½-inch (1-cm) slices	1
4	whole sheets nori (toasted seaweed)	4
6 oz	cooked crabmeat	175 g
¼	cucumber, cut into ¼-inch (.5 cm) julienne strips	¼
	soy sauce and wasabi for dipping	

1. Rinse the rice. In a saucepan with a tight-fitting lid, add the rice and cold water. Let stand for 15 minutes. Bring the water and rice to a boil, cover and reduce the heat and cook about 10 minutes until the water is absorbed.
2. Reduce heat to low, and simmer another 5 minutes. Remove from heat and let the rice stand, covered, for 5 minutes. Transfer the rice to a large platter.

Mix together the vinegar, sugar, salt and mirin, and pour over rice while mixing with a fork. Cool to room temperature.

3. In a small bowl, combine wasabi powder and water.

4. Lay one sheet of seaweed on work surface and, with dampened hands, spread 1 cup (250 ml) of rice over the seaweed, leaving a 1-inch (2.5-cm) strip along the top.

5. Using ¼ of the wasabi mixture, paint a stripe on the rice, 1-inch (2.5-cm) above the bottom edge. Arrange ¼ of the crab over the stripe. Arrange ¼ of the avocado slices next to the crab and then ¼ of the cucumber next to the avocado.

6. Beginning at bottom edge, carefully roll the seaweed and its contents jelly-roll style. Moisten the top free seaweed edge to seal.

7. Continue in same manner for the remaining three sheets.

8. Using a sharp knife, slice into 1-inch (2.5-cm) pieces.

9. Serve with soy sauce and wasabi for dipping.

Makes 32 pieces.

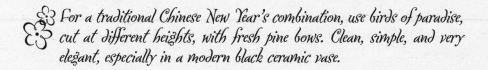

For a traditional Chinese New Year's combination, use birds of paradise, cut at different heights, with fresh pine bows. Clean, simple, and very elegant, especially in a modern black ceramic vase.

Sashimi

Always use fresh ocean fish for your sashimi, tuna being my first choice. Serve with grated radish and carrots and an extra dab of wasabi, for those who like it hot.

1 lb	fresh tuna	500 g
1 cup	grated raw carrot	250 ml
1 cup	grated giant white radish	250 ml
1 tbsp	wasabi	15 ml
2 tsp	water	10 ml
½ cup	Japanese soy sauce	125 ml

1. Partially freeze tuna to make it easier to slice. With a sharp knife, slice tuna into very thin slices. Cover and refrigerate.
2. Divide carrot and radish evenly and arrange on four chilled salad plates. Lay slices of tuna on top.
3. In a small dish, mix wasabi and water to make a paste and spoon a dollop onto each plate.
4. Pour soy sauce into four bowls. Serve beside salad plates for dipping tuna.

Makes 4 servings.

Hint – Other fish such as sea bass, striped bass, or red snapper may be used.

Vegetable Thai Bundles

Crunchy peanuts within the bundles and spicy peanut dipping sauce make this the fastest-disappearing snack I've ever served. Put out little plates so everyone can slather on the delicious sauce with abandon.

Dipping Sauce

½ cup	smooth peanut butter	125 ml
¼ cup	lime juice	50 ml
¼ cup	fish sauce or soy sauce	50 ml
5	cloves garlic, finely chopped	5
2 tbsp	sugar	25 ml
1 tbsp	grated fresh ginger	15 ml
1 tsp	finely chopped lemon grass	5 ml
½ tsp	chili paste	2 ml
½ tsp	grated lime zest	2 ml

Bundles

¾ lb	shrimp, cooked and chopped	375 g
½ cup	bean sprouts, chopped	125 ml
½ cup	grated carrot	125 ml
½ cup	diced jicama	125 ml
3	green onions, chopped	3
¼ cup	chopped, unsalted, roasted peanuts	50 ml
¼ cup	chopped fresh mint	50 ml
3 tbsp	chopped fresh cilantro	45 ml
1 tbsp	chopped fresh basil	15 ml
20	6-inch (15-cm) round sheets rice paper	20

1. In a food processor, measure the peanut butter, lime juice, fish sauce, garlic, sugar, ginger, lemon grass, chili paste and lime zest. Process until smooth. Spoon mixture into a bowl. Set aside.

2. In a bowl combine shrimp, bean sprouts, carrot, jicama, green onion, peanuts, mint, cilantro, basil and 3 tbsp of the Dipping Sauce. Toss gently to coat well. Set filling aside.

3. Fill a large pan with hot water. Cover rice paper sheets with a damp tea towel. Line a baking sheet with waxed paper.

4. Using one rice paper sheet at a time, dip into the hot water for 10 seconds, until pliable. Place on a dry tea towel. Fold bottom third of rice paper up.

5. Place 1½ tbsp of the filling in the center of the folded part of the rice paper sheet. Shape the filling into a 2½-inch cylinder. Fold the sides of the rice paper sheet over the filling.

6. Working from the bottom, roll the rice paper sheet tightly around the filling, making a spring roll shape. Use a little water to seal the seams. Place bundle seam side down on baking sheet .

7. Repeat with the remaining rice paper and filling.

8. To serve, mound bundles on a platter with Dipping Sauce in a bowl.

Makes 20 servings.

Shrimp Toasts

These are perfect finger food. I started making them for friends and soon I had to keep the recipe handy as people continually fell in love with them. It is now one of my most treasured recipes. They can be prepared in advance and popped into the cooking oil right from the freezer.

1 lb	shrimp, shelled and deveined	500 g
4	water chestnuts, finely chopped	4
1	green onion, finely chopped	1
1 tbsp	fresh ginger root, finely chopped	15 ml
1 tsp	sesame oil	5 ml
1 tsp	sake or dry sherry	5 ml
1 tsp	salt	5 ml
1	egg white, beaten until foamy	1
1 tbsp	cornstarch	15 ml
¼ cup	cold water	50 ml
12	slices sandwich bread, crusts trimmed	12
	vegetable oil for frying	

1. In a food processor or blender, combine shrimp, water chestnuts, green onion, ginger and sesame oil. Add sake or sherry and salt. Process with four to five on/off motions until finely chopped. Add egg white and blend.
2. Dissolve cornstarch in water and blend into shrimp mixture
3. Spread shrimp mixture on bread slices. Cut each slice of bread into four triangles.
4. Freeze or refrigerate until just before serving.
5. In a deep fryer or deep skillet, heat oil to 375°F (190°C). Slip bread triangles into oil shrimp side down. Cook 1 to 2 minutes and turn. Cook 1 minute more, until bread is golden.
6. Remove from oil, drain on paper towel.
   Serve immediately.

Makes 48 squares.

Imperial Rolls with Hot Chinese Mustard

Don't hesitate to try these. Wrappers are available at Chinese food stores.

¾ lb	ground pork shoulder	375 g
¼ cup	chopped dried mushrooms	50 ml
¼ cup	arrowroot noodles,	50 ml
	cut in 2-inch (5-cm) pieces	
2 tbsp	lukewarm water	25 ml
3	shredded small carrots	2
2 cups	shredded cabbage	500 ml
1	medium onion, finely chopped	1
1	clove garlic, finely chopped	1
1	egg, slightly beaten	1
1 tbsp	soy sauce	15 ml
½ tsp	ground ginger	2 ml
25	frozen spring roll wrappers	25
	(10 inches/25 cm diameter)	
	vegetable oil to deep-fry	

1. In a skillet, cook ground pork, stirring, until browned.
2. In a small bowl, soak mushrooms in hot water to cover for 10 minutes; drain.
3. In a separate bowl, soak noodles in lukewarm water about 10 minutes until liquid is absorbed.
4. In a large bowl, combine mushrooms, noodles, carrots, cabbage, onion, garlic, pork, egg, soy sauce and ginger. Mix well.
5. Place 2 tbsp (25 ml) of mixture on each wrapper. Fold in sides and roll up.
6. Deep-fry at 375°F (190°C) for 3 minutes; remove and place on paper towel. Deep-fry a second time about 4 minutes, until outside is golden brown. Drain on paper towel.
Serve hot.

Makes 25 rolls.

Hot Chinese Mustard

½ cup	dry mustard	125 ml
¼ cup	rice vinegar	50 ml
¼ cup	water	50 ml
pinch	salt	pinch
pinch	granulated sugar	pinch

1. In a small saucepan, combine mustard, vinegar, water, salt and sugar. Bring to a boil and reduce heat. Simmer, stirring, about 2 minutes, until thickened.
2. Pour into a container. Cover and store in refrigerator. Keeps for up to 2 months.

Makes 1 cup (250 ml).

Have fun making Chinese appetizers. They can be as colorful and varied as characters in a Chinese opera.

Deep-Fried Wontons with Sweet and Tangy Dipping Sauce

Wontons are perfect finger food and are ideal to serve with cocktails. Put out a few bowls of Chinese mustard and your own plum sauce and you'll make your guests very happy. When you shop for Chinese ingredients, ask for the thin wonton wrappers.

1 tsp	cornstarch	5 ml
1 tsp	sake or dry sherry	5 ml
½ lb	ground pork	250 g
½ lb	raw shrimp, shelled, deveined and coarsely chopped	250 g
1 tbsp	vegetable oil	15 ml
2	large dried Chinese mushrooms, finely chopped	2
4	green onions, finely chopped	4
¼ cup	water chestnuts or bamboo shoots, finely chopped	50 ml
¼ cup	rich chicken stock	50 ml
1 tsp	salt	5 ml
½ tsp	granulated sugar	2 ml
¼ tsp	grated fresh ginger root	1 ml
24	wonton wrappers	24
	peanut oil for frying	

1. In a medium bowl, combine cornstarch and sake; mix well. Add pork and shrimp. Stir well to coat.
2. In a large skillet, heat oil. Add shrimp and pork mixture, stir-fry about 5 minutes, or until pork is no longer pink. Cool mixture.
3. Soak mushrooms in cold water to cover for 3 minutes; drain. Stir into pork mixture. Add onion, water chestnuts, stock, salt, sugar and ginger root; mix well.

4. Place a spoonful of shrimp filling on each wonton wrapper. Moisten wrapper edges with water. Fold in triangle around filling. Bring two corners of folded edge together and pinch.
5. Heat peanut oil in wok or deep skillet to 375°F (190°C). Deep-fry wontons a few at a time for 1 to 2 minutes until very pale golden. Drain on paper towel. Cool.
6. Fry second time to deep gold. Drain on paper towel.

Makes 24 wontons.

Sweet and Tangy Dipping Sauce

1 cup	orange juice, freshly squeezed	250 ml
½ cup	brown sugar	125 ml
⅓ cup	cider vinegar	75 ml
¼ cup	ketchup	50 ml
2 tbsp	light soy sauce	25 ml
2 tbsp	cornstarch	25 ml
1 tbsp	tomato paste	15 ml
2 tsp	Worcestershire sauce	10 ml
¼ tsp	hot pepper sauce	1 ml

1. In a saucepan, combine orange juice, brown sugar, vinegar, ketchup, soy sauce, cornstarch, tomato paste, Worcestershire sauce and hot pepper sauce; mix well.
2. Bring to a boil; stir constantly about 3 minutes until thick and clear.
3. Cool and serve.

Makes 2 cups (500 ml).

Pungent Peking Chicken Bites
with Dipping Sauce

These delightful morsels travel well, and I often take a jar of the Dipping Sauce and a plastic bag full of "bites" to my cottage. They reheat beautifully.

2 lb	chicken breasts, skinless, boneless	1 kg
2	eggs, beaten	2
½ cup	all-purpose flour	125 ml
¼ cup	beer or water	50 ml
1 tsp	salt	5 ml
	vegetable oil for deep-frying	

1. Cut chicken breasts into 1-inch (2.5-cm) cubes.
2. In a small bowl, combine eggs, flour, beer or water and salt; blend well.
3. In a deep skillet or deep-fryer, heat oil to 375°F (190°C). Dip chicken in batter and slip into hot oil. Deep-fry, turning once, about 5 to 6 minutes until coating is golden brown.
4. Drain on paper towel and keep warm. Serve with Dipping Sauce.

Hint – Anything today can be rented, but try and use some of your own things to give a more homey, natural look. Use your own glassware and fine crystal for small parties, but for larger ones the risk of breakage and the time involved in washing up make it too complicated.

Dipping Sauce

1	can (14 oz/398 ml) pineapple, unsweetened, crushed	1
1	clove garlic, finely chopped	1
½ cup	brown sugar, lightly packed	125 ml
¼ cup	vinegar	50 ml
3 tbsp	cornstarch	45 ml
1½ tbsp	soy sauce	20 ml
½ tsp	grated fresh ginger root	2 ml

1. In a saucepan, combine pineapple, garlic, sugar, vinegar, cornstarch, soy sauce and ginger; mix well.
2. Cook, stirring, about 10 minutes until sauce thickens. Serve warm or cold.

Makes 6 to 8 servings.

Chun King Chinese Pork Slices

You can also use this as a divine luncheon dish to serve with Chinese asparagus salad. Make it ahead of time so you can slice it and serve it cold with hot sweet Russian or Chinese mustard.

¼ cup	red currant jelly or jam	50 ml
¼ cup	sherry	50 ml
2 tbsp	soy sauce	25 ml
1	clove garlic, finely chopped	1
1 tsp	five-spice powder	5 ml
2	pork tenderloins (1 lb/500 g each)	2

1. In a large bowl, combine jelly or jam, sherry, soy sauce, garlic and five-spice powder.
2. Add tenderloins, turning to coat.
3. Cover and marinate in refrigerator overnight, turning once or twice.
4. Preheat oven to 325°F (160°C).
5. Remove meat from marinade and place in a shallow casserole. Brush with marinade.
6. Cover and bake, basting frequently, for 1 to 1¼ hours, until meat is tender and no longer pink. Uncover during last 30 minutes.

Makes 4 to 6 servings.

 For a casual summer buffet, fill a large glass water pitcher with as many cosmos as you can fit in it. Let the cosmos fall and bend as they will over the lip of the base. Remember to fill the vase completely so the water line can't be seen. This magnifies the stems and makes the arrangement clean and complete.

Roast Duck with Hoisin Sauce in Chinese Pancakes

You no longer need dine in Chinese restaurants to have Golden Peking Duck. The little pancakes are like pita bread. Stuffed with the sliced duck and its wonderful sauces, they make a munchie to drool over. Try them and see.

1	duck (4 to 5 lb/2 to 3 kg)	1
	juice of ½ lemon	
½ tsp	ground ginger	2 ml
½ tsp	white pepper	2 ml
¼ tsp	cinnamon	1 ml
¼ tsp	nutmeg	1 ml
¼ tsp	salt	1 ml
pinch	ground cloves	pinch
½ cup	hoisin sauce	125 ml
2 tbsp	light soy sauce	25 ml
1 cup	shredded green onion	250 ml

1. Preheat oven to 425°F (220°C).
2. Clean duck and remove excess fat; discard neck and giblets. Pierce skin well.
3. Squeeze lemon juice inside cavity and over skin of duck.
4. Combine ginger, pepper, cinnamon, nutmeg, salt and cloves. Sprinkle half of seasoning mixture inside duck and the remainder on the skin.
5. Place duck breast side up on a roasting rack in a shallow roasting pan and sear in oven for 30 minutes.
6. Reduce temperature to 350°F (180°C). Pierce skin again and roast for 50 to 60 minutes, or until juices run clear when duck is pierced. During last 30 minutes, baste duck with a combination of 1 tbsp (15 ml) hoisin sauce and the soy sauce.
7. Let duck rest 15 minutes. Cut into very thin slices.
   To serve, place some of remaining hoisin sauce, shredded green onion, and duck inside a Chinese Pancake and roll up.

Makes 16 servings.

Chinese Pancakes

2 cups	all-purpose flour	500 ml
¾ cup	boiling water	175 ml
2 tsp	sesame oil	10 ml

1. Place flour in a large bowl. Pour boiling water over flour and stir with a wooden spoon until it clumps together.

2. Knead on a floured work surface until dough is soft and smooth, about 5 minutes. Form dough into ball, cover with an inverted bowl, and let stand for 30 to 60 minutes.

3. With your hands, roll dough into a cylinder, then cut it into 16 equal pieces. Again, using the lightly floured work surface, flatten ball of dough with a rolling pin into 3-inch (7.5-cm) rounds.

4. Brush half the rounds with sesame oil, making sure to coat the edges. Place unbrushed rounds on oiled ones and use rolling pin to flatten them into eight thin pancakes, about 8 inches (20 cm) in diameter.

5. Heat a heavy, ungreased, small skillet. Cook pancakes, one at a time, over medium heat 1 to 2 minutes until small bubbles appear on surface. Turn and cook on other side until a few golden spots appear.

6. Remove from skillet and gently pull apart into two pancakes. Pile pancakes on a place and cover with plastic wrap so they won't dry out.

7. To reheat, wrap in foil, and heat in a 350°F (190°C) for 10 minutes. Or steam, unwrapped in steamer for 5 minutes. Or place in microwave covered with plastic wrap or waxed paper at medium for 3 to 4 minutes, or until warm.

Makes 16 pancakes.

Hint – Five-Spice Powder – This pungent Chinese blend is equal parts star anise, ginger, cinnamon, cloves and fennel seed. Use sparingly to add interest to roast meats and poultry, toasted nuts, salad dressing with sesame oil, gingerbread, apple sauce and spice cookies.

Rainbow Chopped in Crystal Fold

Doesn't that sound unbelievable? The crystal fold is a lettuce leaf, the rainbows are the chopped vegetables, but still it remains totally Land of Oz. When you serve these, make sure you put them on plates as they are inclined to drip!

4 cups	peanut oil	1 l
1 cup	rice vermicelli, broken	250 ml
½ lb	pork loin, finely chopped	250 g
2	pieces (2-inch/5-cm) Chinese sausage, finely chopped	2
3	green onions, finely chopped	3
1	medium carrot, finely chopped	1
1	stalk celery, finely chopped	1
2 tsp	oyster sauce	10 ml
1 tsp	soy sauce	5 ml
¼ tsp	salt	1 ml
½ tsp	cornstarch	2 ml
1 tbsp	cold water	15 ml
	lettuce leaves	

1. In a large skillet or wok, heat oil until very hot. Add vermicelli; cook about 3 seconds until it puffs up and floats on the surface. Remove and drain on paper towel.
2. Add pork to oil and cook for about 1 minute. With slotted spoon, remove the pork. Pour out oil, leaving just a coating on the bottom of the pan.
3. Add sausage, onions, carrot and celery. Stir in pork, oyster sauce, soy sauce and salt. Cook and stir for 2 to 3 minutes.
4. Dissolve cornstarch in cold water. Stir into hot mixture and cook for an additional 30 seconds, until thickened.
5. Spoon mixture onto lettuce leaves. Fold the leaves over and eat with fingers like a taco.

Makes 4 servings.

Beet Dip

When I first tasted this, I hesitated to ask for the recipe because I find cooking beets a nuisance. But when I heard that raw beets went straight into the food processor, I was all ears. The color is so beautiful it demands to be presented in a special way. I often serve it in small, hollowed-out eggplants (don't forget to cut a strip off the bottom of each so they lie flat on your serving platter). Or fill a radicchio leaf and surround it with exotic dipping vegetables, such as jicama, daikon and snow peas. If there's any left over, slather it on a rare roast beef sandwich.

1	green onion	1
¼ lb	beets, peeled and quartered	125 g
1	bunch watercress, washed, stems removed and chopped	1
6 oz	cream cheese	175 g
2 tsp	lemon juice	10 ml
1 tsp	prepared horseradish, drained	5 ml
½ tsp	dried dill	2 ml

1. In a food processor, process onion and beets until finely chopped. Add the watercress and process 5 seconds. Add the cream cheese, lemon juice, horseradish and dill and process until well blended.
2. Spoon into container and refrigerate until ready to use. Serve with raw vegetables.

Makes 1 cup (250 ml).

Brandade de Morue

My introduction to this dish came in Languedoc where my daughter was at chef's school. *Morue* means salt cod. The Provençal term *brandade*, meaning vigorously stirred, is now conveniently done by the food processor. And like many dishes from that region in France, it's loaded with healthy garlic. Startlingly white, it looks fabulous garnished with red peppers and served in a pretty crock.

1 lb	salt cod	500 g
½ cup	milk	125 ml
½	onion, thinly sliced	½
2	whole cloves	2
1	potato, boiled and peeled	1
1 cup	olive oil, heated	250 ml
¾ cup	heavy or whipping cream, heated	175 ml
2	cloves garlic, finely chopped	2
	white pepper to taste	

1. Place cod in a large glass or ceramic dish. Cover with water and soak at least 24 hours or up to 36 hours. Change the water three or four times. Drain cod.
2. In a large heavy saucepan, combine cod, milk, onion and cloves. Add water to cover the cod; bring to a boil. Remove the saucepan from the heat and let stand for 30 minutes. Drain, discarding the onion and cloves.
3. In a food processor, combine cod and potato. Process just to blend.
4. With machine running, add olive oil, then cream, in a steady stream. Add garlic and pepper and process just to blend.
5. Spoon into a bowl or crock. Serve lukewarm with toast points.

Makes 4 cups (1 l).

Tapenade D'Antibes

If you've been lucky enough to travel in Provence, you'll recognize this dark, lusty spread. As an olive lover, this traditional tapenade recipe is my favorite. It's also versatile: you can mix it with mayonnaise, drizzle it over a tomato and basil salad, add it to spice up vegetables in a pita pocket, or use it to fill tiny tomatoes or chilled baby potatoes.

2 cups	black olives, pitted	500 ml
1 cup	green olives, pitted	250 ml
½ cup	fresh basil leaves	125 ml
3	anchovy fillets	3
2 tbsp	parsley	25 ml
2	cloves garlic	2
2 tbsp	olive oil	25 ml

1. In a food processor or blender, combine olives, basil, anchovies, parsley and garlic. Process 15 seconds.
2. With machine running, gradually add olive oil. Continue to process 20 to 30 seconds, or until a smooth paste forms.
3. Transfer to a covered container and store in refrigerator up to 2 weeks.

Makes 2 cups (500 ml).

Tapenade de Marseilles

The name comes from *tapeno*, the Provençal word for capers, an essential ingredient which is often omitted from this traditional recipe. Pile it high into an earthenware crock and watch it disappear. Colleen, who is not crazy about olives (to put it mildly), tempered this recipe of ground Mediterranean olives and olive oil with tuna. Serve it on toasts or warm onion focaccia, use it as a stuffing for deviled eggs, or (a favorite of mine) mix it with cooked eggplant and serve on grilled breads.

1½ cups	pitted black olives	375 ml
2	cans anchovy fillets, drained (1.75 oz/50 g each)	2
½ cup	drained capers	125 ml
½ cup	drained canned tuna fish	125 ml
2	large cloves garlic, peeled	2
1	bay leaf, crumbled	1
2 tbsp	brandy, optional	25 ml
¼ cup	olive oil	50 ml
	freshly ground black pepper	

1. In a blender or food processor, process olives, anchovies, capers, tuna, garlic, bay leaf (and brandy if using). With machine running, gradually add oil and process until smooth. Season with pepper to taste.
2. Turn into a crock or serving bowl. Cover and refrigerate until serving time.

Makes 2½ cups (625 ml).

Hot Crabmeat Dip

This one's for winter, although you can serve it any time of year, especially if you are doing an Indian party. The rich curry flavor starts people thinking of elephants and the Taj Mahal. But I think of this in connection with skiing; of dipping breadsticks or toast into the golden goodness while waiting for the aches to start and the dinner to cook.

1	pkg (8 oz/250 g) cream cheese	1
1 cup	cooked crabmeat	250 ml
1	medium onion, finely chopped	1
1 tsp	lemon juice	5 ml
1 tsp	Worcestershire sauce	5 ml
1½ tsp	curry powder	7 ml
½ tsp	salt	2 ml
¼ tsp	freshly ground black pepper	1 ml
	toast triangles	

1. In a small saucepan, combine cream cheese, crabmeat, lemon juice, Worcestershire sauce, curry powder, salt and pepper.
2. Heat, stirring to break up crabmeat, and mix thoroughly, about 3 to 4 minutes, until bubbling.
3. Serve with toast triangles for dipping.

Makes 2 cups (500 ml).

Dipsidoodle Crab Dip

This is a pretty pink color that speaks of spring and demands mounds of baby mushrooms, thin young zucchini, and tender green onions as accompaniment.

2 cups	cooked crabmeat	500 ml
1 cup	mayonnaise	250 ml
5	water chestnuts	5
3	cloves garlic	3
1 tsp	tomato chili sauce	5 ml
1 tsp	Worcestershire sauce	5 ml
½ tsp	salt	2 ml
¼ tsp	hot pepper sauce	1 ml
¼ tsp	freshly ground black pepper	1 ml
2	green onions, finely chopped	2

1. In a blender or food processor, combine crabmeat, mayonnaise, water chest-nuts, garlic, chili sauce, Worcestershire sauce, salt, hot pepper sauce and black pepper.
2. Process with on/off motion for 1 to 2 minutes, until smooth.
3. Transfer to a small bowl and fold in green onions.
4. Cover and refrigerate 1 hour to chill thoroughly before serving.

Makes 2 cups (500 ml).

Baba Ganouj with Cayenne Pita Toasts

You can buy this at many take-out counters, but nothing says lovin' like making it yourself. Barbecuing the eggplant gives it that wonderful roasted flavor, but an oven broiler will also do the trick. Colleen scoops out a large baked onion to serve this dip as an hors d'oeuvre. Or use one small onion per person to serve as a starter course.

2	medium eggplants	2
1	lemon, peeled, halved, seeded	1
¼ cup	tahini (sesame paste)	50 ml
2	cloves garlic, coarsely chopped	2
½ tsp	salt	2 ml
2 tbsp	olive oil	25 ml
1 tbsp	finely chopped parsley	15 ml
½ tsp	paprika	2 ml

1. Preheat oven to broil.
2. Prick eggplants all over; place on a baking sheet and broil, turning frequently, about 12 minutes, until skin is slightly charred and eggplant is soft.
3. Remove eggplant from oven, peel and cube.
4. In a food processor or blender, place lemon, tahini, garlic and salt. Process 30 seconds. Add eggplant and process only a few seconds more, leaving eggplant chunky.
5. To assemble, place baba ganouj on a plate and garnish with olive oil, parsley and paprika. Serve with pita toasts.

Makes 4 to 6 servings.

Hint – *Mash 20 cloves of garlic in a food processor at one time. Roll into a log and wrap well. Freeze. Slice off what you want when you need it. Return balance of unused garlic to the freezer.*

Tzatziki

Why make this when you can get it at any Greek take-out counter? Fresher flavor, for starters, not to mention far better texture from the mounds of shredded cucumber and, of course, garlic. I turn this dip into a marinade for barbecued salmon steaks. It's also a healthy and piquant garnish for chilled soups when you tire of plain old sour cream.

1	English cucumber, peeled and grated	1
1 cup	yogurt	250 ml
1	clove garlic, finely chopped	1
1 tbsp	chopped fresh dill	15 ml
pinch	salt	pinch

1. With your hands, squeeze water from the cucumber. Place cucumber in a bowl.
2. Combine cucumber, yogurt, garlic, dill and salt; mix well.
3. Spoon into a small dish or crock. Cover and chill. Serve as a dip for vegetables or pita bread.

Makes 1½ cups (375 ml).

Indian Dip with Crisp Curried Crackers

I serve this in an earthenware bowl to play up the rich brown colors. With heaps of curried crackers, this is the ultimate Sunday-afternoon-football kind of dip.

1 cup	mango chutney	250 ml
1 cup	chunky peanut butter	250 ml
¾ cup	refried beans	175 ml
1	jalapeño pepper, seeded and chopped	1
2 tsp	ground coriander	10 ml
2 tsp	ground cumin	10 ml
¼ tsp	cayenne pepper	1 ml
¼ tsp	hot pepper sauce	1 ml
½–1 cup	chicken stock	125-250 ml

1. In a food processor, purée the chutney. Set aside.
2. In a medium saucepan, heat peanut butter, beans, jalapeño, coriander, cumin, cayenne and hot pepper sauce until combined.
3. Add hot mixture to the chutney; process until smooth.
4. With motor running, gradually add chicken stock until desired consistency.
5. Spoon into an earthenware crock and serve warm with curried crackers. May be kept refrigerated for up to 1 week.

Makes 4 cups (1 l).

Curried Crackers

½ cup	butter	25 ml
1½ tsp	curry powder	7 ml
1	box (6 oz/170 g) cracker bread (Lavosh)	1

1. Preheat oven to 275°F (140°C).
2. In a small saucepan, melt the butter and add the curry powder. Mix well.
3. Brush both sides of the cracker bread with curry mixture.
4. Place on a cookie sheet and bake 15 to 20 minutes, until golden.
5. Remove from oven, cool and break into pieces. Serve with dip.

Purposeful leftovers – Baguettes and pita bread turn into chips by tossing them with spices and baking until crisp. Recycle with flair!

Quick Pâté

I've loved this recipe for years, but when I started feeling guilty about oodles of cream cheese and butter going into my well-exercised body, I decided to rethink the ingredients. This is my new "low-fat" Quick Pâté. Its moist, robust flavors come from slow-cooked onions, pear and apple (instead of you-know-what). It's still quick to make, and you can eat it by the potful without feeling cheated.

¼ cup	sweet butter	50 ml
2	medium onions, chopped	2
1	large apple, peeled, cored and sliced	1
1	large pear, peeled, cored and sliced	1
½ lb	chicken livers	250 g
½ tsp	salt	2 ml
½ tsp	ground nutmeg	2 ml
¼ tsp	white pepper	1 ml
1 tbsp	Cognac or sherry	15 ml

1. In a medium-sized skillet, melt butter. Add onions, apple, pear and sauté about 5 minutes until tender.
2. Add livers; sauté about 10 minutes, until brown. Cool slightly.
3. Transfer liver mixture to food processor or blender. Add salt, nutmeg and pepper. Process until smooth. Add Cognac or sherry; process until blended.
4. Turn into crock or serving bowl. Refrigerate. Serve with toasts.

Makes 2 cups (500 ml).

Give your whole party a festive almost picnic patina by setting pâtés, breads, rolls, pickles, condiments and butters on a table covered with pine boughs or other fragrant evergreens. If you can find two large half barrels for the beer and the wine, fill them with ice and dot the inside with chrysanthemum blooms. As the ice melts, the flowers will float and look like a country garden.

Peppercorn Pâté with Madeira

When a friend of mine returned from Portugal and made this pâté from her imported Madeira, I was thrilled by the awesome taste.

⅓ cup	butter	75 ml
1	large Bermuda onion, finely chopped	1
2	cloves garlic, finely chopped	2
1 lb	chicken livers	500 g
1 tbsp	chopped fresh tarragon, or 1 tsp (5 ml) dried	15 ml
1 tsp	salt	5 ml
½ tsp	freshly ground black pepper	2 ml
1 tsp	dried thyme leaves	5 ml
¼ tsp	cayenne pepper	1 ml
¼ tsp	ground cloves	1 ml
¼ tsp	ground allspice	1 ml
¼ cup	Madeira	50 ml
1 tsp	cracked black or green peppercorns	5 ml

1. In a skillet, heat butter, add onion and garlic; sauté 10 minutes, until softened.
2. Add chicken livers and sauté 5 to 7 minutes, or until no longer pink. Sprinkle with tarragon, salt, pepper, thyme, cayenne pepper, cloves and allspice.
3. Transfer chicken livers to blender or food processor; purée until smooth. Add Madeira and process to combine.
4. Pack pâté into 2-cup (500 ml) crock and top with cracked peppercorns. Refrigerate one day before serving.
5. Allow pâté to stand at room temperature 30 minutes before serving.

Makes 8 servings.

Diet Chopped Liver

Makes a great quick lunch for friends. I usually serve it on shredded Romaine lettuce with a really mustardy deviled egg.

2 lb	chicken livers	1 kg
1 lb	beef liver	500 g
2 tbsp	vegetable oil	25 ml
4	chopped medium onions	4
3	hard-cooked eggs	3
½ tsp	salt	2 ml
¼ tsp	freshly ground black pepper	1 ml
	toast triangles	
	shredded lettuce	

1. Preheat oven to 375°F (190°C).
2. On a lightly greased baking sheet, arrange chicken and beef livers. Bake in oven for 10 minutes, or until brown. Drain excess liquid from liver while baking.
3. In a large skillet, heat oil; add onions and sauté until soft. Cook.
4. In a meat grinder or food processor, combine liver, onion, eggs, salt and pepper. Grind or chop with an on/off motion about 2 minutes, until roughly chopped.
5. Serve on toast topped with shredded lettuce.

Makes 2 cups (500 ml).

An all hors d'oeuvre menu makes for a marvelous evening of mixing and munching among your guests. Offer a full bar for this kind of party as most people will want to choose their own drinks. But do have lots of white wine cooling and red wine breathing.

Artichoke Bottoms with Parmesan Cheese

The tinier the better for these. They make a luxurious addition to any buffet party.

12	cooked, small artichoke bottoms	12
2 tbsp	olive oil	25 ml
2 tbsp	soft sweet butter	25 ml
⅔ cup	Parmesan cheese, freshly grated	150 ml
1 tbsp	chopped fresh parsley	15 ml

1. Preheat oven to 450°F (220°C).
2. In a shallow baking dish, combine olive oil and 1 tbsp (15 ml) butter.
3. Arrange artichoke bottoms in a single layer, cut side up. Dot with remaining butter.
4. Sprinkle with cheese.
5. Bake for 12 minutes until cheese turns golden brown.
6. Place on paper towel for 1 minute to drain. Sprinkle with parsley. Serve hot.

Makes 4 servings.

Swedish Meatballs

I usually serve these on toothpicks. They look great with their little feathers of dill.

2	eggs, lightly beaten	2
1 cup	milk	250 ml
½ cup	dry bread crumbs	125 ml
3 tbsp	butter	45 ml
½ cup	onion, finely chopped	125 ml
1 lb	medium ground beef	500 g
¼ lb	ground pork	125 g
1 tsp	salt	5 ml
¾ tsp	dried dill	4 ml
¼ tsp	allspice	1 ml
pinch	nutmeg	pinch
pinch	ground cardamom	pinch
3 tbsp	all-purpose flour	45 ml
⅛ tsp	freshly ground black pepper	0.5 ml
1 cup	beef stock	250 ml
½ cup	cream	125 ml
	fresh dill sprigs	

1. In a large bowl, combine eggs, milk and bread crumbs.
2. In a skillet, heat 1 tbsp (15 ml) butter; add onions and sauté 5 minutes until softened.
3. Add sautéed onions to crumb mixture along with ground beef, pork, salt, ¼ tsp (1 ml) dill, allspice, nutmeg and cardamom; mix well.
4. Cover and chill 1 hour.
5. Preheat oven to 325°F (160°C).
6. Shape meat mixture into balls, each about 1-inch (2.5-cm) in diameter. Heat remaining butter and sauté the meatballs, half of them at a time, until brown. Transfer to an 8-cup (2-l) casserole.
7. Remove skillet from heat; remove all but 2 tbsp (25 ml) drippings from pan. To drippings in skillet add flour, and pepper. Stir to make a smooth paste.

8. Gradually stir in beef stock; bring to a boil, reduce heat, stirring constantly about 3 minutes until smooth.
9. Stir in cream and remaining dill; pour sauce over meatballs.
10. Cover and bake for 30 minutes until bubbling.
    Garnish with fresh dill sprigs.

Makes 6 servings.

Scampi Allegro (Garlic Shrimp)

These can be prepared the night before a party and popped under the broiler at the crucial moment. They make a great beginning for an Italian supper. Your guests can nibble on the scampi while you prepare your favorite pasta.

2 lb	large raw shrimp	1 kg
3	large cloves garlic, chopped	3
¼ cup	vegetable oil	50 ml
¼ cup	melted sweet butter	50 ml
2 tbsp	chopped fresh parsley	25 ml
2 tbsp	lemon juice	25 ml
½ tsp	salt	2 ml
¼ tsp	freshly ground black pepper	1 ml

1. Shell and devein shrimps, leaving tails on. With a knife, split lengthwise, if desired.
2. Combine garlic, oil, butter, parsley, lemon juice, salt and pepper.
3. Place shrimp in a single layer on a foil-lined jelly roll pan. Pour garlic mixture over shrimps. Cover and marinate, in refrigerator, overnight.
4. Broil in same pan, 3 inches (7 cm) from heat, 2 minutes per side, until shrimps are pink. Remove to a warm platter.
5. Spoon marinade remaining in pan over top. Serve immediately.

Makes 4 servings.

Beef Empanadas

These are slightly sweet, super savory, somewhat hot little meat turnovers. They freeze perfectly, ready to be popped into the oven.

Dough

2 cups	all-purpose flour	500 ml
⅓ cup	granulated sugar	75 ml
1½ tsp	ground cinnamon	7 ml
¼ tsp	salt	1 ml
¾ cup	sweet butter	175 ml
1	egg yolk	1
2½ tbsp	milk	30 ml
2 tbsp	Madeira	25 ml

Filling

½ tsp	sweet butter	2 ml
1½ tbsp	onion, finely chopped	20 ml
½ lb	medium ground beef	250 g
⅓ cup	peeled pears, finely chopped	75 ml
¼ cup	peeled peaches, finely chopped	50 ml
¼ cup	green pepper, finely chopped	50 ml
¼ cup	tomatoes, finely chopped, peeled and seeded	50 ml
1 tbsp	Madeira or sherry	15 ml
1 tsp	chopped chives	5 ml
1 tsp	salt	5 ml
1 tsp	chili powder	5 ml
1	egg, lightly beaten	1
1 tsp	granulated sugar	5 ml
½ tsp	ground cinnamon	2 ml

1. In a large bowl, combine flour, sugar, cinnamon and salt for empanada dough. With a pastry blender or two knives, cut in butter until mixture is crumbly and resembles small peas.
2. Blend together egg yolk, milk and Madeira. Pour into flour mixture and mix with a fork until dough is formed. Chill 1 hour.
3. In a skillet, heat butter. Add onion and sauté 1 minute. Add beef and cook, stirring, 2 minutes, or until brown. Transfer to a bowl. Add pears, peaches, green pepper, tomatoes, Madeira or sherry, chives, salt and chili powder; mix well.
4. Preheat oven to 400°F (200°C).
5. Roll out dough to ¼-inch (5-mm) thickness. Cut into 4-inch (10-cm) rounds.
6. Place 1 tsp (5 ml) meat filling on each round. Fold round in half and seal edges by pressing with a fork. Prick several times. Brush with beaten egg and sprinkle with sugar and cinnamon. Place on a baking pan or cookie sheet. Bake in oven for 20 minutes, or until brown. Serve hot.

Makes 3 dozen.

Tuna Empanada Squares

This recipe comes from my daughter Joanne's Argentinean mother-in-law but I'm the one who makes it for all my grandchildren's birthday parties—much to the adult guests' delight. The spicy tuna filling is delicious without being heavy and the dough has all the richness and flakiness of a short empanada crust without all the work. Amazingly versatile, too: you can bake and freeze, or freeze and bake.

Dough

2 cups	all purpose flour	500 ml
pinch	turmeric	pinch
pinch	cayenne pepper	pinch
¼ tsp	salt	1 ml
¾ cup	sweet butter	175 ml
1	egg yolk	1
2 tbsp	milk	25 ml
2 tbsp	Madeira	25 ml
1	egg, lightly beaten (for later use)	1

Filling

2	green onions, sliced	2
1	onion, sliced	1
1	scotch bonnet pepper, seeded	1
1	clove garlic	1
2 tbsp	oil	25 ml
½ cup	black olives, chopped	125 ml
2	eggs, hard-boiled, chopped	2
2	cans oil-packed tuna, undrained (6.5 oz/184 g)	2
2 tsp	fresh thyme	10 ml
1 tsp	tumeric	5 ml
½ tsp	salt	2 ml
¼ tsp	freshly ground black pepper	1 ml

1. In a large bowl, combine flour, turmeric, cayenne pepper and salt. With a pastry blender or 2 knives, cut in butter until mixture is crumbly and resembles small peas.
2. Blend together egg yolk, milk and Madeira. Pour into flour mixture and mix with fork until dough is formed. Chill for 1 hour.
3. In a food processor or blender, combine onions, pepper and garlic. Process 1 minute until very finely minced.
4. In a large skillet, heat oil. Add minced onion mixture and sauté 4 minutes until soft.
5. Turn mixture into a bowl and add olives, eggs, tuna (with ¼ cup/50 ml of oil from the can), thyme, turmeric, salt and pepper; stir to combine.
6. Preheat oven to 375°F (190°C).
7. Roll out half the dough to ½-inch (1-cm) thickness and pat into a greased 8x8-inch (20x20-cm) pan.
9. Spread filling evenly over dough and cover with remaining dough, rolled. Brush with beaten egg. Bake in oven for 25 minutes, or until brown. Serve warm or at room temperature, cutting into 32 bite-size pieces.

Makes 32 servings.

Mushroom Caps Stuffed with Pecans

I serve these at room temperature nestled on a bed of lettuce at cocktail parties, where my rule is finger food only. They can be prepared well in advance and stored in the refrigerator until it's time to cook them.

25	medium mushrooms	25
¼ cup	sweet butter	50 ml
1	clove garlic, finely chopped	1
½ cup	pecans, finely chopped	125 ml
¼ cup	chopped fresh parsley	50 ml
¼ tsp	dried thyme	1 ml
½ tsp	salt	2 ml
¼ tsp	freshly ground black pepper	1 ml
2 tbsp	heavy or whipping cream	25 ml

1. Preheat oven to 350°F (180°C).
2. Remove mushroom stems, finely chop them, and set aside. Wipe caps with damp cloth and arrange in a shallow baking dish, hollow side up.
3. In a skillet, over medium heat, melt butter; add mushroom stems, garlic, pecans, parsley, thyme, salt and pepper. Cook until moisture evaporates, about 5 minutes.
4. Stir in whipping cream until mixture is combined, about 1 minute. Remove from heat.
5. Heap mixture into mushroom caps and bake 10 minutes, until heated through.

Makes 25 appetizers.

Hint – Lemon juice brings out the flavor of all fruit. It will also help mushrooms stay white if you add a few drops of lemon juice before cooking them.

Salads

Salads

Misted leaves of lettuce, blushing radishes, glistening cucumbers, gold and white spears of endive. These fresh and delicate gems have an attraction all their own, and most good cooks know how to handle them.

Keep it simple, keep it fresh. Most of my salad recipes are geared to more than a supporting role, either as a main course for lunch or an individual course at dinner.

Main Course Salads

Positive Power Salad with Canyon Ranch Dressing
Hot Chêvre Salad with Bacon
Hot Watercress Salad
Panzanella Salad
Oriental Noodle and Chicken Salad
Fried Chicken Salad with Cashews
Dilled Chicken Salad
Chinese Chicken Salad in a Lettuce Leaf
Steak Salad with Classic Dressing
Poppyseed Crusted Tuna Salad with Sundried Tomatoes
Seafood Spinach Fettuccine Salad

Side Salads

Wild Rice Salad with Raisins and Madeira
Indonesian Rice Salad
Curried Basmati Rice and Apple Salad
Rice Salad with Tamari Sauce
Summer Corn and Bulgur Salad
Couscous Salad with Sugar Snap Peas and Portobello Mushrooms
Minted Lentil Salad
Quinoa Salad
Chinese Asparagus Salad
Savoy Cabbage and Spinach Salad
Green Bean and Brie Salad
Ginger String Bean Salad
Marinated Green Bean Salad
Hot and Spicy Potato Salad
Tuscan Bean Salad
Cheese Salad with Endive
Salad Romano with Tarragon Vinaigrette
Mango Salad
Dilly Cucumbers and Red Onions

Positive Power Salad

A few years back, my husband gave me a week at Canyon Ranch, a spa in Arizona. I came back with muscles firmed up, and with this recipe. I served this to a crowd of 3,000 people at a political luncheon, and was thanked royally for the change from traditional fare. Jicama is usually available in smart supermarkets, Mexican grocers or Chinese fruit markets.

⅓ cup	sunflower seeds	15 ml
2 cups	broccoli, coarsely chopped	500 ml
2 cups	mushrooms, thinly sliced	500 ml
1½ cups	cauliflower, coarsely chopped	375 ml
1½ cups	diced jicama	375 ml
1 cup	diced carrots	250 ml
½ cup	diced yellow squash	125 ml
½ cup	diced zucchini	125 ml
½ cup	alfalfa sprouts	125 ml
¼ cup	green onion tops,. finely chopped	50 ml
2	diced apples	2
½ cup	raisins	125 ml
½ cup	almonds, coarsely chopped	125 ml
1 cup	diced Mozzarella cheese	250 ml
¼ cup	Canyon Ranch Dressing	50 ml

1. In a pan, toast sunflower seeds in a 325°F (160°C) oven for 8 to 10 minutes, until lightly browned.
2. In a large salad bowl, combine broccoli, mushrooms, cauliflower, jicama, carrots, squash, zucchini, sprouts, green onions, apples, raisins, almonds and cheese.
3. Pour dressing over top and toss thoroughly. Sprinkle sunflower seeds on top.

Makes 8 servings.

Canyon Ranch Dressing

½ cup	red wine vinegar	125 ml
¼ cup	vegetable oil	50 ml
2	cloves garlic, finely chopped	2
1 tbsp	Dijon mustard	15 ml
2 tsp	granulated sugar	10 ml
2 tsp	Worcestershire sauce	10 ml
1½ tsp	dried tarragon	7 ml
1 tsp	dried basil	5 ml
¾ tsp	dried oregano	4 ml
¾ tsp	salt	4 ml
	juice of 1 lemon	
1 cup	water	250 ml

1. In a blender or food processor, combine vinegar, oil, garlic, mustard, sugar, Worcestershire sauce, tarragon, basil, oregano, salt and lemon juice. Process using an on-off motion for 1 minute, until well-blended. Add water and mix well.
2. Refrigerate in a jar with a tight-fitting lid for 24 hours to allow the flavor to develop before using. Will keep for up to 2 weeks. Shake before using.

Makes 2 cups (500 ml).

Choose a crisp, dry Sauvignon Blanc from California to complement this salad.

Hot Chêvre Salad with Bacon

This salad stands alone at lunch and is also an elegant and delicious dish to serve for a formal dinner party. Try a Pouilly Fumé from the Loire Valley or a California Sauvignon Blanc.

2 oz	diced slab bacon	50 g
1	head leaf lettuce	1
1	head radicchio	1
1	bunch watercress	1
2	Belgian endives	2
2	ripe tomatoes	2
2 tbsp	raspberry vinegar	25 ml
⅓ cup	olive oil	75 ml
	salt, freshly ground black pepper and chopped chives	
⅔ lb	goat cheese	170 g
18	thin slices French stick, 2 inches (5 cm) in diameter	

1. Preheat oven to 350°F (180°C).
2. In a skillet, sauté bacon until crisp. Drain bacon bits on paper towel and keep warm.
3. Wash and trim lettuce, radicchio, watercress and endives. Cut tomatoes into thin wedges. Arrange all attractively on six plates.
4. Combine vinegar, oil, salt, pepper and chives to taste; whisk together and pour over salads.
5. Cut cheese in 18 slices and arrange on bread. Place on a baking sheet. Bake 5 to 7 minutes, until melted.
6. Place three cheese toasts on each salad. Sprinkle with bacon bits. Serve immediately.

Makes 6 servings.

Hot Watercress Salad

A perfect luncheon salad with a hunk of cheese and crusty bread. Sautéed onions and garlic provide its unusual taste and texture; the warmed oil over top wilts the watercress slightly and imparts a wonderfully peppery taste. For an alternative, add cold shredded roast beef or chicken.

2	bunches watercress, washed and stems removed	2
4 tsp	toasted sesame seeds	20 ml
¼ cup	vegetable oil	50 ml
1	onion, thinly sliced	1
2	cloves garlic, thinly sliced	2
2	green onions, including green tops, thinly sliced	2
2 tbsp	soy sauce	25 ml
2 tbsp	white vinegar	25 ml
4 tsp	sugar	20 ml
1 tsp	red pepper flakes	5 ml
½ tsp	freshly ground black pepper	2 ml
¼ tsp	salt	1 ml

1. In a small skillet, heat oil; sauté onion and garlic until golden brown. Set aside.
2. In a large salad bowl, combine green onions, soy sauce, vinegar, sugar, pepper flakes, pepper and salt. Add onion mixture and stir until combined.
3. Add watercress and toss to coat with dressing. Sprinkle with sesame seeds.

Makes 4 servings.

A salad this distinctive deserves an interesting partner — Pouilly Fumé or a young Chablis, for example. The peppery taste of the warmed oil would also go well with a Gewurtztraminer.

Panzanella Salad

The wonderful flavor of vine-ripened summer field tomatoes—and the fact that you can assemble it ahead of time—make this Tuscan bread salad a perfect dish for hot-weather buffets. Throw in some yellow tomatoes if you can find them. If you're tempted to try it in the dead of winter, make sure you use good hothouse tomatoes. At any time, the type of bread is crucial. A delicate white bread will turn to mush, so make sure you use a hearty variety.

½	loaf stale crusty sourdough bread, sliced into 1-inch (2.5-cm) pieces	½
4	anchovies	4
¼ cup	milk	50 ml
3	large tomatoes, peeled and coarsely chopped	3
3	stalks celery, chopped	3
2	eggs, hard-boiled and chopped	2
1	medium red onion, thinly sliced	1
1	can tuna, drained and broken up (optional)	1
½ cup	peeled, chopped cucumber	125 ml
½ cup	basil leaves	125 ml
2 tbsp	capers, drained and chopped	25 ml
2	cloves garlic, minced	2
½ cup	extra virgin olive oil	125 ml
¼ cup	red wine vinegar	50 ml
1 tbsp	balsamic vinegar	15 ml
½ tsp	salt	2 ml
½ tsp	freshly ground black pepper	2 ml

1. Soak the anchovies in milk for 15 minutes. Drain and chop finely.
2. Place bread in a large bowl and cover with cold water; let soak for 10 minutes. With your hands, gently squeeze out as much water as possible. Tear bread into bite-size pieces.

3. In a large bowl, combine bread, anchovies, tomatoes, celery, eggs, onion, tuna (if using), cucumber, basil and capers.
4. In a small bowl, whisk together garlic, oil, vinegar, salt and pepper. Pour over salad. Toss gently to coat. Refrigerate at least 2 hours or up to 8 hours before serving.

Makes 12 servings.

~~~~~~

My favorite wine of all time with this mouth-watering salad is a dry Spanish Rosé from Marques de Caceras. Twist my arm and I'll settle for a dry, lemony Sauvignon Blanc or a floral Semillon.

~~~~~~

Oriental Noodle and Chicken Salad

Pile the noodles high on a large platter and surround them with smaller mounds of chicken, water chestnuts and green onions. A fun salad to serve to a group as each person can create their own combination.

10 oz	thin Oriental egg noodles	248 ml
2 cups	cooked, shredded chicken	500 ml
1 cup	toasted peanuts, coarsely chopped	250 ml
1 cup	bean sprouts	250 ml
1 cup	diagonally sliced carrots	250 ml
1 cup	cucumber, peeled, halved and thinly sliced	250 ml
1 cup	thinly sliced green onions	250 ml
1 cup	water chestnuts, slivered	250 ml

Dressing

½ cup	peanut butter	125 ml
⅓ cup	chicken stock	75 ml
¼ cup	soy sauce	50 ml
3 tbsp	rice wine vinegar	45 ml
2 tbsp	grated fresh ginger	25 ml
2 tbsp	brown sugar	25 ml
3	cloves garlic, finely chopped	3
2 tsp	chili oil	10 ml
¼ cup	heavy or whipping cream	50 ml

1. Cook noodles according to the instructions on the package. Rinse with cold water, drain and set aside.
2. In a food processor or blender, combine peanut butter, chicken stock, soy sauce, vinegar, ginger, sugar, garlic and chili oil. Process until smooth. With the motor running, add the cream in a stream and blend until smooth. Transfer to a bowl.

3. In a large bowl, combine the noodles and 1½ cups (375 ml) of the dressing. Toss gently to coat well. Arrange noodles in the center of a large serving platter; sprinkle with the peanuts. Surround with mounds of chicken, bean sprouts, carrot, cucumber, green onion and water chestnuts. Serve remaining dressing in a pitcher on the side.
4. To serve, allow guests to create their own salad by mixing noodles and garnish to their own wishes.

Makes 4 to 6 main course servings.

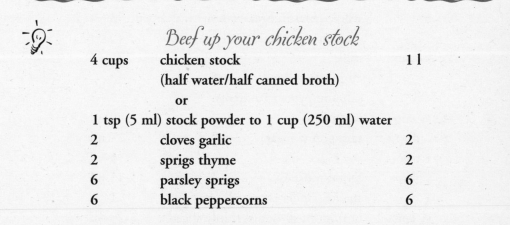

Beef up your chicken stock

4 cups	chicken stock (half water/half canned broth)	1 l
	or	
	1 tsp (5 ml) stock powder to 1 cup (250 ml) water	
2	cloves garlic	2
2	sprigs thyme	2
6	parsley sprigs	6
6	black peppercorns	6

1. Combine stock, garlic, thyme, parsley and pepper in a pot and bring to a boil. Reduce heat and simmer 10 minutes. Strain before using.

For an Eastern flavor, add a strip of lemon rind, 2 slices of fresh ginger root and a pinch of red pepper flakes.

Fried Chicken Salad with Cashews

In addition to being a festive lunch salad, this makes a wonderful light supper for after-theater parties. For a summer dinner, serve this salad with a cold soup beforehand and a fluffy lemony dessert to follow.

3	whole chicken breasts, boned, skinned and cut into ½-inch (1-cm) strips	3
⅓ cup	milk	75 ml
	all-purpose flour, salt and pepper to dredge	
¼ cup	sesame oil	50 ml
2 tbsp	tarragon vinegar	25 ml
1 tsp	soy sauce	5 ml
1 tbsp	Dijon mustard	15 ml
1	shallot, finely chopped	1
½ cup	button mushrooms, thinly sliced	25 ml
1	head curly endive, washed and leaves torn apart	1
2 cups	cherry tomatoes	500 ml
1	purple onion, thinly sliced and separated into rings	1
½ cup	whole cashews	125 ml

1. Dip chicken strips in milk; dredge in flour mixture.
2. In a medium-size skillet, heat oil. Fry strips about 7 minutes, until golden brown; remove and drain on paper towel.
3. Add vinegar to skillet and scrape to deglaze.
4. Pour into a bowl, add soy sauce and mustard; mix well. Stir in shallot and mushrooms and toss to coat.
5. Divide endive and tomatoes evenly onto six plates.
6. To serve, pour mushroom mixture over lettuce and tomatoes. Garnish with fried chicken, onion rings and cashews.

Makes 6 servings.

Dilled Chicken Salad

This chicken salad is a bright and beautiful alternative to the mayonnaise variety that usually turns up. Garnish it with fresh cantaloupe slices and a handful of mint leaves. The dressing makes this dish. It can also do great things for fresh green vegetables cooked al dente: asparagus, young green beans, snow peas or broccoli. For a variation to this dilly dressing, substitute half a teaspoon of curry powder.

2 cups	chicken, cooked and diced	500 ml
1 cup	broccoli florets	250 ml
2 cups	water chestnuts, thinly sliced or jicama, julienned sliced	500 ml
10	green onions, coarsely chopped	10
1 cup	halved seedless green grapes cantaloupe slices and fresh mint	250 ml

Dressing

1 cup	sour cream	250 ml
2 tbsp	soy sauce	25 ml
1 tsp	sesame oil	5 ml
8 to 10 drops	hot pepper sauce	8 to 10 drops
	white pepper to taste	
2 tbsp	chopped fresh dill, or 2 tsp (10 ml) dried dill	25 ml

1. In a large salad bowl, combine chicken, broccoli, water chestnuts, green onions and grapes.
2. In a small bowl, combine sour cream, soy sauce, sesame oil, hot pepper sauce and pepper to taste. Stir in dill.
3. Pour over chicken mixture; toss gently to combine. Chill 1 hour before serving. Garnish with peeled cataloupe slices and fresh mint.

Makes 6 servings.

Chinese Chicken Salad in a Lettuce Leaf

This is like an egg roll, but the roll is a lettuce leaf and that makes it crunchy. You can substitute fresh shrimp for the chicken if you would rather have a seafood salad. I also like to serve this as a first course followed by Gingered Oriental Fish.

2 lb	boneless and skinless chicken breasts, cooked and chopped	1 kg
1 lb	bean sprouts	500 g
1	shredded head lettuce	500 g
3	shredded large carrots	3

Dressing

1	clove garlic, finely chopped	1
2 tbsp	chopped fresh mint or 2 tsp (10 ml) dried	25 ml
	juice of 3 lemons	
⅓ cup	water	75 ml
2 tbsp	sesame oil	25 ml
½ tsp	red pepper flakes	2 ml
1 tbsp	granulated sugar	15 ml
10 to 12	lettuce leaves	10 to 12

1. In a large salad bowl, combine chicken, sprouts, lettuce and carrots.
2. Combine garlic, mint, lemon juice, water, sesame oil, pepper flakes and sugar. Pour over chicken mixture. Toss to mix thoroughly.
3. Wash lettuce and pat dry. Spoon salad onto lettuce leaves; roll up to serve.

Makes 10 to 12 servings.

Steak Salad with Classic Dressing

Admonition! Start with fine beef steaks. Use any cut, but don't attempt to do this with leftover steak or roasts.

2 tbsp	soy sauce	25 ml
1 tbsp	vegetable oil	15 ml
1	clove garlic, finely chopped	1
¼ tsp	freshly ground black pepper	1 ml
1 lb	sirloin steak	500 g
2	large red potatoes, boiled with skins on and coarsely chopped	2
1	medium red onion, cut in rings	1
1	red pepper, thinly sliced	1
½ cup	cooked peas	125 ml
¼ cup	chopped Italian parsley	50 ml
½ cup	Classic Dressing	125 ml

1. In a small bowl, combine soy sauce, oil, garlic and pepper. Brush over both sides of steak; marinate overnight in refrigerator. Remove steak from marinade.
2. Grill, broil or barbecue steak for 3 to 4 minutes on each side, until rare. Cut diagonally, across the grain, into thin slices.
3. In a large bowl, combine hot steak slices, potatoes, onion, pepper, peas and parsley.
4. Pour dressing over top and toss well to coat.

Makes 6 to 8 servings.

Classic Dressing

Ever since I got into the business of making and selling condiments, people have been after me for "The Perfect Salad Dressing." Well, here it is!

½ cup	light cream	125 ml
½ cup	vegetable oil	125 ml
¼ cup	olive oil	50 ml
¼ cup	tarragon or balsamic vinegar	50 ml
1	egg, beaten lightly	1
2 tsp	finely chopped garlic	10 ml
1½ tsp	salt	7 ml
1 tsp	freshly ground pepper	5 ml
1 tsp	Dijon mustard	5 ml
1 tsp	fresh lemon juice	5 ml
½ tsp	dry mustard	2 ml
¼ tsp	sugar	1 ml

1. In a jar with a screw-top lid, combine cream, oils, vinegar, egg, garlic, salt, pepper, Dijon mustard, lemon juice, dry mustard and sugar. Cover tightly; shake well and refrigerate for up to 2 weeks. Always shake before using.

Makes 2 cups (500 ml).

Variations

Anchovy Dressing: Add 2 tbsp (25 ml) finely chopped anchovies to Classic Dressing in place of salt.

Roquefort Dressing: Add 2 tbsp (25 ml) crumbled Roquefort or blue cheese to Classic Dressing.

Herb Classic Dressing: Add 2 tbsp (25 ml) fresh or 2 tsp (10 ml) dried chopped basil, dill, summer savory, parsley, alone or in combination.

Poppyseed Crusted Tuna Salad with Sundried Tomatoes

❧❦❧

Served on a bed of crunchy greens and peppered with fine black poppy seeds, this salad is not only visually interesting—its contrasting flavors and textures please and surprise the palate as well. Just make sure you don't overcook the tuna—when we say 30 seconds per side, we mean it. Time it carefully and you'll have a terrific main course dish for a party luncheon.

24	pieces sundried tomato	24
9	cloves garlic, minced	9
½ cup	olive oil	125 ml
3 tsp	chopped tarragon	15 ml
¼ tsp	salt	1 ml
¼ tsp	freshly ground black pepper	1 ml
¼ cup	poppy seeds	50 ml
3 tbsp	cracked black peppercorns	45 ml
½ tsp	salt	2 ml
1 lb	tuna loin	500 g
1 tbsp	olive oil	15 ml
½ lb	baby greens	250 g

1. Place the sundried tomatoes in a small bowl. Pour boiling water over to cover. Let stand 5 minutes; drain and chop.
2. In a bowl, combine the sundried tomatoes with half the garlic, 3 tbsp (50 ml) of the oil, 2 tsp (10 ml) of the tarragon, salt and pepper. Purée 1½ tbsp (25 ml) of this mixture with remaining oil in food processor or blender. Set aside the purée.
3. In a separate bowl, combine the poppy seeds, cracked peppercorns, salt, remaining garlic and remaining tarragon.
4. Roll tuna in poppy seed mixture so that all sides are evenly coated.

5. Heat heavy-bottomed skillet until smoking; pour in olive oil. Sear tuna for 30 seconds on each side, until crust is crispy, but tuna is still pink and soft in the center. Remove the tuna from the pan.
6. With a very sharp knife, cut tuna into slices about ¼ inch (.5 cm) thick.
7. Arrange baby greens among four plates and divide tuna evenly in a fan shape. Spoon remaining sundried tomato mixture at bottom of the fan; drizzle with reserved sundried tomato purée/oil.

Makes 4 servings.

Hint – *Tuna is the sea's macho equivalent of beef. An unstoppable well-muscled swimmer, it has a dense texture with large, generous flakes. Lightly oiled or marinated, tuna steaks fare well with a hot grill or boiler, and loins of tuna can be braised or roasted like beef. The only danger is overcooking.*

Seafood Spinach Fettuccine Salad

The green of the spinach fettuccine and the fresh touch of dill give this salad a look and a taste that make luncheon guests ask for seconds. Make a little extra because it is very appetizing. Serve for a leisurely summer lunch with many glasses of cool, white wine.

½ lb	peeled small raw shrimp	250 g
¼ lb	bay scallops	125 g
1 lb	fresh spinach fettuccine	500 g
few drops	olive oil	few drops
3	fresh ripe tomatoes, peeled seeded and coarsely chopped	3
3	green onions, chopped	3
½ tsp	salt	2 ml
½ tsp	freshly ground black pepper	2 ml
	juice of ½ lemon	
⅓ cup	vegetable oil	75 ml
2 tbsp	finely chopped fresh parsley	25 ml
2 tbsp	finely chopped fresh dill	25 ml
2	cloves garlic, finely chopped	2

1. In a pot of salted boiling water, cook shrimp and scallops for about 3 minutes, until shrimp are pink. Remove and drain. Plunge into cold water to stop the cooking.
2. In a large pot of salted boiling water, cook fettuccine about 10 minutes, until al dente. Drain well. Add olive oil and toss through pasta to prevent sticking.
3. In a large bowl, combine shrimp, scallops, pasta, tomatoes, onions, salt, pepper, lemon juice, oil, parsley, dill and garlic. Toss together.
4. Refrigerate about 2 hours to chill thoroughly.

Makes 4 servings.

Wild Rice Salad with Raisins and Madeira

The orange rind and yellow raisins soaked in Madeira add a special flavor to this high-fiber, healthy salad. I like to serve it with Pecan Chicken so I can toss the toasted pecans over the rice and chicken. It's also superb with roasted duck from the Chinese market, which I then throw on my barbecue to crisp up even more.

2½ cups	stock	725 ml
4 oz	wild rice	114 ml
½ cup	bulgur	125 ml
1½ tsp	salt	7 ml
¼ cup	Madeira or sherry	50 ml
⅓ cup	golden raisins	75 ml
2 tbsp	sweet butter	25 ml
6	green onions, chopped	6
2	stalks celery, sliced	2
1	clove garlic, minced	1
	rind of 2 oranges	
¼ cup	orange juice	50 ml
2 tbsp	chopped parsley	25 ml
1 tbsp	lemon juice	15 ml
½ tsp	freshly ground black pepper	2 ml
⅓ cup	toasted, chopped pecans	75 ml

1. In large saucepan, combine stock and 1 tsp of the salt; bring to a boil. Stir in wild rice, bring to a boil, reduce heat, cover and simmer for 40 minutes. Stir in bulgur. Cover and continue cooking for about 15 minutes.
2. Meanwhile, in a small saucepan combine Madeira and raisins. Boil for 2 minutes. Set aside.

3. In a skillet over medium-high heat, melt butter. Add green onions, celery and garlic; cook 2 minutes. Stir in rind, orange juice, parsley, lemon juice, pepper, remaining salt, and raisin mixture. Cook 2 minutes. Remove from heat; keep warm.
4. Drain wild rice and bulgur, and place in a large bowl. Toss with the vegetable-orange juice mixture and pecans. Serve warm or at room temperature.

Makes 6 servings.

Hint – Wild rice is not rice at all, but a grass seed. Nutty and rich in flavor, it's high in B vitamins and low in fat—one cup contains just 135 calories.

Indonesian Rice Salad

I make this salad ahead of time and throw in the cashews at the last minute. It's always on the menu when I serve sesame baked salmon for a summer backyard supper.

2 cups	cooked brown rice	500 ml
2	green onions, finely chopped	2
1	green pepper, coarsely chopped	1
1	stalk celery, thinly sliced	1
1 cup	bean sprouts	250 ml
½ cup	raisins	125 ml
¼ cup	toasted cashews	50 ml
¼ cup	toasted sesame seeds	50 ml
1 tbsp	chopped fresh parsley	15 ml
	lettuce	

Dressing

3 tbsp	vegetable oil	45 ml
2 tbsp	orange juice	25 ml
2 tbsp	lime juice	25 ml
2 tsp	soy sauce	10 ml
1 tsp	sesame oil	5 ml
½ tsp	grated fresh ginger root	2 ml
½	clove garlic, finely chopped	½
¼ tsp	salt	1 ml
¼ tsp	freshly ground pepper	1 ml

1. In a large bowl, combine rice, green onions, green pepper, celery, bean sprouts, raisins, cashews, sesame seeds and parsley. Toss thoroughly.
2. In a blender or food processor, combine vegetable oil, orange juice, lime juice, soy sauce, sesame oil, ginger and garlic. Process until smooth. Season with salt and pepper.
3. Pour dressing over salad and toss. Chill about 2 hours. Serve on a bed of lettuce.

Makes 6 servings.

Curried Basmati Rice and Apple Salad

This is the perfect accompaniment to a picnic of barbecued chicken, and both the rice and dressing can be made a day ahead for extra convenience. When adding cooked rice to a salad, make sure it's dry. (I often put it on a baking sheet and pop it in a 300°F oven for 10 minutes.) I've also added slices of barbecued chicken to turn it into a main-course luncheon salad. The ingredients make a pretty combination, so use a beautiful bowl to show it off. Remember that basmati rice should always be rinsed before cooking and is best when soaked in cold water for 10 minutes; the result is long separate grains when cooked.

4 cups	cooked Basmati rice	1 l
1	large Granny Smith apple, cored and diced	1
1	stalk celery, diced	1
8	radishes, slivered	8
4	green onions, chopped	4
⅓ cup	raisins, plumped in hot water	75 ml

Dressing

¼ cup	vegetable oil	50 ml
2 tbsp	cider vinegar	25 ml
2 tbsp	mango chutney	25 ml
1½ tsp	curry powder	7 ml
½ tsp	salt	2 ml
¼ tsp	freshly ground black pepper	1 ml

1. In a serving bowl, combine rice, apple, celery, radishes, onions and raisins.
2. In a small bowl, whisk together the dressing ingredients; pour over the salad and toss to mix well. Serve at room temperature.

Makes 6 servings.

Rice Salad with Tamari Sauce

A hearty and satisfying salad that can become a lunch if you add a soup to the menu. The raisins and nuts give this salad an exotic taste. Serve with thick slices of whole wheat breads.

1 cup	brown rice	250 ml
1¾ cup	boiling water	425 ml
½ cup	raisins	125 ml
2	green onions, chopped	2
¼ cup	toasted sesame seeds	50 ml
1 cup	fresh bean sprouts	250 ml
1 cup	toasted cashews	250 ml
1	large green pepper, coarsely chopped	1
1	stalk celery, sliced diagonally	1
2 tbsp	chopped fresh parsley	25 ml
	lettuce	

Dressing

¼ cup	fresh orange juice	50 ml
½ cup	vegetable oil	125 ml
1 tbsp	sesame oil	15 ml
¼ cup	tamari sauce	50 ml
2 tbsp	dry sherry	25 ml
	juice of 1 lime	
1	clove garlic, finely chopped	1
1 tsp	grated fresh ginger root	5 ml
	salt and freshly ground pepper to taste	

1. In a large saucepan, combine rice with water. Cook over medium heat 30 minutes. Drain and let cool.

2. In a bowl, combine rice, raisins, onions, sesame seeds, bean sprouts, cashews, green pepper, celery and parsley. Toss thoroughly.
3. Into a blender or food processor, measure orange juice, oils, tamari sauce, sherry, lime juice, garlic and ginger root. Process until smooth. Season with salt and pepper to taste.
4. Pour over salad and toss. Chill about 2 hours. Serve on a bed of lettuce.

Makes 10 to 12 servings.

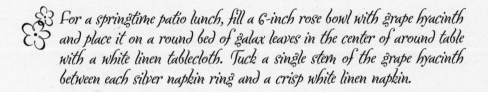 *For a springtime patio lunch, fill a 6-inch rose bowl with grape hyacinth and place it on a round bed of galax leaves in the center of around table with a white linen tablecloth. Tuck a single stem of the grape hyacinth between each silver napkin ring and a crisp white linen napkin.*

Summer Corn and Bulgur Salad

This is my favorite side dish when I barbecue burgers. I like to throw the corn on the barbecue as well for that extra roasted flavor. It's my fall harvest version of tabbouleh—an end of summer celebration of corn, apples and tomatoes, served around the fireplace for a casual supper.

1 cup	boiling stock, chicken or vegetable	250 ml
1 cup	bulgur	250 ml
¼ cup	olive oil	50 ml
1	clove garlic, finely chopped	1
1	medium Granny Smith apple, chopped	1
2 tbsp	lemon juice	25 ml
4	plum tomatoes, peeled and coarsely chopped	4
3	green onions, thinly sliced	3
3	ears corn, boiled or barbecued, kernels removed from cob	3
½ cup	chopped fresh basil	125 ml
½ tsp	salt	2 ml
½ tsp	freshly ground black pepper	2 ml

1. In a large bowl, pour boiling water over bulgur; add olive oil and garlic and stir well. Let stand 30 minutes until all water is absorbed. Fluff with a fork.
2. In a small bowl, combine apple and lemon juice.
3. Add apple mixture, tomatoes, green onions, corn, basil, salt and pepper to bulgur. Toss to mix well. Chill 1 hour or up to 2 days.

Makes 6 servings.

Couscous Salad With Sugar Snap Peas And Portobello Mushrooms

Serve this salad as soon as it's made. Try it with lamb kebabs at a casual get-together.

¼ lb	portobello mushrooms, stems removed, wiped clean and cut in 1x¼ inch (2.5x.5 cm) slices	125 g
1½ cups	stock, chicken or vegetable	375 ml
¼ cup	finely chopped shallots	50 ml
3 tbsp	lemon juice	45 ml
½ tsp	freshly ground black pepper	2 ml
1 cup	couscous	250 ml
⅓ cup	coarsely chopped cilantro	75 ml
2 tbsp	olive oil	25 ml
¼ lb	sugar snap peas	125 g
¼ tsp	salt	1 ml
1 tsp	red wine vinegar	5 ml
1	head red leaf lettuce, washed and dried	1

1. In a saucepan, combine stock, half the shallots, 2 tbsp (25 ml) of the lemon juice and black pepper. Bring to a boil; stir in couscous and half the cilantro. Cover pan and remove from heat; let stand 15 minutes, until all the liquid is absorbed.
2. Meanwhile, in a large heavy-bottomed skillet, heat 1 tbsp (15 ml) of the oil. Add the mushrooms and remaining shallots; cook about 4 minutes, until they begin to brown. Stir in the sugar snap peas and the salt. Cook for 2 more minutes, until peas are bright green and tender crisp. Remove skillet from heat.
3. In a large bowl, combine couscous and the mushroom mixture; stir with a fork.
4. In a small bowl, combine the remaining oil, vinegar, remaining lemon juice and remaining cilantro. Pour over salad and toss gently to coat.
5. On large platter or individual plates, arrange lettuce leaves and mound salad on top. Serve at once.

Makes 6 servings.

Minted Lentil Salad

This salad is the perfect partner for a roasted lamb, or as part of a vegetarian meal.

1½ cups	dried green lentils	375 ml
1	carrot, peeled	1
1	stalk celery	1
¼	onion	¼
1	clove garlic	1
1	bay leaf	1
½ tsp	salt	2 ml
3 tbsp	lemon juice	45 ml
2 tbsp	olive oil	25 ml
	rind of 1 lemon	
1	red pepper, roasted and sliced	1
1	yellow pepper, roasted and sliced	1
2	green onions, finely chopped	2
2 tbsp	chopped fresh parsley	25 ml
2 tbsp	chopped fresh mint	25 ml
4 oz	feta cheese, crumbled	114 ml

1. In a large saucepan, combine lentils, carrot, celery, onion, garlic, bay leaf and salt. Cover with water so that lentils are 2 inches beneath water's surface. Bring to a boil, reduce heat and simmer for about 20 minutes, until the lentils are tender. Drain lentils and discard carrot, celery, onion, garlic and bay leaf.
2. In a small bowl, combine lemon juice, olive oil and rind.
3. In a large bowl; combine lentils, lemon juice mixture, roasted peppers, green onions, parsley and mint. Toss gently to coat. Sprinkle with feta. Chill for 1 hour. Serve at room temperature.

Makes 6 servings.

Quinoa Salad

This grain-based dish is high in protein but low in calories—and easily prepared ahead of time since it gets better as it sits. Chock-full of colorful limes, fresh cilantro and jalapeño peppers, it looks especially good served in a clear crystal dish.

1¾ cup	stock, chicken or vegetable	425 ml
1 cup	quinoa, rinsed well and drained	250 ml
2	carrots, peeled and grated	2
2	jalapeño peppers, seeded and finely chopped	2
½ cup	peeled and diced cucumber	125 ml
	rind of 1 lime	
⅓ cup	lime juice	75 ml
¼ cup	coarsely chopped cilantro	50 ml
2 tbsp	chopped shallot	25 ml
2 tbsp	corn oil	25 ml
¼ tsp	salt	1 ml
¼ tsp	freshly ground black pepper	1 ml

1. In a saucepan, bring the stock to a boil. Add quinoa; bring to a boil, reduce heat, cover, and simmer 10 to 15 minutes, or until quinoa is tender and translucent and the stock is absorbed. Cool.
2. In a large bowl, toss together quinoa, carrots, jalapeño, cucumber, rind, lime juice, cilantro, shallot, corn oil, salt and pepper. Toss gently to coat. Cover and refrigerate at least 1 hour or up to 2 days.

Makes 6 to 8 servings.

Chinese Asparagus Salad

Make this just before serving as it does not improve with age. You can add a border of thinly sliced radishes and a good dab of Russian mustard. Sprinkle with sesame seeds for that added Oriental look and flavor.

2 lb	fresh asparagus, each stalk ½-inch (1-cm) thick	1 kg
1 tbsp	soy sauce	15 ml
1 tbsp	sesame oil	15 ml
1 tsp	sugar	5 ml
½ tsp	salt	2 ml
4 drops	hot pepper sauce	4 drops
¼ cup	toasted sesame seeds	50 ml

1. Snap tough root end off asparagus. Slice stalks into 1½-inch (1.75-cm) lengths to make 3 cups (750 ml) asparagus pieces.
2. In 2 quarts (2 l) of rapidly boiling, salted water, blanch asparagus for 1 minute. Drain immediately, running cold water over asparagus to stop cooking and set color. Spread on a double thickness of paper towel and pat dry.
3. In a glass bowl, combine soy sauce, sesame oil, sugar, salt and hot pepper sauce. Mix until sugar is completely dissolved.
4. Add asparagus. Toss to coat each asparagus piece with dressing.
5. Chill 1 to 2 hours. Sprinkle with toasted sesame seeds before serving.

Makes 4 servings.

Savoy Cabbage and Spinach Salad

Doesn't it sound intriguing? I serve this hearty salad with a sandwich of Liptauer cheese on freshly sliced black bread, topped with a slice of Black Forest ham and a bowl of hot consommé.

1 lb	fresh spinach, washed, dried and torn into bite-sized pieces	500 g
3 cups	shredded Savoy cabbage	750 ml
1 cup	bean sprouts	250 ml
1	small red onion, thinly sliced	1
1 cup	slivered almonds, toasted	250 ml

Dressing

1 cup	vegetable oil	250 ml
3 tbsp	mayonnaise	45 ml
2 tbsp	cider vinegar	25 ml
2 tbsp	soy sauce	25 ml
2	cloves garlic, finely chopped	2

1. In a bowl, combine spinach, cabbage, sprouts, onion and almonds.
2. In a small bowl, combine oil, mayonnaise, vinegar, soy sauce and garlic. Pour over salad; toss to coat thoroughly.
3. Serve at once.

Makes 6 to 8 servings.

Green Bean and Brie Salad

Serve as a side dish to any delicately flavored main course, such as a simple grilled salmon, or solo as a light luncheon. The ingredients provide an opportunity for a pretty arrangement of fanned green beans and garnishes of red and yellow cherry tomatoes.

½ lb	fresh green beans	250 g
½ lb	mixed greens (frisée, baby greens, Belgian endive, arugula, etc.), washed, dried, and torn into bite-sized pieces	250 g
½ lb	Brie cheese, cut into 12 pieces, 1x¼ inch	250 g
1	red pepper, roasted and thinly sliced	1
4 tbsp	sesame oil	50 ml
1 tbsp	white wine vinegar	15 ml
1 tbsp	chopped shallot	15 ml
pinch	each salt, pepper, sugar and wasabi	pinch
2 tsp	toasted sesame seeds	10 ml

1. Trim beans and blanch in boiling water about 3 minutes, until tender crisp. Drain and rinse under cold water.
2. Place beans, greens, cheese and red pepper in a large bowl.
3. In a small bowl, combine sesame oil, vinegar, shallot, salt, pepper, sugar, and wasabi. Pour over salad. Toss until thoroughly coated.
4. Divide evenly on four plates. Sprinkle with toasted sesame seeds. Serve at once.

Makes 4 servings.

Hint – The original hors d'oeuvre or simple snack was a collection of cheese, crackers and bread. But there are many more interesting things you can do with cheese, such as frying it, marinating it or spearing it with fruit.

Ginger String Bean Salad

Lots of toasted almonds and the wonderful Oriental taste of fresh ginger make this a delicious hot salad. Shop diligently for thin young beans. You'll want to use the dressing with other crisp vegetables such as broccoli and spinach, cauliflower, and even red cabbage.

⅓ cup	slivered almonds	75 ml
1 lb	fresh green beans	500 g
1 tbsp	finely chopped fresh ginger root	15 ml

Dressing

2 tsp	dry mustard	10 ml
1 tsp	cold water	5 ml
4 tsp	white vinegar	20 ml
1 tbsp	sesame oil	15 ml
1 tbsp	light soy sauce	15 ml
1 tsp	sugar	5 ml
1 tsp	salt	5 ml

1. Toast almonds on baking sheet in medium oven until golden. Let cool.
2. Trim beans and cut into pieces about 2 inches (5 cm) long. Blanch beans in boiling water about 4 minutes until tender but still crisp. Drain and rinse with cold water to stop cooking. Place in bowl.
3. Add ginger root and almonds; toss to mix.
4. In a small mixing bowl, place mustard powder and gradually stir in water to make a smooth paste. Add vinegar, sesame oil, soy sauce, sugar and salt; mix well.
5. Pour over bean mixture and toss until thoroughly coated. Serve at room temperature.

Makes 3 to 4 servings.

Marinated Green Bean Salad

Use the tenderest, greenest, youngest beans you can find, and put them in the tomato sauce marinade for 1 or 2 days. When they are ready, you have a salad that adds immeasurably to an antipasto buffet or as the first course of a pasta dinner.

1 lb	green beans, trimmed	500 g

Marinade

1 cup	tomato sauce	250 ml
½ tsp	cinnamon	2 ml
¼ tsp	nutmeg	1 ml
pinch	ground allspice	pinch
pinch	ground cloves	pinch

1. In a saucepan of lightly salted boiling water, blanch beans for 2 minutes. With a slotted spoon, remove to a bowl of ice water and chill thoroughly.
2. In a bowl, combine tomato sauce, cinnamon, nutmeg, allspice and cloves; mix well.
3. Drain beans thoroughly. Pour sauce over beans. Toss gently to coat.
4. Cover and refrigerate 1 to 2 hours before serving. Toss again and serve.

Makes 4 to 6 servings.

Hint – Combine leftover salad in a blender with bouillon and tomato juice to make a delicious hot or cold gazpacho-like soup.

Hot and Spicy Potato Salad

Like the non-mayonnaise chicken salad, this is a welcome change for guests. The dressing is also perfect with fresh green salads, like young beans when they first appear in the market, snappy and full of moisture.

12	small red potatoes with skins, cooked until just tender	12
2 lb	fresh green beans, stems removed cut in half diagonally	1 kg
1	medium jicama or Chinese radish, julienne-cut	1
2 cups	rice, pitted black olives, sliced	500 ml
12	green onions, finely chopped, or 1 red onion separated into rings	12

Dressing

⅔ cup	olive oil	150 ml
⅓ cup	sherry	75 ml
¼ cup	cider vinegar	50 ml
½ cup	crumbled Gorgonzola or blue cheese	125 ml
½ tsp	Worcestershire sauce	2 ml
½ tsp	salt	2 ml
¼ tsp	coarsely ground black pepper	1 ml
1	can (1.75 oz/50 g) anchovy fillets with oil drained	1

1. Cut cooked potatoes in half.
2. In a steamer basket over boiling water, steam green beans about 4 minutes, until tender crisp; then plunge them immediately into cold water and drain thoroughly.
3. In a large bowl, combine potatoes, beans, jicama, olives and green onions. Chill for about 2 hours.

4. In a blender or food processor, combine oil, sherry, vinegar, cheese, Worcestershire sauce, salt, pepper and anchovy fillets. Process about 1 minute until smooth. Pour over chilled potato mixture. Toss gently to coat.

Makes 12 servings.

Hint – New Ideas for Super Salads

Green beans, walnuts and Feta cheese.

Eggplant, tomatoes, green olives and almonds.

Peas, apple and green onions.

New potatoes, Roquefort cheese and bacon.

Warm mushrooms, black olives, anchovies and Gorgonzola cheese.

Tomatoes, peppers, mushrooms, onions, hardboiled eggs and crumbled bacon.

Cauliflower, black olives, capers and anchovies.

Apples, red onion, Brie and chopped walnuts.

Pears, watercress, raspberries and cheese.

Chicken, Gruyere, bacon and avocado.

Hot lamb and chevre on baby greens.

Snow peas, pine nuts, roasted red peppers and grilled sausage.

Tuscan Bean Salad

This salad owes its flavor as much to the kind of beans used as it does to the inclusion of onions, parsley, olive oil and spices. Serve it to your guests with a lamb roast or Chicken Saag.

1½ cups	dried white beans	375 ml
½ cup	olive oil	125 ml
2 cups	thinly sliced onions	500 ml
1½ tsp	salt	7 ml
½ tsp	freshly ground black pepper	2 ml
2 tbsp	minced parsley	25 ml

1. Wash beans. Put in a saucepan, cover with cold water, and bring to a boil. Remove from heat; cover and let soak 1 hour. Drain.
2. Cover beans with fresh water and bring to a boil. Reduce heat, cover, and simmer 1½ hours, or until tender. Drain.
3. Heat oil in a skillet. Add onions, sauté about 10 minutes, until light brown. Remove from heat and combine with beans, salt and pepper.
4. Transfer to glass bowl. Chill at least 2 hours, preferably overnight.
5. Sprinkle with parsley and serve cold.

Makes 6 to 8 servings.

Cheese Salad with Endive

There are only a few months of the year when Belgian endive is not available in North America. This comes with its own vinaigrette and makes an excellent salad almost year-round.

6	Belgian endives	6
¼ lb	Bel Paese cheese, cubed*	125 g
⅓ cup	olive oil	75 ml
1 tbsp	lemon juice	15 ml
1 tbsp	red wine vinegar	15 ml
½ tsp	salt	2 ml
¼ tsp	freshly ground black pepper	1 ml
¼ tsp	dried oregano leaves	1 ml
	Italian parsley	

1. With a sharp knife, slice endive crosswise into 1-inch (2.5-cm) pieces. In a bowl, combine endive and cheese.
2. Combine oil, lemon juice, vinegar, salt, pepper and oregano; mix well. Pour over endive and cheese. Toss lightly. Divide evenly and spoon on to four salad plates.
   Garnish with sprigs of Italian parsley

Makes 4 servings.

* Fontina cheese may be substituted for Bel Paese, if desired.

Hint – Quick Winter Salad

Core and thinly slice an unpeeled pear along with sliced Parmesan on a bed of baby greens. Lace with a walnut vinaigrette.

Salad Romano (or Locarno?) with Tarragon Vinaigrette

I pose the question because this salad owes its personality to Swiss cheese. You can substitute an Italian cheese, but I find the Gruyère to be a perfect salad ingredient. This is a hearty year-round salad, and I find myself using it for parties in the snowy months, for the combination of mushrooms, celery and cheese give that nice stick-to-the-ribs consistency.

½ lb	Gruyère cheese, cut in julienne strips	250 g
2	stalks celery, thinly sliced	2
½ lb	fresh mushrooms, thinly sliced	250 g
¼ cup	chopped fresh parsley	50 ml
2 tbsp	Tarragon Vinaigrette	25 ml

1. In a large salad bowl, toss together cheese, celery, mushrooms and parsley. Pour Tarragon Vinaigrette on top; toss well.
2. Let stand 15 minutes before serving. Toss again.

Makes 6 servings.

Tarragon Vinaigrette

One of the most prized and surprising tastes in the world comes from tarragon. It is used for many things, especially for tarragon chicken and for flavoring salad dressing. Here's the definitive vinaigrette to round out your year-round dressings.

½ cup	chopped fresh parsley	125 ml
½ cup	olive oil	125 ml
⅓ cup	wine vinegar	75 ml
¼ cup	chopped capers	50 ml
1 tbsp	chopped fresh tarragon, or 1 tsp (5 ml) dried	15 ml
2 tsp	Dijon mustard	10 ml
2 tsp	salt	10 ml
1 tsp	freshly ground black pepper	5 ml
1	clove garlic, finely chopped	1
1 tsp	Worcestershire sauce	5 ml

1. In a jar with a tight-fitting lid, combine parsley, oil, vinegar, capers, tarragon, mustard, salt, pepper, garlic and Worcestershire sauce. Secure lid; shake well.
2. Store in refrigerator up to 2 weeks. Shake well before using.

Makes 1 cup (250 ml).

Mango Salad

Not a drop of oil in this recipe—which always tempts me to make a gooey chocolate cake for dessert. A refreshing palate cleanser, it's also a great way to ease the heat from Louisiana Cajun Shrimp. Don't be a snob about using iceberg lettuce; it's really the best for this salad.

1	iceberg lettuce, shredded	1
1	large, ripe mango	1
¼ cup	fresh cilantro, chopped	50 ml
	juice of 2 limes	
½ cup	chopped peanuts, roasted and lightly salted	125 ml

1. Divide lettuce among four plates.
2. Slice mango and toss with cilantro. Place on top of lettuce.
3. Sprinkle each salad with lime juice and peanuts.

Makes 4 servings.

Dilly Cucumbers and Red Onions

I make this salad frequently. My family likes it best when I drain off the marinade and fold in sour cream.

1	English cucumber, cut into ¼-inch (5-mm) slices	1
1	red onion, thinly sliced	1

Marinade

½ cup	white vinegar	125 ml
¼ cup	water	50 ml
¼ cup	granulated sugar	50 ml
2 tbsp	vegetable oil	25 ml
1 tbsp	chopped fresh dill, or 1 tsp (5 ml) dried dill weed	15 ml
1 tsp	salt	5 ml
¼ tsp	white pepper	1 ml

1. Combine cucumber and onion in a bowl.
2. In a small bowl, combine vinegar, water, sugar, oil, dill, salt and pepper. Pour over cucumber mixture; toss to coat thoroughly.
3. Chill for at least 2 hours, stirring occasionally.

Makes 4 to 6 servings.

Variation

Creamed Dill Cucumber and Onions: Thoroughly drain marinade from cucumber mixture, then fold in ½ cup (125 ml) sour cream or yogurt. Sprinkle with chopped dill to serve.

Dilly Onions: Double the onions and omit the cucumber. Serve with cheeses and breads.

Soups

Soups

Soup served from a large, elegant tureen gets a dinner or lunch off to a wonderfully intriguing start. When the lid comes off the tureen and the steam rises and fills the nostrils with rich and rare scents of vegetables, meats, and herbs, all kinds of memories are stimulated. If you are interested in antiques, spend a rainy day visiting the little antique stores in your town, where you can usually find one or two soup tureens for sale. If cooking and entertaining is your pleasure, even three or five tureens that take your fancy are not too many.

Hearty Soups

Thai Fish Soup
Corn and Crab Soup
Special Corn Chowder
Very Vegetable Soup
Beef Consommé Bordeaux
Minestrone Alla Genoese
Tuscan Bread Soup
Pear and Leek Soup
Smooth Pumpkin Soup with Dark Rum and Walnuts
Country Lentil Soup
Krupnik Soup

Chilled Soups

West Indies Avocado Soup
Chilled Persian Yogurt Soup
Soup for Summer
Zesty Summertime Soup
Gazpacho
Chilled Zucchini Soup

Thai Fish Soup

Show off with this simple recipe. Measure out the ingredients beforehand, then invite your friends into the kitchen for a glass of wine while you put it all together. The aromas will sharpen everyone's appetite. All you need to add for a hearty repast are bowls of steamed rice.

2 tbsp	vegetable oil	25 ml
3	cloves garlic, finely chopped	3
1	leek, white only, julienned	1
1 tbsp	finely chopped ginger root	15 ml
¼ tsp	hot pepper flakes	1 ml
1 tbsp	curry powder	15 ml
1	red pepper, julienned	1
1 cup	unsweetened coconut milk	250 ml
4	tomatoes, peeled, seeded and chopped	4
1 tsp	grated lemon rind	5 ml
3 cups	water	750 ml
2 tbsp	soy sauce	25 ml
	juice of ½ lemon	
1 lb	halibut or other white fish fillets, cut into chunks	500 g
½ lb	scallops	250 g
½ lb	shrimp, peeled, deveined, cut in half	250 g
¼ tsp	salt	1 ml
¼ tsp	pepper	1 ml
¼ cup	chopped cilantro	50 ml
2 tbsp each	chopped fresh basil, mint, chives	25 ml each

1. In large saucepan, heat oil over medium heat. Add garlic, leek, ginger and pepper flakes. Cook about 3 minutes or until softened but not browned.
2. Add curry powder; cook, stirring for 1 minute. Stir in red pepper, coconut milk, tomatoes and lemon rind. Bring to boil.

3. Add water, soy sauce and lemon juice. Bring to boil, reduce heat and simmer gently 15 minutes.
4. Add halibut, scallops, shrimp, salt and pepper. Cook gently 5 minutes or until fish is just cooked through.
5. In a small bowl, mix cilantro, basil, mint and chives. Divide herb mixture among soup bowls. Pour soup over herbs.

Makes 4 main course or 6 appetizer servings.

Corn and Crab Soup

This simple, classic recipe was handed down from my dear 90-year-old aunt, and yes, it does call for a canned product. But rest assured that the tastes of crab, ginger and corn are subtle and distinctive. Served with bowls of toasted almonds, it's one helluva soup with almost no effort.

1	can creamed corn (19 oz/540 ml)	1
1 cup	chicken stock	250 ml
½ lb	crab meat	250 g
2 tbsp	soy sauce	25 ml
1 tbsp	grated fresh ginger	15 ml
¼ tsp	sesame oil	1 ml

1. In a large saucepan, combine corn, chicken stock, crab, soy sauce, ginger and sesame oil. Bring to a boil, lower heat and simmer 10 minutes. Serve immediately.

Makes 4 servings.

Special Corn Chowder

This recipe started with our driving to and from the summer cottage with an eye on the fields of farmers' corn. When the corn was as high as an elephant's eye, it would go on sale by the roadside, and I always purchased far too much. So I made corn chowder with the excess. At first I had to recruit friends to help me shuck the corn. Now they phone up to ask when I'm making it and can they help!

6	cobs corn (2 cups/500 ml of kernels)	6
¼ lb	slab bacon, chopped	125 g
1 tbsp	sweet butter	15 ml
2	stalks celery, finely chopped	2
1	medium onion, finely chopped	1
1	medium potato, peeled and diced	1
4 cups	chicken stock	1 l
¼ cup	all-purpose flour	50 ml
¼ tsp	white pepper	1 ml
2 cups	milk	500 ml
1 cup	heavy or whipping cream	250 ml

1. With a sharp knife, cut kernels from corn cobs; set them aside.
2. In a large saucepan, heat bacon and butter. Cook, stirring about 4 minutes, until fat renders from bacon.
3. Add celery, onion and potato. Sauté about 7 minutes, until potato is tender.
4. Stir in corn kernels. Stir and cook 2 minutes longer.
5. Add stock, bring to a boil, reduce heat, and simmer for about 40 minutes.
6. Combine flour, pepper, and ½ cup (125 ml) milk; stir until smooth. Gradually pour into corn mixture, stirring until mixture begins to thicken. Stir in remaining milk and cream.
7. Heat to warm through, but do not boil.
   Soup freezes well before or after the addition of milk and cream.

Makes 12 cups (3 l).

Very Vegetable Soup

This is the fastest vegetable soup recipe I've ever used, and yet it has a great look and a taste that says you slaved over it for hours.

5	carrots, finely chopped	5
4	stalks celery with leaves, finely chopped	4
2	onions, finely chopped	2
2	cobs fresh sweet corn, kernels removed	2
4 cups	chicken stock	1 l
1	can (28 oz/796 ml) Italian tomatoes	1
1 tsp	salt	5 ml
½ tsp	freshly ground black pepper	2 ml
½ tsp	dried oregano	2 ml

1. In a large saucepan, combine carrots, celery, onion, corn, stock, tomatoes, salt, pepper and oregano.
2. Bring to a boil, reduce heat, and simmer, stirring occasionally to break up tomatoes, for 45 minutes, until vegetables are tender.
3. Ladle into warm soup bowls and serve.

Makes 4 to 6 servings.

Beef Consommé Bordeaux

This rich beef consommé is like the Vin du Pays: deep, dark and spicy. The spice comes from the cinnamon, which is unusual in a soup and particularly interesting. Float the egg whites on the top of each bowl and garnish with chopped chives.

4 cups	clear beef stock or consommé	1 l
1	cinnamon stick, 1-inch (2.5-cm) long	
1 cup	dry red wine	250 ml
1 cup	boiling water	250 ml
2	eggs, separated	2
½ tsp	salt	2 ml
¼ tsp	freshly ground black pepper	1 ml
pinch	cayenne	pinch
	chopped chives	

1. In a large saucepan, heat broth; add cinnamon stick. Bring to a boil, reduce heat, and simmer 5 minutes.
2. Stir in red wine and boiling water; simmer 5 minutes longer.
3. In a small bowl, lightly beat egg yolks.
4. In another bowl, beat egg whites until stiff.
5. Remove cinnamon stick and pour yolks slowly into broth, stirring constantly. Season with salt, pepper and cayenne.
6. Ladle immediately into warmed bouillon cups. Float a dollop of beaten egg white on each serving, and sprinkle with chopped chives.

Makes 6 servings.

Minestrone Alla Genoese

From the great northern Italian seaport of Genoa comes this meal-in-a-pot soup. Serve it to your guests late at night or in combination with a simple salad and plenty of Italian bread. It's packed with macaroni, beans, spinach and other veggies and looks really Picassoesque in a bowl. Pass the pepper mill when you serve.

2 tbsp	olive oil	25 ml
4	medium carrots, grated	4
4	medium potatoes, diced	4
2	medium onions, coarsely chopped	2
2	leeks, thinly sliced	2
2 cups	shredded raw spinach	500 ml
6 cups	beef stock	1.5 l
1	can (19 oz/540 ml) Italian plum tomatoes	1
3 cups	cooked kidney beans	750 ml
1 to 2 tsp	salt	5 to 10 ml
¼ tsp	freshly ground black pepper	1 ml
¼ cup	chopped fresh parsley	50 ml
½ tsp	dried basil leaves	2 ml
½ tsp	dried oregano leaves	2 ml
2	cloves garlic, finely chopped	2
4	slices bacon, chopped	4
1½ cups	macaroni	375 ml
	grated Parmesan cheese	

1. In a large soup kettle, heat oil. Add carrots, potatoes, onions, leeks and spinach; cook over medium heat 5 minutes, until onions are limp.
2. Stir in stock, tomatoes, beans, salt and pepper. Bring to a boil, reduce heat, cover, and simmer 1 hour, until potatoes are tender.
3. In a blender or food processor, combine parsley, basil, oregano, garlic and bacon. Purée about 2 minutes, until a paste forms. Stir into soup.

4. Add macaroni. Bring to a boil, reduce heat, cover and simmer 15 minutes, or until macaroni is tender.
   Serve with grated Parmesan cheese.

Makes 12 servings, about 20 cups (5 l).

Hint – There is a special way to shuck corn which I've developed over the years. Pinch the leaves and the cornsilk firmly together and pull down to the stem. But don't try to take too much at once or you won't get a nice clean strip. And try not to let your guests become too competitive over the number of ears they shuck. Quality, not quantity, is what you are after. Of course, you could establish a prize for the cleanest 20 ears.

Friends who have watched my rather slow process of removing kernels from the cobs with a small, hard-edged knife, have searched the world of kitchen technology for a better way. I have a drawer full of these devices—everything from a tiny, complicated lathe to what looks like a simple paint scraper. None do the job as well as a knife, but then maybe that's because I'm used to it.

Tuscan Bread Soup

My friend Ethel brought this recipe back from a trattoria in Florence —and now it's mine. I make batches of it in August when the summer tomatoes are crying out to be used. Defrosting it is the thrill of the month come November. This is a soup that improves with age, so if you can resist, let it sit for a day or two before serving. Then warn your friends and family that the garlic gives it a real punch. Garnish with a few slices of thinly sliced Parmesan and an extra twist of the pepper mill. It makes good use of bread ends, so start popping them into the freezer from now on.

1 tbsp	olive oil	15 ml
1	small onion, chopped	1
5	large cloves garlic, crushed	5
7	large ripe fresh tomatoes, peeled and quartered	7
3 tbsp	tomato paste	40 ml
⅛ tsp	cayenne pepper	5 ml
2 tbsp	coarsely chopped fresh basil	25 ml
1 lb	day-old bread (rye, whole wheat) cubed	500 g
5 cups	chicken stock	1.25 l
½ tsp	salt	2 ml
¼ tsp	freshly ground black pepper	1 ml

1. In a large pot, heat oil and sauté onion and garlic about 10 minutes until soft but not brown.
2. Add tomatoes, tomato paste and cayenne and simmer 20 minutes.
3. Add basil, bread, stock, salt and pepper. Simmer 10 to 15 minutes, stirring occasionally to break up the bread.
4. Spoon into soup bowls and serve.

Makes 4 to 6 servings.

Pear and Leek Soup

I refused to leave my friend Michaela's kitchen until I got this recipe.

⅓ cup	sweet butter	75 ml
3 cups	sliced leeks	750 ml
4	pears, peeled, cored and coarsely chopped	4
6 cups	chicken stock	1.5 l
1 tsp	ground savory	5 ml
¼ tsp	white pepper	1 ml
1 tbsp	lemon juice	15 ml
1	pear, peeled, cored and sliced	
	blue cheese	

1. In a large saucepan, heat butter. Add leeks; sauté 10 minutes, until softened.
2. Add chopped pears, chicken stock, savory and pepper. Bring to a boil, reduce heat, and simmer 20 minutes, until pears are softened. Stir in lemon juice.
3. In batches, purée in blender or food processor, until smooth.
   Soup may be served hot or cold. If serving hot, return to saucepan and heat through. If serving cold, pour into large bowl and chill.
   Garnish with pear slices and crumbled blue cheese.

Makes 8 servings.

At Thanksgiving, bundle up tall cornstalks and surround them with pumpkins, bushels of apples, and clusters of bittersweet. Make one of these displays especially large and impressive and put it just outside the front door to let your guests know they're in for a treat.

Smooth Pumpkin Soup with Dark Rum and Walnuts

I have a garden full of pumpkins and squash, so I have plenty on hand year-round in my freezer. One of my favorite ways to serve them is in this creamy, delicious, slightly tipsy soup, and my favorite time of year is just before Halloween, when the frost is on the pumpkins. This is an elegant soup to precede a holiday dinner.

¼ cup	finely chopped walnuts	50 ml
⅓ cup	sweet butter	75 ml
¼ cup	all-purpose flour	50 ml
1 tsp	salt	5 ml
½ tsp	white pepper	2 ml
pinch	cinnamon	pinch
3 cups	milk	750 ml
2 cups	mashed or puréed cooked pumpkin or squash	500 ml
⅓ cup	heavy or whipping cream	75 ml
2 tbsp	dark rum	25 ml

1. Place walnuts on a baking sheet. Toast in a 350°F (180°C) oven for about 5 minutes.
2. In a large saucepan, melt butter; stir in flour, salt, pepper and cinnamon until blended. Gradually add milk, whisking constantly until mixture is smooth.
3. Bring to a boil and cook, whisking, until mixture is thickened.
4. Whisk in pumpkin and cream. Cook about 2 minutes longer to heat through. Stir in rum.
5. Ladle into hot soup bowls. Garnish with toasted chopped walnuts.

Makes 6 to 8 servings.

Country Lentil Soup

This meal-in-a-bowl combines vegetables, grains and protein in one dish. And with its crouton topping bubbling with baked cheese, it will bring back fond memories of your French onion soup days.

1 cup	dried lentils	250 ml
6 cups	chicken stock	1.5 l
2	slices bacon	2
2 tbsp	olive oil	25 ml
1	onion, chopped	1
2	cloves garlic, finely chopped	2
1	stalk celery, diced	1
2 tbsp	finely chopped fresh parsley	25 ml
3	tomatoes, peeled and chopped	3
½ tsp	salt	2 ml
½ tsp	pepper	2 ml
½ cup	short tubular pasta	125 ml
2 tbsp	butter	25 ml
6	slices bread, cut into desired shape	6
¾ cup	Romano cheese, freshly grated	175 ml

1. Rinse lentils and place in a large heavy-bottomed pot. Cover with stock and bring to a boil. Reduce heat and simmer for 30 to 40 minutes, until lentils are tender.
2. Meanwhile, in a large skillet, cook bacon. Add olive oil, onion, garlic, celery and parsley. Cook, stirring 15 minutes until onions are golden. Stir into cooked lentils.
3. Stir in tomatoes, salt, pepper and pasta; simmer 10 to 12 minutes until pasta is al dente.
4. In a skillet over moderate heat, melt butter. Cook bread slices 2 minutes on each side until golden brown.
5. Ladle soup into ovenproof bowls and top each with croutons and 2 tbsp (25 ml) cheese. Place under broiler for 2 minutes until cheese is melted.

Makes 6 servings.

Krupnik Soup

A comforting soup to come home to after an invigorating day in the country. The barley, mushrooms and diced potatoes go well with a sandwich of tangy cheese and crisp apple slices.

⅔ cup	pearl barley	150 ml
8 cups	water	2 l
1 tsp	salt	5 ml
3 tbsp	sweet butter	50 ml
1	onion, diced	1
1	red potato, diced	1
8 oz	mushrooms, sliced	250 g
4 oz	Shitake mushrooms, sliced	125 g
4 tsp	chopped fresh thyme	20 ml
¼ tsp	freshly ground black pepper	1 ml

1. Wash barley and place in large saucepan. Cover with water and salt and bring to boil. Reduce heat and simmer for 2 hours, until tender.
2. Meanwhile, in a frying pan, heat butter. Add onion, potato, and mushrooms and cook 10 minutes, until tender.
3. Stir the vegetables into the barley and add 2 tsp (10 ml) of the thyme and pepper and simmer for another 10 minutes.
4. Ladle into hot soup bowls and serve, garnishing with the remaining thyme.

Makes 8 servings.

Hint – To get the smell of onions off your hands, rub them with a little ground coffee. (Better to smell of coffee than of onions!)

West Indies Avocado Soup

No cooking. Quick and easy. Doesn't that say summer? I'll wager none of your guests will figure out the combination of ingredients that give this soup its mysterious appeal. Decorate each bowl with a thin slice of lime.

1	ripe avocado	1
2 cups	chicken stock	500 ml
1 cup	light or table cream	250 ml
2 tbsp	white rum	25 ml
½ tsp	curry powder	2 ml
½ tsp	salt	2 ml
	juice of 1 lime	
pinch	white pepper	pinch

1. Peel avocado and cut into pieces.
2. In a blender or food processor, combine avocado, stock, cream, rum, curry powder, salt, lime juice and white pepper. Process 1 to 2 minutes, until smooth and creamy.
3. Chill 1 hour before serving.

Makes 4 servings.

Chilled Persian Yogurt Soup

The shredded cucumber is what makes this soup so interesting. Serve the garnishes separately so everyone can reinvent their own dish. With side dishes of grated hard-boiled egg, dill, mint, pistachios or walnuts, this soup will get a lazy Sunday lunch off to an entertaining start.

4 cups	plain yogurt	1 l
1 cup	buttermilk	250 ml
1 cup	chicken stock	250 ml
1	English cucumber, peeled, seeded and grated	1
¾ cup	seedless raisins	175 ml
2	cloves garlic, finely chopped	2
¼ tsp	salt	1 ml
¼ tsp	freshly ground black pepper	1 ml
1 tbsp	coarsely chopped mint	15 ml
1 tbsp	coarsely chopped dill	15 ml
2	eggs, hard-boiled, peeled and crumbled	2
1 cup	pistachios, toasted and coarsely chopped	250 ml

1. Whisk together yogurt, buttermilk and stock until smooth.
2. Add cucumber, raisins, garlic, salt and pepper and refrigerate at least 1 hour.
3. Pour into chilled bowls and have guests garnish their own soup with mint, dill, eggs and pistachios.

Makes 8 servings.

Soup for Summer

The world's fastest soup—a cup, a cup, a cup and it's done. The tiniest dollop of unsweetened whipped cream, a quick zest of orange rind and you're ready for anything, from a blistering hot day to a wedding banquet. Have some more fun by challenging your friends to guess the ingredients.

2 cups	orange juice	500 ml
2 cups	tomato juice	500 ml
2 cups	white wine	500 ml

In a pitcher, mix orange juice, tomato juice and white wine. Chill for at least 1 hour. Serve cold.

Makes 8 servings.

Zesty Summertime Soup

Sort of a sophisticated gazpacho. The buttermilk tends to tone it down to an inviting pink.

4	green onions, cut into pieces	4
1	green pepper, seeded and coarsely chopped	1
1	small cucumber, peeled, seeded and cut into chunks	1
1 cup	tomato juice	250 ml
2 cups	buttermilk	500 ml
½ tsp	Worcestershire sauce	2 ml
few dashes	hot pepper sauce	few dashes

1. In a blender or food processor, combine onions, half the pepper, cucumber and tomato juice; process 1 to 2 minutes, until smooth and puréed. Pour into a refrigerator container.
2. Stir in buttermilk, Worcestershire and hot pepper sauce.
3. Chill at least 2 hours, or until ready to serve. Serve in chilled soup bowls. Garnish with remaining green pepper, diced.

Makes 5 cups (1.25 l).

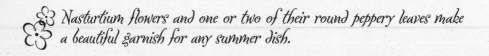 *Nasturtium flowers and one or two of their round peppery leaves make a beautiful garnish for any summer dish.*

Gazpacho

I serve this Spanish classic in a tall glass with a dash of vodka for zip. It's sort of my own version of the Bloody Mary. This is also the way Chef Rademacher of Lausanne serves it to her Swiss clientele. If the group you've got coming is a little standoffish, consider retaining the dash of vodka and serve this in a bowl.

5	medium ripe tomatoes, peeled, seeded and coarsely chopped	5
3	cloves garlic	3
3	slices bread, crusts removed and cubed	3
1	cucumber, peeled, seeded and coarsely chopped	1
1	green pepper, seeded and coarsely chopped	1
2 cups	tomato juice	500 ml
2 cups	water	500 ml
¼ cup	olive oil	50 ml
1 tsp	salt	5 ml
few dashes	hot pepper sauce	few dashes
	freshly ground black pepper	
	diced cucumber, avocado and green pepper	

1. In batches in a food processor, combine tomatoes, garlic, bread, cucumber, green pepper, tomato juice, water, olive oil and vinegar. Process until puréed. Season with salt, pepper and hot pepper sauce.
2. Pour into container, cover and chill at least 1 hour until serving time.
3. Garnish with diced cucumber, avocado and green pepper.

Makes 9 cups (2.25 l).

Chilled Zucchini Soup

My friends call this my summertime soup, and it must be served well chilled. I use my most colorful bowls as background for the pale green soup and float snipped chives on the top.

⅓ cup	sweet butter	75 ml
1 lb	zucchini (4 medium), thickly sliced	500 g
1	medium onion, coarsely chopped	1
1	clove garlic, coarsely chopped	1
1 to 2 tsp	curry powder	5 to 10 ml
1 tsp	ground cumin	5 ml
½ tsp	salt	2 ml
2 cups	chicken stock	500 ml
3 cups	buttermilk	750 ml
	paprika	

1. In a large saucepan, heat butter. Add zucchini, onion and garlic; sauté for 15 minutes.
2. Stir in curry powder, cumin and salt. Cook 5 minutes longer, or until zucchini is softened. Stir in chicken stock.
3. In batches, purée mixture until smooth in a food processor or blender.
4. Pour into a large bowl. Stir in buttermilk. Chill.
5. Serve in chilled bowls or mugs. Garnish with a sprinkling of paprika.

Makes 6 servings.

Main Courses

Main Courses

It can be a sitdown, formal dinner with the elegance of the opera. It can be a buffet in the kitchen. It can be an outdoor barbecue with anything from grilled salmon to a Sloppy Joe. It can be your finest china and crystal or gaily painted pottery and beer steins. It can be a night at the symphony with beautifully blended and harmonized dishes or a potluck dinner in the country that is like a farmers' fair. It can be anything your imagination runs to. The thing to concentrate on is how you feel, what kind of dinner you want to put together, and then plan your dishes to carry the event. How are you to dress your dishes? In a sizzling copper pan, direct from the heat? Floating on a platter of rich sauce and vegetables? In an elaborate casserole? It is so exciting, the possibilities so endless, that you almost don't know where to start.

Fish and Seafood

Gingered Fish Oriental
Fillet of Sole East Indian
Cold Sole with Orange, Lime and Green Pepper Rings
Cod with Saffron
Swordfish with Tomato and Onion Relish
Grilled Curried Mahi Mahi
Roast Sesame Salmon Fillets
Sake Salmon Steaks
Sophisticated Salmon Patties or Salmon Loaf
Gingered Scallops in Lettuce Leaf
Bay Scallops with Hot and Sweet Red Pepper
Shrimps in Lobster Sauce
Gon-Bow Shrimps (Shrimps with Hot Sauce)
Szechwan Garlic Prawns
Spicy Sweet Grilled Shrimp
Naked Shrimp Thai
Louisiana Cajun Shrimp
Tandoori Shrimp
Sour Cream Jumbo Shrimp Curry
Crabcakes with Chili Mayo and Citrus Salsa

Chicken

Chicken in Black Bean Sauce
Chinese One-Pot Supper
Mahogany Chicken Wings with Parsnip Chips
Chicken with Oranges and Hot Chili Peppers
Ginger Chicken with Sweet Red Peppers and Cashews
Stir-Fried Chicken with Walnuts
Chinese Lemon Chicken
General Tsao's Chicken
Chinese Roast Chicken
Mediterranean Chicken with Dried Fruit and Couscous
Jerk Wings with "Cool-Down" Apricot Tamarind Sauce
Caribbean Chicken with Dark Rum
Chicken Provencal
Chicken Saag
Plum Sauce Chicken Breasts
Poulet aux Deux Moutardes
Chicken Diable
Minted Chicken Breasts
Grilled Chicken with Apple and Rosemary
Crisp Baked Almond Chicken
Pecan Chicken with Red Pepper Coulis
Sesame Baked Chicken
Chicken Fingers with Three Dipping Sauces
Chicken Burgers or Chicken Loaf

Beef

Fillet Roast of Beef with Pepper Sauce
Rare Beef Tenderloin in Oyster Sauce
Oriental Beef Shishkebabs
Cabbage Rolls
Brisket in Ginger Ale
German Pot Roast
French Country Meatloaf

Lamb

Spicy Lamb Chops in a Tomato Rosemary Marinade
Indian Lamb Chops in a Snappy Yogurt Marinade
Lamb Calcutta
Lamb Tajine
Swedish Lamb Roast
Lamb Basted
Barbequed Butterfly Lamb
Lamb Burgers or Lamb Loaf

Pork

Tiffany's Barbecued Ribs
Chinese Barbequed Wings and Ribs with Orange
Ginger Pork Cubes
Peanut Pork Satay
Canadian Bacon with Raisin Glaze
Tourtiere or French Canadian Meat Pie

Veal

Sweetbreads au Porto
Veal and Mushroom Ragout

Fish and Seafood

My home town is on a lake. I often envy my friends who live on the Atlantic or Pacific coasts and have all that freshly caught seafood at their command. On the other hand, you probably have good fresh fish stores dotted around your city. So if your nose is good and you know what to sniff for, you can achieve some really good fish dishes to dazzle your guests.

I find that fish dishes on their own are partyish, but if you want to do honor to old King Neptune with some special decorations, you can fill large shells with the salt and pepper. Another trick is to use what I call beach flowers for your table: anemones or big African daisies. Use the anemones for the vibrant blues and purples and reds, the daisies for the pastels. Mixed together, they are striking. You can drape your rooms with ropes and add bollards to the decor.

Notes

Gingered Fish Oriental

This fish looks just great intact on a platter. It can marinate all day if you wish and will improve with every passing moment. Once cooked, the meat drops away easily from the bones. Serve it covered with lots of stir-fried Chinese vegetables and a mass of soft Japanese noodles strewn with cilantro. Serve a fruity Sauvignon Blanc or an Alsatian Gewurtztraminer. A well-hopped Pilsener or a Dortmunder lager will stand up well to the spiciness

1	whole snapper (4 to 5 lbs/2 to 2.5 kg) with head or any fresh fish	1
¼ cup	light soy sauce	50 ml
¼ cup	sesame oil	50 ml
¼ cup	dry sherry	50 ml
2 tbsp	grated fresh ginger root	25 ml
⅛ tsp	crushed red pepper flakes	0.5 ml
3	cloves garlic, finely chopped	3
4	green onion brushes*	4

1. Place fish in a large shallow baking dish. Combine soy sauce, sesame oil, sherry, ginger root, red pepper and garlic. Pour over fish, cover tightly with foil, and marinate in refrigerator 4 hours, turning once.
2. Preheat oven to 350°F (180°C).
3. Bake fish in marinade (still covered) for 45 minutes, or until it flakes easily with a fork. Garnish with green onion brushes.

Makes 6 to 8 servings.

* To make green onion brushes: Wash green onions. Trim off root end and enough green to leave a 4-inch (10-cm) piece. At about 1-inch (2.5-cm) from ends, cut lengthwise slits in both ends. Put green onions in ice water and place in refrigerator for 30 minutes to allow cut ends to spread.

Fillet of Sole East Indian

When you look at the myriad recipes the East Indians have for fish, you begin to realize how much ocean surrounds the Subcontinent and how many rivers, besides the Ganges and the Shalimar, run through it. This is a mild little dish with lots of personality, and can be served with Indian Rice and oodles of chutneys, fresh fruits and chopped onions.

1 lb	sole fillets	500 g
2 tbsp	melted sweet butter	25 ml
1 tsp	curry powder	5 ml
½ tsp	ground cumin	2 ml
½ tsp	salt	2 ml
¼ tsp	freshly ground black pepper	1 ml
2	limes, rind and juice	2
½ cup	dry white wine	125 ml

Sauce

2 tbsp	sweet butter	25 ml
20	medium mushrooms, thinly sliced	20
1	shallot, finely chopped	1
2 tbsp	all-purpose flour	25 ml
¼ tsp	dry mustard	1 ml
¼ cup	milk	50 ml
¼ cup	light or table cream	50 ml

1. In a bowl, combine melted butter, curry powder, cumin, salt, pepper, lime rind and juice. Dip sole fillets into butter mixture.
2. Place sole in a large skillet. Pour wine over sole. Bring to a boil, reduce heat, and poach gently for 5 minutes, or until fish flakes easily with a fork.
3. Place sole in a shallow baking dish in a single layer. Reserve poaching liquid; set aside.
4. Preheat oven to 350°F (180°C).

5. Melt butter in a saucepan; add mushrooms and shallots; sauté about 2 minutes.
6. Stir in flour and mustard. Whisk in milk, cream and ½ cup (125 ml) poaching liquid. Cook, stirring, over medium heat about 5 minutes, until thickened.
7. Pour over sole. Bake for 20 minutes, until sauce is bubbly.
   Garnish with lime slices and chopped chives.

Makes 4 servings.

This mild curry requires something simple—a sweet white such as Orvieto Abbocato or Australian Traminer Riesling

---

Hint – The seated dinner party is probably the most satisfying form of entertaining. It appeals to all senses and produces that glowing spirit of goodwill which is the aim of social gatherings. Candles are the most beautiful lighting you can use, but be sure that they supply adequate lighting. If the room is poorly lit, it gives an aura of gloom. Besides, people like to see what they are eating.

Cold Sole with Orange, Lime and Green Pepper Rings

The orange, lime and green pepper rings make this a most attractive summer dinner plate, and it is also a natural for a buffet menu, as the longer it sits the better it gets.

6	small fillets of sole	6
¼ cup	sweet butter	50 ml
¾ cup	vegetable oil	175 ml
	flour for dredging	
1 tsp	salt	5 ml
	freshly ground black pepper	
1	medium onion, thinly sliced and separated into rings	1
1	clove garlic, finely chopped	1
1	medium green pepper, sliced into thin rings	1

Dressing

½ cup	orange juice	125 ml
	juice of 2 limes	
¼ tsp	hot pepper sauce	1 ml
½ tsp	salt	2 ml
¼ tsp	freshly ground black pepper	1 ml

Garnish

	orange slices	
	lime slices	
1 tbsp	grated orange rind	15 ml

1. In a large skillet over medium heat, heat butter and 2 tbsp (25 ml) oil. Coat fish with flour and sauté until browned on both sides. Season with salt and pepper.

2. Arrange fillets on a platter. Garnish with onion rings, garlic and green pepper rings.
3. In a small bowl, combine orange juice, lime juice, hot pepper sauce, salt and pepper. Pour over warm fish.
4. Cover and refrigerate 12 to 24 hours.
5. Garnish with orange and lime slices and orange rind at serving time.

Makes 6 servings.

The acid and herbal notes of the citrus and peppers in this dish go well with a crisp Fumé Blanc from California or a nice Sauvignon Blanc from France.

Hint – Star Anise – This pungent licorice-flavored dried fruit comes from a tree in the Magnolia family. Add whole stars to any spiced, braised dishes, to hot fruit or wine punch, creamed soup (add during last 15 minutes of cooking), to the liquid used for cooking rice, or to stud a roasted ham.

Cod with Saffron

This can work with haddock, halibut, or, as called for here, that old North Atlantic standby—freshly caught cod. Use a big skillet and thrill to how saffron threads will color and flavor a dish in moments. Serve hot with finely chopped onions, chopped and seeded tomatoes, a pepper mill, and your favorite rice, to absorb the wonderful sauce.

2 lb	cod fillets (½-inch/1-cm thick)	1 kg
¼ cup	olive oil	50 ml
2 tbsp	chopped fresh parsley	25 ml
2 tbsp	lemon juice	25 ml
2 tsp	all-purpose flour	10 ml
1 tsp	salt	5 ml
½ tsp	saffron threads	2 ml
¼ tsp	freshly ground black pepper	1 ml
1	clove garlic, finely chopped	1
½ cup	hot water	125 ml
1	small onion, finely chopped	1
1	tomato, peeled, seeded and coarsely chopped	1
	freshly ground black pepper	

1. In a large skillet off the heat, combine oil, parsley, lemon juice, flour, salt, saffron, pepper and garlic; mix well. Add cod fillets, turning over in the mixture to coat with the seasonings.
2. Place skillet over low heat; cover and cook about 5 minutes, until top surface of cod turns white.
3. Turn fillets over and pour hot water over top. Bring to a boil and cook 1 minute longer, until fish flakes easily with a fork.
4. Remove from heat and serve. Garnish with chopped onion, tomato and pepper.

Makes 6 servings.

Swordfish with Tomato and Onion Relish

I always use blood oranges in the relish to heighten the vivid colors of this dish. If you have them, use dishes and platters in turquoise and green to keep the ocean theme alive. Classically served with a dry Sauvignon Blanc.

4	swordfish fillets (1-inch/2.5-cm thick)	4

Marinade

1 tbsp	shallots, finely chopped	15 ml
¼ cup	red wine	50 ml
	juice of 1 orange	
½ cup	vegetable oil	125 ml

Relish

2 tbsp	dark brown sugar	25 ml
	juice of 3 oranges and rind of 1	
½ cup	red wine vinegar	
3	oranges, peeled, seeded and sectioned	3
3	tomatoes, peeled, seeded and chopped	3
1	small red onion, finely chopped	1

1. In a shallow baking dish, place swordfish in a single layer.
2. In a small bowl, combine shallots, red wine, orange juice and oil. Pour over the fish; cover and refrigerate at least 4 hours.,
3. In a small saucepan over low heat, combine sugar, orange juice, rind and vinegar. Cook about 10 minutes until the sauce is reduced to about ½ cup (125 ml).
4. Add the oranges, tomatoes, onion and cook another 20 minutes. Set aside.
5. Preheat grill to high. Remove fish from marinade, reserving marinade. Brush the cooking surface with oil. Grill swordfish about 4 to 6 minutes per side, brushing with marinade, until firm. Serve with the relish.

Makes 4 servings.

Grilled Curried Mahi Mahi

Serve on a bed of spicy greens, spinach and kale to complement the curry rub on the fish, and take the opportunity to display all the tropical party souvenirs you've ever picked up. Note that swordfish can be substituted for the mahi mahi. This requires a Sauvignon Blanc with a rich lemony flavor. For more adventurous guests, serve an Alsatian Gewurtztraminer.

| 4 | mahi mahi or swordfish fillets (1-inch/2.5-cm thick) | 4 |

Red Onion Salsa

1	red onion, thinly sliced	1
	juice of 3 limes	
1 tsp	sugar	50 ml
¼ cup	chopped cilantro	250 ml

Curry Mixture

1½ tsp	cumin	8 ml
1½ tsp	paprika	8 ml
¾ tsp	ground coriander	4 ml
¾ tsp	ground ginger	4 ml
½ tsp	salt	2 ml
¼ tsp	turmeric	1 ml
¼ tsp	dry mustard	1 ml
pinch	cayenne pepper	pinch

1. Preheat grill to high.
2. In a medium bowl, combine red onion, lime juice, sugar and cilantro. Let stand 30 minutes.
3. In a small bowl, combine ingredients for curry mixture.
4. Rub curry on both sides of fish. Grill fish 4 to 6 minutes per side or until firm. Serve with Red Onion Salsa.

Makes 4 servings.

Roast Sesame Salmon Fillets

Black and white sesame seeds put a sparkle on this dish for any occasion. I serve it hot with braised red cabbage and leeks with star anise, or at room temperature with Indonesian Rice Salad. Serve either a good quality Burgundy or a fruity California Chardonnay from the Napa or Sonoma Valleys.

6	skinless salmon fillets (1-inch/2.5-cm thick)	6
2 tbsp	soy sauce	25 ml
2 tbsp	sesame oil	25 ml
2 tbsp	honey	25 ml
2	cloves garlic, finely chopped	2
2 tbsp	finely chopped fresh ginger	25 ml
¼ tsp	freshly ground black pepper	1 ml
½ cup	sesame seeds, toasted*	125 ml
1 tsp	coarse sea salt	5 ml
2 tbsp	olive oil	25 ml

1. In a medium bowl, combine soy sauce, sesame oil, honey, garlic, ginger and pepper. Pat salmon dry and rub mixture into salmon. Place on a platter and let stand 30 minutes.
2. Preheat oven to 450°F (230°C).
3. Remove salmon from marinade and coat with sesame seeds; season with salt.
4. In a non-stick, ovenproof skillet, heat oil. Add salmon; cook 1 minute and turn; cook 1 minute longer.
5. Immediately transfer pan to oven and roast 5 to 7 minutes, or until fish flakes with a fork.

Makes 6 servings.

*For maximum effect, use ¼ cup (50 ml) black sesame seeds and ¼ cup (50 ml) white sesame seeds.

Sake Salmon Steaks

This is a favorite of mine for barbecuing. Leave it on for 8 minutes per inch if you like it charred on the outside and rare on the inside. Make sure to marinade overnight so the incredible flavors penetrate right through the fish. Accompanied by sushi rice and a side salad of crunchy cucumbers, it's a party dish in minutes. Swordfish and tuna steaks can easily be substituted. Use dry white vermouth if you're low on sake.

4	salmon steaks (1-inch/2.5-cm thick)	4
¼ cup	soy sauce	50 ml
¼ cup	sake	50 ml
¼ cup	mirin or dry sherry	50 ml
2	cloves garlic, finely chopped	2
1	green onion, finely chopped	1
1 tbsp	finely chopped fresh ginger root	15 ml
1 tbsp	wasabi powder	15 ml
1 tsp	brown sugar	5 ml

1. In a small bowl, combine soy sauce, sake, mirin, garlic, green onions, ginger, wasabi and sugar. Mix well.
2. Place fish in a shallow baking dish and pour marinade over. Cover and marinate in refrigerator overnight.
3. Preheat grill.
4. Remove fish from marinade, reserving marinade and place on a grill. Grill 8 minutes, turning once.
5. Remove and serve with heated marinade.

Makes 4 servings.

The savory intense flavors marry well with a crisp New World Fumé Blanc or Sauvignon Blanc.

Sophisticated Salmon Patties or Salmon Loaf

I advise using a skillet when you make the burgers. Somehow the barbecue does not do justice to the combined flavors of fresh and smoked salmon. For the perfect brunch dish, top each pattie with a freshly poached egg.

2 cups	flaked, cooked, fresh salmon	500 ml
¼ lb	smoked salmon, coarsely chopped	125 g
¾ cup	mashed potatoes (2 medium)	175 g
1	small onion, finely chopped	1
1 tbsp	chopped fresh parsley	15 ml
1 tbsp	fresh lemon juice	15 ml
1 tbsp	chopped fresh dill, or 1 tsp (5 ml) dried	15 ml
¼ tsp	freshly ground black pepper	1 ml
1	egg, slightly beaten	1
¼ cup	light cream	50 ml
2 tbsp	sweet butter	25 ml

1. In a large bowl, combine fresh and smoked salmon, potatoes, onion, parsley, lemon juice, dill and pepper.
2. Combine egg and cream; stir into salmon mixture; mix well.
3. Divide into four portions and shape into burgers with hands.
4. In a large skillet, heat butter and add burgers; cook, turning once, for 8 to 10 minutes, until golden brown.

Makes 4 patties

Variation: Salmon Loaf

1. Preheat oven to 350°F (180°C).
2. Substitute ½ cup (250 ml) fine breadcrumbs for the mashed potatoes. Make salmon mixture. With hands shape it into loaf, about 8x5x3 inches (20x12x7.5 cm). Place in center of a baking pan. Bake in oven for 30 minutes, until firm and golden brown. Serve hot or cold.

Makes 1 loaf.

Gingered Scallops in Lettuce Leaf

Keep this in mind as an after-theater supper. The delicate flavor of the scallops comes through the understated marinade, even at room temperature. And it looks fabulous with its bright orange rinds and white scallops tied up with green chives and nestled in scarlet radicchio cups. A California Chenin Blanc, a French Gewurtztraminer, or a Hermitage Blanc from the Rhône will highlight this dish.

2 lb	sea scallops, rinsed and dried	1 kg
1 cup	orange juice	250 ml
¼ cup	finely chopped fresh ginger	50 ml
2 tbsp	soy sauce	25 ml
2 tbsp	sesame oil, plus more for cooking	25 ml
¾ tsp	freshly ground black pepper	3 ml
16	radicchio leaves	12
	rind of one orange	
2 tbsp	chives, finely chopped or whole, for making bundles	25 ml

1. In a large bowl, combine orange juice, ginger, soy sauce, oil and pepper. Add scallops and toss to coat well. Cover and marinate for 2 hours.
2. Remove scallops from marinade with slotted spoon. Reserve marinade.
3. In a large skillet over medium heat, heat 1 tsp (5 ml) sesame oil. Add a single layer of scallops. Cook until brown, about 2 minutes on each side. Place in a shallow dish.
4. Repeat until all scallops are cooked, wiping and re-oiling pan between batches.
5. In a small saucepan, bring reserved marinade to a boil. Reduce heat and simmer until slightly thickened, about 3 minutes. Pour over scallops and let cool.
6. Place two radicchio leaves on each plate and arrange 3 scallops on each leaf. Sprinkle with orange rind, ginger (from marinade) and chives, or tie each leaf with a chive.

Makes 8 servings.

Bay Scallops with Hot and Sweet Red Pepper

The red of the peppers and the green and white of the scallions make this a pretty dish—and pretty delicious too! Serve over Sesame Rice for a full-flavored accompaniment.

1 lb	bay scallops	500 g
10	dried black mushrooms or 1 (½ oz/14 g) package	10
1	can (10 oz/284 ml) water chestnuts, drained	1
1	can (10 oz/284 ml) bamboo shoots, drained	1
2	sweet red peppers, cut in julienne strips	2
¼ cup	soy sauce	50 ml
¼ cup	rice vinegar	50 ml
2 tbsp	brown sugar	25 ml
½ tsp	crushed dried hot chili peppers	2 ml
2	egg whites	2
2 tbsp	cornstarch	25 ml
¼ cup	vegetable oil	50 ml
4	green onions	4

1. In warm water to cover, soak dried mushrooms for 30 minutes, until plumped. If water chestnuts are large, cut in half horizontally.
2. Combine water chestnuts, bamboo shoots and red peppers. Combine soy sauce, rice vinegar, brown sugar and chili peppers.
3. Drain and thinly slice mushrooms. Add to soy sauce mixture to absorb flavor.
4. In a large bowl, whisk egg whites and cornstarch. Add scallops and toss to coat well. Remove scallops to plate lined with waxed paper and refrigerate 30 minutes.
5. In a wok, heat oil. Stir-fry scallops, a few at a time, for 1 minute, or until opaque. Remove and drain on paper towel.

6. Add water chestnut mixture. Stir-fry 2 minutes.
7. Add mushrooms, sauce and scallops. Stir-fry 2 minutes.
8. Serve immediately. Garnish with green onions.

Makes 4 servings.

You'll never fail with a Chenin Blanc or an Italian Fruili Colli Orientali.

Hint – Woking Sticks – Some, if not all of your friends, will have mastered dining with chopsticks. Simple bamboo sticks are best and easy to obtain. You can stir your wok with a couple of chopsticks too. Never use only one—it's bad form. Besides, you need two in nearly all recipes where you remove the meat and then add the vegetables.

Shrimp in Lobster Sauce

When I first got this recipe from Hazel Mah at her San Francisco restaurant, I said to her in amazement, "You've left out the lobster sauce." She smiled and said, "But my dear Myra, there is no lobster in Shrimp in Lobster Sauce." Hmmm. You figure it out! This rich dish needs a wine with good acidity and lots of fruit. A California Chenin Blanc or a Muller Thurgau from Oregon are ideal.

1 lb	small shrimp, shelled and deveined	500 g
2 tbsp	peanut oil	25 ml
3	cloves garlic, finely chopped	3
4	green onions, thinly sliced	4
¼ lb	ground pork	125 g
1 tbsp	soy sauce	15 ml
1 tbsp	black bean paste	15 ml
1 tbsp	sherry	15 ml
½ tsp	granulated sugar	2 ml
½ tsp	salt	2 ml
¼ tsp	freshly ground pepper	1 ml
½ cup	water	125 ml
2 tsp	cornstarch	10 ml
2	eggs, well beaten	2

1. In a wok, heat oil. Add garlic and green onions. Stir-fry 1 minute.
2. Add pork and stir-fry 3 to 4 minutes, until no longer pink.
3. Stir in shrimp and stir-fry 2 to 3 minutes, or until pink.
4. Combine soy sauce, black bean paste, sherry, sugar, salt and pepper. Stir into wok.
5. Combine water and cornstarch, mix until smooth; stir into wok and cook about 8 minutes, until thickened.
6. Stir in eggs. Remove from heat immediately and serve.

Makes 4 servings.

Con-Bow Shrimp (Shrimp with Hot Sauce)

I like to sprinkle these with salt as soon as they come out of the wok. If you like salt as much as I do, try that. Serve with a dish of soft Chinese noodles and extra hot pepper sauce. The only thing better than a dry Gewertztraminer would be an ice-cold Asian rice beer though, in a pinch, a Budweiser will do.

¾ lb	shrimp, shelled and deveined	375 g
1½ tsp	salt	7 ml
1	egg white, beaten	1
1 tbsp	all-purpose flour	15 ml
2 tsp	cornstarch	10 ml
¼ tsp	baking powder	1 ml
1 cup	peanut oil	250 ml
6	green onions, thinly sliced	6
1 tsp	granulated sugar	5 ml
4 drops	hot pepper sauce	4 drops
	hot chili sauce	

1. Wipe the shrimp with paper tower to dry thoroughly. Sprinkle with 1 tsp (5 ml) salt. In a shallow dish, combine egg white and shrimp.
2. Combine flour, cornstarch and baking powder. Sprinkle over shrimp and toss to coat well. Refrigerate 30 minutes.
3. In a wok, heat oil. Deep-fry shrimp a few at a time, about 2 minutes, until golden brown. With a slotted spoon remove and drain on paper towel.
4. Pour all but 1 tbsp (15 ml) oil out of wok. Add green onions and stir-fry for 1 minute.
5. Stir in sugar, hot pepper sauce and shrimp. Toss all together. Serve immediately with hot chili sauce.

Makes 4 servings.

Szechwan Garlic Prawns

I let this sit overnight in the marinade so the flavors can really soak in. For friends who like it fiery, serve with hot pepper sauce on the side. I fill a big glass bowl with these shrimps and set it on the table for everyone to dip into—a great excuse for finger bowls. For a simple meal, just add bowls of steamed rice and jasmine tea. For extra heartiness, add vermicelli garnished with a julienne of vegetables and shredded fried egg, along with bowls of snow peas and Shiitake mushrooms.

20	large prawns, shelled and deveined (1 lb/450 g)	20
2 tbsp	vegetable oil	25 ml
3	cloves garlic, chopped finely	3
½ tsp	crushed dried chili peppers	2 ml

Sauce

1 tbsp	sugar	15 ml
1½ tsp	salt	7 ml
2 tsp	soy sauce	10 ml
⅓ cup	water	75 ml
2 tbsp	sherry	25 ml

1. In a small bowl, combine sugar, salt, soy sauce, water and sherry, and stir until dissolved.
2. In a wok heat oil. Add garlic, chilies and brown lightly.
3. Add prawns, a few at a time, and stir-fry about 2 minutes, until pink. Remove with a slotted spoon and set aside.
4. Return prawns to wok and add sauce. Stir well and cook another 3 minutes.
5. Serve hot over rice.

Makes 4 servings.

Spicy Sweet Grilled Shrimp

This delectable hot, sweet dish is quick and easy to prepare for a crowd. I barbecue the shrimp along with radicchio and thick slices of Vidalia or Spanish onions which will naturally caramelize over the grill. For extra flavor and presentation, skewer the shrimp on lemon grass. The only appetizer I serve is a bowl of roasted cashews, so people can really dig in when the platters of grilled shrimp arrive. If you can't find guava jelly for the dipping sauce, use apple jelly. The spicy herbal flavors will stand up well with an assertive California Sauvignon Blanc.

1 cup	guava or apple jelly	250 ml
2	cloves garlic, finely chopped	2
	juice of 2 limes	
1 tbsp	Worcestershire sauce	15 ml
1	jalapeño pepper, seeded and finely chopped	1
¼ tsp	crushed, dried chili peppers	1 ml
40	large shrimp, shelled and deveined (2 lbs/1 kg)	40
¼ tsp	salt	1 ml
10	12-inch (30-cm) wooden skewers*	10

1. Preheat grill to high heat.
2. In a small saucepan, combine jelly, garlic, lime juice, Worcestershire, jalapeño and chilies.
3. Cook mixture over medium heat, until jelly melts, about 3 minutes. Remove from heat and set aside.
4. Thread four shrimp on each wet, wooden skewer (shrimp should lay flat). Brush both sides of shrimp liberally with jelly mixture and place on tray. Allow shrimp to marinate for ½ hour. Before grilling, sprinkle with salt.
5. Grill shrimp 3 minutes on each side, brushing on more of the jelly mixture before turning.
6. Serve hot on skewers, with remaining sauce.

Makes 6 servings.

* Soak in cold water for 1 hour before using.

Naked Shrimp Thai

Served atop a bed of shredded leafy lettuce and red cabbage on a black plate, this is one sexy dish—the perfect set-up for a romantic dinner à deux. Start with carrot and ginger soup or chilled cucumber soup followed by a salad and a dessert of cheese and fruit for an uncomplicated and elegant evening.

8	large shrimp, shelled and deveined (1 lb/500 g)	8
¼ cup	white wine vinegar	50 ml
3 tbsp	soy sauce	50 ml
¼ cup	cilantro, washed	50 ml
3	cloves garlic	3
2	jalapeño peppers, seeded and quartered	2
1 tbsp	sugar	15 ml
½ tsp	olive oil	2 ml
1	small red onion	1
4	leaves leaf lettuce, thinly sliced	4
3	cabbage leaves, thinly sliced	3

1. Preheat grill to high heat.
2. In food processor fitted with metal blade, combine vinegar, soy sauce, cilantro, garlic, peppers and sugar. Process until finely chopped. Set dressing aside.
3. Lightly brush shrimp with olive oil.
4. Grill shrimp until they turn pink and are just cooked through; about 6 minutes, turning once.
5. In medium bowl, combine cooked shrimp and red onion; pour dressing on top and toss to mix well.
6. To serve, divide lettuce and cabbage on each of two plates. Top with equal portions of shrimp mixture, and spoon some of the dressing over each.

Makes 2 servings.

Louisiana Cajun Shrimp

This is a favorite Sunday lunch when my kids are over. I serve it in huge soup bowls with crusty herb breads and rice. There's some preparation involved, so if you enjoy cooking at night, get it all done the day before. Then simply throw it together when the hordes arrive. I serve refreshing Mango Salad to cool down the palate after this spicy dish.

1 lb	shrimp, shelled and deveined	500 g
1 tsp	cayenne pepper	5 ml
1 tsp	freshly ground black pepper	5 ml
1 tsp	paprika	5 ml
1 tsp	dried rosemary	5 ml
½ tsp	dried thyme	2 ml
½ tsp	salt	2 ml
¼ tsp	red pepper flakes	1 ml
½ cup	sweet butter	125 ml
1 cup	beer	250 ml
½ cup	bottled clam juice	125 ml
2 tsp	lemon juice	10 ml

1. In a small bowl, combine cayenne, black pepper, paprika, rosemary, thyme, salt and pepper flakes. Set aside.
2. In a large skillet, melt butter and add seasonings. Cook until bubbly.
3. Add the shrimp, coat with the butter mixture and cook 1 minute. Add the beer, clam juice and lemon juice and cook 3 more minutes until shrimp are pink.
4. Serve hot in bowls.

Makes 4 servings.

Cold beer is a must—the only antidote to the exquisite heat in this dish. An American-style ale, with its somewhat cloying sweetness (due to the corn used in its manufacture) would complement the sweet meat of the shrimp perfectly.

Tandoori Shrimp

This is one of my favorite quick party suppers: just toss the shrimp and the marinade over steamed rice and garnish with cilantro leaves and lime wedges for a fragrant, juicy feast.

2 ½ lbs	medium shrimp, peeled and deveined	1.25 kg
	juice of 1 lime	
1¼ cups	plain yogurt	300 ml
2	cloves garlic, crushed	2
1	small onion, peeled and chopped	1
2 tbsp	chopped fresh cilantro	25 ml
1 tbsp	grated, fresh ginger root	15 ml
1 tsp	ground cumin	5 ml
1 tsp	paprika	5 ml
1 tsp	salt	5 ml
½ tsp	freshly ground black pepper	2 ml
½ tsp	cayenne pepper	2 ml

1. Rinse shrimp and pat dry.
2. Place shrimp in a shallow glass dish and sprinkle with lime juice. Set aside.
3. In a blender or food processor, combine yogurt, garlic, onion, cilantro, ginger, cumin, paprika, salt, pepper and cayenne. Process until smooth and frothy.
4. Pour over shrimps; marinate in refrigerator overnight.
5. Preheat broiler.
6. Remove shrimps from marinade, draining well and place on broiler tray. Grill 3 minutes each side or until pink.
7. Serve at once. Garnish with lime wedges and fresh cilantro.

Makes 6 servings.

Sour Cream Jumbo Shrimp Curry

This dish can be assembled well in advance and heated just before you are ready to serve, or you can serve it cold. Absolutely delicious either way.

16	jumbo shrimp	16
2 tbsp	sweet butter	25 ml
⅓ cup	finely chopped onion	75 ml
¼ cup	finely chopped green pepper	50 ml
1	clove garlic, finely chopped	1
10	medium mushrooms, thinly sliced	10
1 cup	sour cream	250 ml
1 tsp	curry powder	5 ml
½ tsp	Worcestershire sauce	2 ml
½ tsp	salt	2 ml
¼ tsp	dry mustard	1 ml
⅛ tsp	white pepper	0.5 ml
¼ cup	toasted slivered almonds	50 ml

1. In a saucepan of lightly salted boiling water, cook shrimp about 3 minutes, until shell turns pink and shrimp curls. Drain and cool for a few moments until easy to handle. Peel off shell, leaving tail in place. Devein and place in a warm bowl; keep warm.
2. In a skillet, heat butter; add onion, green pepper and garlic; sauté about 5 minutes, until softened.
3.. Add mushrooms and sauté 5 minutes longer. Blend in sour cream, curry powder, Worcestershire sauce, salt, mustard and pepper.
4. Serve over warm shrimps. Garnish with toasted almonds.

Makes 4 servings.

Crabcakes with Chili Mayo and Citrus Salsa

I pack these up for irresistible beachside picnics whenever I'm in Biddeford, Maine. The citrus salsa and hot chili mayo look great in colorful little bowls I picked up in Spain. The sweetness of the corn and peppers seems to elicit an extra sweetness from the crab. They also freeze well and can be served hot or cold, so keep extra bite-sized crabcakes on hand for hors d'oeuvres or to sandwich between small onion buns.

3 tbsp	mayonnaise	50 ml
2	eggs	2
1 tbsp	Dijon mustard	15 ml
1 tsp	dry mustard	5 ml
¼ tsp	hot pepper sauce	1 ml
¼ tsp	cayenne pepper	1 ml
½ tsp	salt	2 ml
¼ tsp	freshly ground black pepper	1 ml
1 lb	cooked crabmeat	500 g
1 tbsp	roasted red pepper, chopped	15 ml
⅓ cup	cooked corn	50 ml
1 tbsp	parsley, chopped	15 ml
1 cup	dry breadcrumbs	250 ml
⅓ cup	vegetable oil	50 ml

1. In large bowl, whisk together mayonnaise, eggs, mustards, hot pepper sauce, cayenne, salt and pepper until smooth.
2. Add crab, roasted pepper, corn, parsley and breadcrumbs to egg mixture. Stir well. Shape into 16 2½-inch (6-cm) patties.

3. In a large skillet, heat oil. Cook patties about 3 minutes on each side or until golden brown and cooked through. Drain on paper towels. Keep warm.

Chili Mayonnaise

1	roasted red pepper, peeled and seeded	1
1½ cups	mayonnaise	325 ml
½ tsp	hot pepper sauce	2 ml
1 tbsp	dry mustard	15 ml
½ tsp	cayenne powder	2 ml
½ tsp	chili powder	2 ml

In a food processor or blender, purée red pepper for 1 minute until smooth. Add mayonnaise, mustard, hot sauce, cayenne and chili powder. Place in serving bowl.

Citrus Salsa

1	clove garlic, peeled and coarsely chopped	1
1	lemon, peeled and sectioned	1
1	lime, peeled and sectioned	1
1	orange, peeled and sectioned	1
1	grapefruit, peeled and sectioned	1
2 tbsp	red onion, chopped	25 ml
2 tbsp	chopped cilantro	25 ml
1	tomato, seeded and chopped	1

In a food processor or blender process all ingredients for 15 seconds until coarse. Drain salsa in a sieve for 15 minutes. Place in serving bowl.

Makes 4 servings.

〜〜〜〜〜〜〜〜〜〜〜〜〜〜〜〜〜〜〜〜〜〜〜〜〜

Sauvignon Blanc, Riesling or Gewurtztraminer all go well with the zesty acidity of the Citrus Salsa.

〜〜〜〜〜〜〜〜〜〜〜〜〜〜〜〜〜〜〜〜〜〜〜〜〜

Chicken

There is an elegance to serving stuffed roasted chicken and turkey. These crisp, succulent birds, prepared with an eye to color, accompaniment and an ambiance of fall leaves, conjure up images of autumn days and informal gatherings.

Chicken in Black Bean Sauce

Hot, cold, bone in, bone out—this dish does it all. I serve it fanned out around bunches of French green beans, or hot with coriander rice and red, green and yellow pepper matchsticks. Try a medium-dry white Sauvignon Blanc or Riesling. If you prefer red, go with a youthful St. Emilion or St. Estephe or a full Châteauneuf du Pape

6	boneless, skinless chicken breasts (3 lbs/1.5 kg)	6
¼ cup	black bean sauce with garlic	50 ml
¼ cup	soy sauce	50 ml
2 tbsp	sesame oil	25 ml
1 tsp	hot chili paste	5 ml

1. In a small bowl, combine black bean sauce, soy sauce, sesame oil and chili paste.
2. Reserve half of the sauce and spread the other half over chicken.
3. Cover and refrigerate for 2 hours.
4. Preheat oven to 375°F (190°C).
5. Place chicken on baking sheet and bake for 25 minutes, or until chicken is tender and no longer pink.
6. Heat remaining sauce and pour over chicken. Serve hot or cold.

Makes 6 servings.

Variation: Chicken Salad with Vermicelli

Make a quick and different salad by tossing the chicken with cooked vermicelli (I always cut mine up to make it easier to serve and eat), black bean vinaigrette and multi-colored matchsticks.

1	clove garlic, finely chopped	1
	juice of 1 orange	
¼ cup	rice wine vinegar	50 ml
1 tbsp	sesame oil	15 ml
¼ cup	vegetable oil	50 ml

1. Combine vinaigrette ingredients and pour over chicken and vermicelli.

Chinese One-Pot Supper

Two courses come out of one pot with this recipe—one of my favorites when I want to get out the chopsticks and my prettiest soup tureen and invite friends over for a casual dinner followed by a game of charades. It uses broth instead of oil to cook the seafood and chicken, making it practically fat-free.

4	whole boneless, skinless chicken breasts (2 lbs/1 kg) cut into 1-inch (2.5-cm) cubes	4
½ lb	shrimp, shelled and deveined	250 g
½ lb	sea scallops	250 g
4 cups	chicken stock	1 l
2	green onions, chopped	2
3	slices fresh ginger	3
1	clove garlic, sliced	1
1	strip (2-inch/5-cm) lemon rind	1
2 tbsp	freshly chopped cilantro	25 ml
2 cups	coarsely chopped spinach	500 ml
1 cup	Oriental egg noodles *	250 ml

Oriental Dipping Sauce

¼ cup	balsamic vinegar	50 ml
¼ cup	soy sauce	50 ml
2 tbsp	brown sugar	25 ml
2 tsp	fresh ginger, chopped	10 ml
1	clove garlic, finely chopped	1

1. Prepare, cover and refrigerate chicken, shrimp and scallops, up to 6 hours or until ready to serve.
2. In a small bowl, combine vinegar, soy sauce, sugar, ginger and garlic. Set aside.
3. In a large saucepan, combine stock, onions, ginger, garlic, lemon rind and cilantro. Bring to boil over high heat. Reduce and simmer 5 minutes.

4. Add chicken to simmering stock for 1 minute. Then add shrimp and scallops and cook for 2 more minutes.
5. With a slotted spoon, remove chicken, shrimp and scallops and arrange them on a heated platter.
6. Add spinach and noodles to broth and cook 3 minutes, or until noodles are tender.
7. Ladle into warm soup bowls and serve with chicken, shrimp and scallops and individual bowls of dipping sauce.

Makes 4 servings.

* If using Italian egg noodles, precook them and add to broth.

Mahogany Chicken Wings

I cut off the tips and halve the wings to make eating easier. I also get out the finger bowls for this yummy, sticky dish—which goes perfectly with crispy french fries or parsnip chips.

4 lbs	chicken wings, tips removed	2 kg

Marinade

1 cup	hoisin sauce	250 ml
¾ cup	plum sauce	175 ml
½ cup	soy sauce	125 ml
½ cup	dry sherry	125 ml
½ cup	honey	125 ml
⅓ cup	cider vinegar	75 ml
6	green onions, finely chopped	6
6	cloves garlic, finely chopped	6
2 tbsp	fresh ginger, peeled and finely chopped	25 ml

1. In a large bowl, combine all ingredients except chicken. Reserve 1 cup marinade for dipping. Add chicken and toss to coat well. Cover and refrigerate for 24 hours.
3. Preheat oven to 400°F (200°C).
4. Remove chicken from marinade and place on foil-lined baking sheets. Bake for 50 to 55 minutes, basting once, until chicken turns a mahogany color. Serve warm with dipping sauce.

Makes 6 servings.

Parsnip Chips

I serve these whenever my grandchildren visit: the parsnips are baked, not fried, and it's a sneaky way to get them to eat vegetables. Serve them hot from the oven while they're sweet and crispy. Kids love 'em!

2 tbsp	olive oil	25 ml
¼ tsp	salt	1 ml
¼ tsp	freshly ground black pepper	1 ml
pinch	cayenne pepper	pinch
4	parsnips, peeled and very thinly sliced	4

1. Preheat oven to 400°F (200°C).
2. In a medium bowl, combine oil, salt, pepper and cayenne. Add parsnips and toss to coat well.
3. Place chips on a baking sheet and bake in oven 5 minutes. Turn and bake another 5 minutes. Serve immediately.

Makes 4 servings.

Chicken With Oranges and Hot Chili Peppers

Great color and fun—but not for the timid. Do warn your friends to watch out for the hot chili peppers. Tossed with chopped green onions, this makes a great casual supper. Add ribs and rice and you've got a zesty Chinese meal. The orange peel can be baked ahead to use in this recipe, or to toss into salads or rice. Keeps well for months in an airtight container.

3	whole boneless, skinless chicken breasts (1½ lbs/750 g), cut into 1-inch (2.5-cm) cubes	3
	rind of 4 oranges	
3 tbsp	oil	50 ml
2	green onions, finely chopped	2
2 tsp	finely chopped fresh ginger root	10 ml
12	dry chili peppers	12
2 tbsp	water	25 ml
2 tbsp	sugar	25 ml
2 tbsp	soy sauce	25 ml
1 tbsp	liquid honey	15 ml
3	green onions, cut into ¼-inch (5-mm) matchsticks	3

1. Preheat oven to 200°F (95°C).
2. Remove pith from orange rind and cut into ¼-inch (5-mm) matchsticks.
3. Place rind matchsticks on baking sheet and cook for 2 hours, until they are dry and begin to crisp. Set aside.
4. In a large skillet, heat oil on very high heat until just smoking. Add chicken and sauté 3 minutes until golden brown. Remove and set aside.
5. Add green onion and ginger and cook for about 1½ minutes until flavors begin to develop.

6. Add reserved rind, chicken, chilies, water, sugar, soy sauce, honey, and cook, stirring until heated through, about 2 minutes.
7. Serve over hot rice and garnish with green onions.

Makes 6 servings.

A Vienna-style or Marzenbier lager, with its residual sweet maltiness, is a perfect potable with this chicken dish.

Ginger Chicken with Sweet Red Peppers and Cashews

This is a very hearty stir-fry and one that will give your guests a really satisfied feeling. For a lively acidity to accompany the ginger, try a flavorful Sancerre Rosé or even the more popular white version.

1 lb	boneless, skinless chicken breasts	500 g
¼ cup	soy sauce	50 ml
¼ cup	sake or dry sherry	50 ml
1 tbsp	peanut oil	15 ml
1	piece (1½-inch/3.5-cm) ginger root, peeled and chopped	1
4	green onions, sliced	4
2	cloves garlic, finely chopped	2
3 tbsp	water	45 ml
1 tbsp	hoisin sauce	15 ml
½ tsp	salt	2 ml
⅛ tsp	freshly ground black pepper	0.5 ml
2	red peppers, cut into thin slices	2
2	green peppers, cut into thin slices	2
½ cup	toasted cashew nuts	125 ml

1. With a sharp knife, slice chicken on the diagonal into thin slices. In a bowl, combine soy sauce and sake; marinate chicken in mixture for 1 hour.
2. In a wok heat oil. Add ginger root, green onions and garlic; stir-fry 2 minutes.
3. Drain chicken, reserving marinade; add chicken to wok and stir-fry 2 minutes, or until no longer pink. Stir in reserved marinade, water, hoisin sauce, salt and pepper. Add red and green peppers. Cook 2 minutes longer.
4. Add cashew nuts. Toss and serve immediately.

Makes 4 servings.

Stir-Fried Chicken with Walnuts

If you prefer some other nut, feel free to add your own favorites: cashews, pecans, or peanuts. Just keep the quantities the same. Serve this with hot steamed snowpeas.

1 lb	boneless chicken breasts, cut in 1-inch/2.5-cm pieces	500 g
1	egg white, beaten until frothy	1
1 tbsp	cornstarch	15 ml
1 cup	peanut oil	250 ml
1 cup	walnut halves	250 ml
2	dried hot chili peppers, broken in small pieces	2
4	cloves garlic, peeled and halved	4
3	pieces (½-inch/1-cm each) ginger root, peeled	3
1 tbsp	soy sauce	15 ml
1 tbsp	sherry	15 ml

1. In a glass bowl, combine chicken and egg white. Sprinkle cornstarch on chicken and toss to coat well. Refrigerate 30 minutes.
2. In a wok, heat oil. Deep-fry chicken a few pieces at a time, about 1 minute, or until golden brown. Remove from wok and drain on paper towel. Pour all but 2 tbsp (25 ml) oil out of wok.
3. Add peppers, garlic and ginger root; stir-fry 2 minutes. Remove with slotted spoon and discard.
4. Return chicken and walnuts to wok. Stir in soy sauce. Stir-fry 1 minute. Stir in sherry. Serve immediately.

Makes 4 servings.

A dry Sauvignon Blanc or dry sparkling wine performs an excellent balancing act with the peanut oil.

Hint – The great thing about a stir-fry is that you might as well have everyone out into the kitchen to watch you put the dinner together and to chat while you work. Most stir-fries take only a few minutes—if you've done all the preparation beforehand. Nearly everything for a stir-fry can be prepared the day before or well in advance of your tour de cuisine.

Chinese Lemon Chicken

This is another of my favorite Chinese recipes from my friend, the fabled Hazel Mah. I tried unsuccessfully for months to duplicate the taste in my own kitchen and then discovered Chinese yellow lump sugar candy was the secret ingredient. It can be purchased at most Chinese grocers.

4	whole chicken breasts, halved, skinned and boned	4
2¾ cups	chicken stock	675 ml
1 lb	Chinese yellow lump sugar candy	500 g
1½	cups lemon juice	375 ml
1	lemon, halved lengthwise and thinly sliced	1
1 tsp	salt	5 ml
2	medium onions, thinly sliced	2
¼ cup	corn starch	50 ml
¼ cup	water	50 ml
1	egg, slightly beaten	1
¼ cup	all-purpose flour	50 ml
¼ cup	vegetable oil	50 ml

1. In a saucepan, combine chicken stock, sugar candy, lemon juice, lemon slices and salt. Heat to simmering, stirring about 10 minutes, until sugar candy is dissolved.
2. Add onions to sauce. Combine cornstarch and water; stir until smooth. Stir into lemon sauce. Cook, stirring constantly, about 3 minutes, until sauce is thickened.
3. Cut chicken breasts into bite-sized pieces.
4. Place beaten egg and flour in separate shallow dishes. Dip chicken pieces in egg and dredge with flour.
5. In a skillet, heat oil. Add chicken pieces to skillet a few at a time; cook 3 to 4 minutes. Remove to a warm platter; keep warm. Repeat with remaining chicken.
6. Place on a warm platter; pour sauce over chicken.

Makes 8 servings.

General Tsao's Chicken

The late, great General was both a political figure and a poet who lived in China, 155 to 220 A.D. He may have owed his longevity (in those days!) to his love of good food. Here's his recipe for chicken to prove it!

1 lb	boneless chicken breasts, cut into 1-inch/2.5-cm pieces	500 g
3 tbsp	soy sauce	45 ml
1 tbsp	cornstarch	15 ml
1	egg white, beaten until frothy	1
1 cup	vegetable oil	250 ml
3	dried hot chili peppers, broken in half	3
2	cloves garlic, finely chopped	2
1	piece (1-inch/2.5-cm) ginger root, peeled and finely chopped	1
1 tbsp	white wine vinegar	15 ml
1 tbsp	white wine	15 ml
1 tsp	cornstarch	5 ml
1 tbsp	brown sugar	15 ml
1 tsp	sesame oil	5 ml
½ tsp	salt	2 ml

1. Place chicken pieces into a glass bowl. Combine 1 tbsp (15 ml) soy sauce and 1 tbsp (15 ml) cornstarch. Blend in beaten egg white. Pour over chicken and toss to coat well. Marinate in refrigerator for 1 hour.
2. In a wok, heat oil. Deep-fry chicken, a few pieces at a time, about 1 minute, or until golden brown. Remove and drain on paper towel. Pour all but 2 tbsp (25 ml) oil out of wok.
3. To the wok add chili peppers, garlic and ginger; stir-fry 2 minutes.
4. In a small bowl, combine remaining soy sauce, vinegar, white wine and 1 tsp (5 ml) cornstarch; mix until smooth. Stir in sugar, sesame oil and salt. Pour into wok and cook, stirring, about 2 minutes, until thickened.
5. Return chicken pieces to wok. Mix well and serve immediately.

Makes 4 servings.

Chinese Roast Chicken

The ginger, soy sauce, garlic and wine make this a handsome and tasty bird of Chinese persuasion. Serve it with sweet-scented rice and a salad or a vegetable stir-fry.

1	chicken (2 to 3 lbs/1 to 1/5 kg)	1
½ cup	soy sauce	125 ml
¼ cup	sake or dry sherry	50 ml
2 tbsp	brown sugar	25 ml
1	piece (1-inch/2.5-cm) ginger root, peeled and finely chopped	1
2	cloves garlic, finely chopped	2
4	green onions, finely chopped	4

1. Place chicken in a medium bowl. Combine soy sauce, sake, brown sugar, ginger root, garlic and onions. Pour over chicken. Cover and refrigerate overnight.
2. Preheat oven to 325°F (160°C).
3. Place chicken on a rack in a roasting pan and bake in oven, basting frequently with marinade, for 1 hour, until tender and no longer pink.

Makes 4 servings.

Choose a light- to medium-bodied fruity red such as Pinot Noir or Dolcetto d'Alba.

Hint – As a thickening agent, 1 tbsp cornstarch equals 2 tbsp flour.

Mediterranean Chicken with Dried Fruits and Couscous

My friend Simon Kattar, the owner/chef of A la Carte Kitchens, passed on this recipe—a one-pot supper that is awe-inspiring in its subtlety of flavors and natural hues. Experiment with a fruity medium-bodied white, such as Alsatian Pinot Blanc or a red youthful Bordeaux..

4	boneless chicken breasts, halved (1½ lbs/750 g)	4
2 tsp	sweet butter	10 ml
1	onion, finely chopped	1
2 cups	boiling chicken stock	500 ml
¼ cup	raisins	50 ml
¼ cup	dried apricots, slivered	50 ml
¼ cup	dried prunes, chopped	50 ml
1 tsp	grated orange rind	5 ml
½ tsp	coriander seeds, toasted	2 ml
1	bay leaf	1
½ tsp	salt	2 ml
¼ tsp	freshly ground pepper	1 ml
1 cup	couscous	250 ml

1. In a medium size skillet, melt butter. Add chicken; sauté for 2 minutes per side, until golden. Remove chicken from skillet. Set aside.
2. Add onion to skillet; sauté for 3 minutes, until softened.
3. Add stock, raisins, apricots, prunes, orange rind, coriander seeds, bay leaf, salt and pepper to skillet. Stir in couscous; mix well.
4. Return chicken breasts to skillet. Bring to boil, reduce heat, cover and simmer for 15 minutes, until liquid is absorbed and chicken is tender and no longer pink.
5. Serve immediately.

Makes 4 servings.

Jerk Wings with "Cool-Down" Apricot Tamarind Sauce

This is an essential part of the midnight supper I serve on New Year's Eve. But remember: the longer it sits in the marinade, the hotter it gets. For me, 1½ hours is just right. For those who like hot wings, these will knock Buffalo wings out of the ballpark. The cooling balancer to this dish is the Apricot Tamarind sauce, created by Helen Willinsky, author of *Jerk: Barbecue from Jamaica*. (I often make double the amount to throw over lamb, ribs or pork tenderloins.)

2 lbs	chicken wings, tips removed	1 kg

Marinade

5	green onions, chopped	5
1	onion, chopped	1
1	Scotch bonnet pepper, seeded	1
3 tbsp	soy sauce	50 ml
1 tbsp	oil	15 ml
1 tbsp	vinegar	15 ml
2 tsp	fresh thyme	10 ml
2 tsp	sugar	10 ml
1 tsp	salt	5 ml
1 tsp	allspice	5 ml
1 tsp	freshly ground black pepper	5 ml
½ tsp	ground nutmeg	2 ml
½ tsp	cinnamon	2 ml

Tamarind Sauce

1 cup	tamarind nectar	250 ml
¼ cup	apricot jam	50 ml
2 tbsp	honey	25 ml
1 tbsp	Dijon mustard	15 ml

1. In shallow dish, place chicken wings in a single layer.
2. In a food processor or blender, combine all the marinade ingredients. Process 2 minutes, until very finely minced.
3. Spoon over chicken; cover and marinate in refrigerator for 1½ hours, turning occasionally.
4. Preheat oven to 400°F (200°C).
5. Remove chicken from marinade and arrange in a shallow baking dish.
6. Bake chicken in oven for 45 minutes until crisp.
7. In a small saucepan, combine the tamarind nectar and jam and bring to a boil. Boil for 4 minutes, until thickened. Stir in honey and mustard, mixing well. Serve hot or at room temperature with wings.

Makes 4 servings.

A frosty pitcher of your favorite ale is the only way to go. Try a brown ale with its spicy nuttiness or something more acidic like Berliner Weissebier or even a Belgium Witbier. Nothing will beat a chilled Red Stripe.

Caribbean Chicken with Dark Rum

This is a spring dish for the fresh cherry season and the time of island festivals, bongo drums, and dark rum. Unless you do your own cherry preserves, don't attempt this out of season. Canned cherries don't seem to cut it.

4	pieces chicken, legs or breasts (2 lb/1 kg)	4
1 tsp	salt	5 ml
½ tsp	paprika	2 ml
2 tbsp	vegetable oil	25 ml
1 tbsp	sweet butter	15 ml
1 tbsp	all-purpose flour	15 ml
1 tsp	granulated sugar	5 ml
¼ tsp	ground allspice	1 ml
¼ tsp	ground cinnamon	1 ml
¼ tsp	dry mustard	1 ml
2 cups	fresh cherries, pitted and halved	500 ml
1 cup	chicken stock	250 ml
1 cup	unsweetened crushed pineapple, including juice	250 ml
2 tbsp	brown sugar	25 ml
2 tbsp	dark rum	25 ml

1. Preheat oven to 350°F (180°C).
2. With a sharp knife, disjoint or cut each piece of chicken in half. Sprinkle chicken pieces with ½ tsp (2 ml) salt and paprika.
3. In a large skillet, heat vegetable oil and butter. Add chicken pieces; cook, turning, about 10 minutes, until golden. Remove chicken to a shallow casserole or baking dish; set aside.
4. To pan drippings in skillet, stir in flour, sugar, allspice, cinnamon and mustard. Add cherries, chicken stock, pineapple, brown sugar and rum; mix well and bring to a boil.
5. Pour over chicken, cover and bake in oven for 50 minutes or until tender. Remove cover and bake 10 minutes longer.

Makes 4 servings.

Chicken Provençal

My daughter Joanna came back from a year in the south of France with this recipe. Its burst of red and orange color reminds me of Provence in the fall. Not to mention that it serves loads of people effortlessly. Poach the chicken and roast the peppers a day ahead; marinate the chicken overnight, and the next day just serve. All you need to add is a selection of hot breads to mop up the sauce. Try a young Chianti or a medium-bodied Crozes Hermitage with this classic dish.

6	boneless, skinless chicken breasts, halved (3 lbs/1.5 kg)	6
4 cups	chicken stock or water	1 l
¼ cup	balsamic vinegar	50 ml
¼ cup	olive oil	50 ml
½ tsp	salt	2 ml
½ tsp	freshly ground black pepper	2 ml
2	cloves garlic, finely chopped	2
½ cup	fresh basil, coarsely chopped	125 ml
1½ cups	Kalamata olives, halved	375 ml
3	peppers (red, green and yellow), roasted, peeled and seeded	3

1. In large, deep skillet bring chicken stock to boil.
2. Poach chicken breasts in stock for 8 minutes, turning once. Remove and set aside.
3. In a large bowl, combine vinegar, oil, salt, pepper, garlic, basil and half the olives.
4. Add chicken to marinade. Cover and let sit overnight, turning often.
5. Remove chicken from marinade and arrange on platter with peppers and remaining olives. Serve at room temperature.

Makes 6 servings.

Chicken Saag

If your friends love to linger over dinner, then this dish will be as good at ten p.m. as it was hours earlier. "Saag" is the East Indian name for the spicy green vegetable purée that gives the dish its character. Serve it with all kinds of fruit chutneys and fresh melons—cranshaw, cataloupe, honeydew—strewn with leaves of fresh mint.

8	half chicken breasts	8
5 cups	rich chicken stock	1.25 l
1	onion, quartered	1
2	stalks celery, including leaves	2
6	sprigs parsley	6
3	garlic cloves, peeled	3
½ lb	fresh spinach, washed, trimmed and coarsely chopped	250 g
1	stalk broccoli, washed, trimmed and coarsely chopped	1
¼ cup	clarified butter	50 ml
1 cup	finely chopped onions	250 ml
1 tbsp	finely chopped fresh ginger root	15 ml
1 tsp	salt	5 ml
½ tsp	ground coriander	2 ml
½ tsp	garam masala*	2 ml
¼ tsp	ground cumin	1 ml
¼ tsp	turmeric	1 ml
½ cup	sour cream	125 ml

1. In a large skillet or saucepan, combine 4 cups (1 l) chicken stock with the onion, celery, parsley and garlic. Bring to a boil. Add chicken breasts and poach about 20 to 25 minutes, until tender. Remove from stock, cool, then skin and bone, but keep the breasts halves in one piece. Return to cooking liquid to keep warm.

2. While chicken breasts are poaching, prepare sauce. In food processor or blender, combine ½ cup (125 ml) chicken stock and a handful of spinach; process until chopped. Add another handful of spinach and process. Repeat until all spinach has been chopped. Remove to a large bowl.

3. Add remaining ½ cup (125 ml) chicken stock to processor. Add broccoli in batches and chop. Add to spinach.

4. In a heavy skillet, heat clarified butter. Add onions; sauté until softened. Add ginger and continue to sauté until golden brown. Stir in salt, coriander, garam masala, cumin and turmeric and sauté 2 minutes.

5. Stir in the spinach and broccoli mixture, bring to a boil, reduce heat, and simmer, uncovered, 20 to 25 minutes, until most of the liquid has evaporated.

6. Just before serving, stir in sour cream. Do not reheat. To serve, arrange poached chicken breasts on attractive platter and spoon sauce over.

Makes 8 servings.

Garam Masala

A principal spice blend of Northern Indian cookery. To be used in pilafs and onion-based sauces for meat and poultry.

2	cinnamon sticks, in pieces	2
3	bay leaves, crumbled	3
2 tsp	cumin seeds	10 ml
1½ tsp	coriander seeds	7 ml
1 tsp	cardamom seeds	5 ml
1 tsp	black peppercorns	5 ml
½ tsp	whole cloves	2 ml
½ tsp	ground mace	2 ml

1. Heat heavy frying pan on medium heat, and when hot put in whole spices. Dry roast until color darkens, shaking often. Remove from heat and cool.

2. Add mace and grind in a clean coffee grinder.

3. Store in airtight container for 3 to 4 months.

A youthful red—Côte Rotie or a California Cabernet Sauvignon, for example—will complement the fruit and spices.

Plum Sauce Chicken Breasts

You may never have seen a purple cow, but when you make this, you are going to see a purple chicken. A beautiful, appetizing purple chicken. It is truly elegant, and when decorated with green and yellow pepper halves, filled with extra plum sauce, it is exotic. Equally good served hot or cold. Garnish with a single yellow oncidium orchid spray on a dark dinner platter or, if using a white or glass serving platter, garnish with a mauve denrobium orchid.

8	half chicken breasts	8
¼ cup	all-purpose flour	50 ml
½ tsp	paprika	2 ml
½ tsp	salt	2 ml
¼ tsp	freshly ground black pepper	1 ml
pinch	cayenne	pinch
¼ cup	sweet butter	50 ml
½ cup	dry white wine	125 ml

Plum Sauce

8	blue Italian plums (1 cup/250 ml), pitted	8
2	slices fresh ginger root, finely chopped	
2 tbsp	brown sugar	25 ml
2 tbsp	rice or wine vinegar	25 ml
2 tbsp	soy sauce	25 ml
½ cup	cold water	125 ml
1 tbsp	cornstarch	15 ml
½ tsp	cinnamon	2 ml

1. Bone and skin chicken breasts.
2. In a shallow dish, combine flour, paprika, salt, pepper and cayenne. Roll each breast half in flour mixture to coat it completely.
3. In a large skillet, heat butter. Add chicken breasts. Cook, turning once or twice, for about 5 minutes, until lightly browned on all sides. Add wine, cover, and simmer for 5 minutes.

4. Transfer chicken pieces to a casserole. Pour pan juices over chicken. Set aside.
5. Preheat oven to 350°F (180°C).
6. In a food processor, finely chop plums and ginger. In a 4-cup (1-l) saucepan, combine chopped plum mixture, brown sugar, vinegar and soy sauce. Cook, stirring, over medium heat, about 5 minutes, until soft.
7. Combine water, cornstarch and cinnamon; stir until smooth. Stir into plum mixture. Cook, stirring constantly, about 2 minutes, until thick.
8. Pour over chicken in casserole. Cover and bake in oven for 20 to 25 minutes, or until chicken is tender and no longer pink.

Makes 8 servings.

Serve a wine that won't clash with the aromatic ingredients in this recipe, such as a floral Semillon from California or Australia.

Hint – You are giving a party. You set the pace, and the guests take your actions as their cue. Don't be afraid to mix dinner guests up. Inviting people for dinner is a lot like making a salad. A lot of different ingredients go into a bowl, and the net result is a wonderful time. Too much of the same thing makes for a boring salad and a dull evening.

Poulet aux Deux Moutardes

This is a quick, easy, and very impressive dish, as long as you have all the ingredients on hand. Once you know you are going to be strapped for time, plan on something like this. It's a great way to be able to put in a full day and still be the complete host or hostess in the evening. Serve with sautéed mushrooms and a salad. Bring on your favorite medium-bodied red Burgundy.

4	pieces chicken legs or breasts (2 lb/1 kg)	4
2 tbsp	all-purpose flour	25 ml
1 tsp	salt	5 ml
½ tsp	white pepper	2 ml
2 tbsp	sweet butter	25 ml
2 tbsp	peanut oil	25 ml
4	shallots, chopped	4
	bouquet garni	
1 cup	chicken stock	250 ml
¼ cup	dry vermouth	50 ml
2 tbsp	Dijon mustard with tarragon	25 ml
1 tsp	dry mustard	5 ml
½ cup	heavy or whipping cream	125 ml

1. Combine flour, ½ tsp (2 ml) salt and ¼ tsp (1 ml) pepper. Dredge chicken with seasoned flour.
2. In a large skillet, heat butter and oil. Add chicken pieces; sauté, turning, about 10 minutes, until golden brown.
3. Add shallots, bouquet garni, stock and vermouth. Scrape down pan. Bring to a boil, reduce heat, and simmer, covered, about 30 minutes, until tender. Remove bouquet garni and discard. Place chicken on warm serving platter and keep warm.
4. Whisk mustards and cream into skillet. Simmer gently for 2 minutes. Season with remaining salt and pepper. Return chicken to sauce to heat thoroughly.

Makes 4 servings.

Chicken Diable

Quick and easy, little or nothing to chop or mix. Just put it together and wait for the excellent results. Serve with rice and chutneys and a cucumber and yogurt salad.

4	pieces chicken, legs or breasts (2 lb/1 kg)	4
¼ cup	sweet butter	50 ml
½ cup	honey	125 ml
¼ cup	Dijon mustard	50 ml
1 tbsp	curry powder	15 ml
1 tsp	salt	5 ml

1. Preheat oven to 350°F (180°C).
2. In a shallow baking dish, arrange chicken pieces.
3. In a small saucepan, melt butter. Stir in honey, mustard, curry powder and salt. Pour honey mixture over chicken , turning pieces so they are coated.
4. Cover and bake in oven for 45 minutes.
5. Uncover and bake, basting frequently with sauce, for 15 minutes longer, until chicken is tender and golden.

Makes 4 servings.

On a country picnic bring along an extra wine carafe. Spend the morning walking through the fields, picking wildflowers such as buttercups, Queen Anne's lace, lupines and anything else that catches your eye. Arrange them loosely in the carafe, and your picnic table becomes a pretty reminder of your carefree morning.

Minted Chicken Breasts

Looks great. Tastes even better. The scent of the mint is irresistible. Why we mentally reserve mint for lamb only, I will never know. There are so many other eating joys we can achieve with this special herb.

6	half chicken breasts (3 lb/1.5 kg)	6
⅓ cup	sweet butter	75 ml
2 tbsp	vegetable oil	25 ml
1	lemon, grated rind and juice	1
1 tsp	salt	5 ml
¼ tsp	freshly ground black pepper	1 ml
	chicken stock	
2 tbsp	all-purpose flour	25 ml
½ cup	light cream	125 ml
2 tbsp	chopped fresh mint, or	25 ml
	2 tsp (10 ml) dried	
1 tbsp	chopped parsley	15 ml
1 tsp	dried thyme leaves	5 ml
1 tsp	granulated sugar	5 ml
1 tsp	paprika	5 ml

1. In a large skillet, heat 2 tbsp (25 ml) butter and oil. Add chicken breasts; cook, turning, 5 to 10 minutes, until golden brown.
2. Add lemon rind and juice, salt and pepper. Reduce heat, cover and simmer 30 minutes. Remove chicken breasts and place in a single layer on a baking pan.
3. Pour any remaining juice from skillet into a measuring cup. Skim off fat. Add enough chicken stock to make 1 cup (250 ml).
4. In the same skillet, combine remaining butter and flour; stir in chicken stock mixture and cream. Cook over medium heat, stirring, about 5 minutes, until thickened. Stir in mint, parsley and thyme.
5. Just before serving, preheat oven to 500°F (260°C).
6. Sprinkle chicken with sugar and paprika. Place chicken in oven just long enough for surface to become brown and crisp.
7. Remove to serving platter. Pour hot sauce over top and serve.

Makes 6 servings.

Grilled Chicken with Apple and Rosemary

The sweet smell of apples cooking will whet everyone's appetite. A sure wine bet is a rich Chardonnay from the Napa Valley or a red Italian Dolcetto di Avada. For an autumn dinner, bouquets of rosemary popped into small pumpkins down the center of the table will add even more color and aroma.

6	whole boneless, skinless chicken breasts, halved (3 lbs/1.5 kg)	6
½ cup	apple juice	125 ml
¼ cup	white wine vinegar	50 ml
¼ cup	vegetable oil	50 ml
1 tbs	chopped fresh rosemary	15 ml
¾ tsp	freshly ground black pepper	4 ml
¼ tsp	salt	1 ml
	grated rind of ½ lemon	
2	cloves garlic, finely chopped	2
6	Granny Smith apples, cored and cut into ½-inch (1-cm) slices	6

1. In shallow baking dish, combine apple juice, vinegar, oil, rosemary, pepper, salt, lemon rind and garlic.
2. Add chicken and apples, coating well with marinade. Cover and marinate in refrigerator overnight.
3. Preheat grill to high heat.
4. Remove chicken and apples from marinade; discard marinade.
5. Grill chicken 10 minutes. Baste, turn and continue to cook for another 8 to 10 minutes, or until chicken is tender and no longer pink. Remove chicken to warm serving platter.
6. Grill apples, turning once, about 6 minutes, or until apples are tender crisp.
7. Place apples around chicken and serve.

Makes 6 servings.

Crisp Baked Almond Chicken

I have made pans and pans of this for proms, sweet sixteen and surprise parties, and it is always a hit. You can serve it for a picnic or a sitdown dinner party with the most impressive guests. It tastes as good as it looks.

4	pieces chicken, legs or breasts	4
	(2 to 3 lbs/1 to 1.5 kg)	
¼ cup	all-purpose flour	50 ml
⅓ cup	sweet butter, melted	75 ml
1 tsp	celery salt	5 ml
1 tsp	paprika	5 ml
1 tsp	salt	5 ml
½ tsp	curry powder	2 ml
½ tsp	dried oregano leaves	2 ml
½ tsp	freshly ground black pepper	1 ml
¾ cup	sliced almonds	175 ml
1 cup	sour cream	250 ml
3 tbsp	fine dry breadcrumbs	45 ml
1 tbsp	soft sweet butter	15 ml

1. Preheat oven to 350°F (180°C).
2. Dredge chicken with flour. Combine melted butter, celery salt, paprika, salt, curry powder, oregano and pepper. Coat chicken with seasoned butter.
3. In a shallow baking dish, arrange chicken in a single layer. Sprinkle with almonds, cover and bake in oven for 45 minutes. Uncover.
4. Pour pan drippings into a bowl. Skim off fat. Combine ¼ cup (50 ml) drippings and sour cream; mix well. Pour sour cream mixture over chicken.
5. Mix soft butter into breadcrumbs. Sprinkle over sour cream. Bake, uncovered, 10 minutes longer, until almonds and crumbs are brown and chicken is tender.

Makes 4 servings.

Pecan Chicken with Red Pepper Coulis

This is the best chicken dish I've ever tasted. Also one of the best-looking. I like to plate before serving as a simple drizzling of the red pepper coulis elicits a round of "wows" before everyone dips in. The nuttiness of the crisp coating goes well served on a bed of crisp watercress. A garnish of lightly sautéed summer squash completes the presentation. Since this is a favorite, I sometimes vary the sauce to a tangy tomato or spicy mustard.

4	boneless, skinless chicken breasts, halved (2 lbs/1 kg)	4
½ cup	white wine	125 ml
2 tbsp	Dijon mustard	25 ml
1 tbsp	olive oil	15 ml
½ cup plus 1 tbsp	flour	140 ml
1	egg	1
1 tbsp	water	15 ml
¼ cup	pecans, ground	50 ml
2 tbsp	breadcrumbs	25 ml
¼ tsp	salt	1 ml
¼ tsp	freshly ground black pepper	1 ml
2 tbs	butter	25 ml

1. In a shallow dish, marinate chicken in the wine, mustard and oil. Cover and refrigerate overnight.
2. Preheat oven to 375°F (190°C).
3. In a shallow dish, place ½ cup (125 ml) of the flour. In another dish, lightly beat the egg and water together. In a third dish, combine pecans, bread crumbs, 1 tbsp (15 ml) flour, salt and pepper.
4. Remove chicken from the marinade; dip each piece in the flour, then egg wash, then pecan mixture, coating each piece well. Set aside.
5. In a large skillet, heat butter. Add chicken breasts and sauté about 2 minutes each side, or until lightly browned.
6. Arrange chicken in a single layer on baking pan. Bake for 8 minutes. Keep warm.

Red Pepper Coulis

3	red peppers, roasted, peeled and seeded	3
1 tbsp	balsamic vinegar	15 ml
¼ tsp	salt	1 ml
¼ tsp	freshly ground black pepper	1 ml

1. In a food processor or blender, combine peppers, vinegar, salt and pepper. Process 30 seconds, or until smooth.
2. Drizzle red pepper sauce over the chicken and serve.

Makes 4 servings.

Choose a medium-bodied red—a youthful Rioja such as Marquis de Riscal, for example—that won't drown the subtle flavors in this dish.

Hint – One pound of unshelled nuts is equal to ½ pound shelled.

Sesame Baked Chicken

I have dined on this when my mother-in-law served it in her home. I have served it at my own buffet parties. I have made it for literally hundreds of people traveling out of town on a theater party, and I've never had a piece left over, just well-picked bones. You won't believe what buttermilk does for chicken when you let it soak up all that goodness overnight. The sesame seed coating mixture is also great for your veal chops and butterfly pork chops.

8	pieces chicken, legs or breasts (4 lbs/2 kg)	8
2½ cups	buttermilk	625 ml
¾ cup	sweet butter, melted	175 ml
2 tbsp	lemon juice	25 ml
2	cloves garlic, finely chopped	2
1½ cups	fine dry breadcrumbs	125 ml
½ cup	sesame seeds	125 ml
½ tsp	salt	2 ml
¼ tsp	white pepper	1 ml
2 tbsp	freshly grated Parmesan cheese	25 ml

1. In a shallow baking dish, arrange chicken pieces. Pour buttermilk over chicken. Cover and refrigerate overnight. Next morning, pour off buttermilk and pat chicken dry.
2. When ready to cook, preheat oven to 450°F (220°C).
3. In a shallow dish, combine butter, lemon juice and garlic. In another dish combine breadcrumbs, sesame seeds, salt, pepper and Parmesan.
4. Dip chicken in butter mixture, then roll in breadcrumb mixture to coat each piece well. Arrange chicken in a single layer in baking pan. Drizzle any remaining butter over chicken.
5. Bake for 10 minutes. Reduce heat to 350°F (180°C) and continue to bake, basting occasionally with drippings, for 1 hour, until golden brown and tender.

Makes 8 servings.

Chicken Fingers with Three Dipping Sauces

I love these sauces because I love to dip. The plum sauce has a sweet garlic hit; the tomato a jalapeño heat; and the honey mustard is sharp and tangy. (All three are great condiments to have on hand for rib basting, to serve with sliced pork tenderloin, poached chicken or grilled shrimp.) Parmesan cheese adds a kick to the chicken fingers. Casual and fun, this is a great make-ahead dish that freezes well. Perfect after a day on the slopes. Serve with cold beer.

4	whole, boneless, skinless chicken breasts, halved (2 lbs/1 kg)	4
1	egg	1
1 tbsp	water	15 ml
½ cup	dry breadcrumbs	125 ml
¼ cup	cornmeal	50 ml
¼ cup	grated Parmesan cheese	50 ml
1 tsp	paprika	5 ml
½ tsp	salt	2 ml
½ tsp	freshly ground black pepper	2 ml
½ tsp	dried basil	2 ml
½ tsp	dried oregano	2 ml
¼ cup	all-purpose flour	50 ml

1. Preheat oven to 375°F (190°C).
2. Slice chicken into ½-inch (1-cm) strips. Set aside.
3. In a shallow dish, whisk together egg and water.
4. In another shallow dish, combine breadcrumbs, cornmeal, Parmesan and seasonings.
5. Coat chicken fingers with flour, a few pieces at a time, and shake off excess.
6. Dip chicken in the egg mixture, then in the breadcrumb mixture.
7. Place on baking sheet and bake in oven for 5 minutes or until just cooked through.

Makes 24 strips.

Make sauces ahead and serve them warm with chicken.

Hot Tomato Sauce

3 tbsp	butter	50 ml
1	small onion, finely chopped	1
1	clove garlic, finely chopped	1
1	jalapeño pepper, seeded and finely chopped	1
½ cup	ketchup	125 ml
	juice of ½ lemon	
½ tsp	hot pepper sauce	2 ml

1. In a small saucepan, heat butter on medium heat. Add onion, garlic and jalapeño; sauté until softened, about 3 minutes.
2. Add ketchup, lemon juice and hot pepper sauce and cook until heated through.

Plum Sauce

½ cup	plum jam	125 ml
1	clove garlic, finely chopped	1
1 tsp	fresh ginger, grated	5 ml
¼ cup	white wine vinegar	50 ml
1 tbsp	soy sauce	15 ml
1 tbsp	water	15 ml

1. In a small saucepan, combine all ingredients on medium heat and bring to a boil.
2. Continue boiling about 3 minutes until sauce is thickened.

Honey Mustard Sauce

2 tbsp	dried mustard	25 ml
1 tsp	grainy mustard	5 ml
¼ cup	brown sugar	50 ml
¼ cup	honey	50 ml
¼ cup	cider vinegar	50 ml
¼ tsp	salt	1 ml

1. In a small saucepan, combine all ingredients on medium heat and bring to a boil.
2. Continue boiling about 3 minutes until sauce is thickened.

Chicken Burgers or Chicken Loaf

If you are barbecuing, paint these burgers with butter to keep them from sticking. Otherwise, the cream does the job of keeping the breast meat moist and delicious. Nothing goes with a great burger like a charming Bordeaux.

2 lb	boneless chicken breasts	1 kg
2	eggs	2
1½ cups	light cream	375 ml
½ cup	fine dry breadcrumbs	125 ml
½ cup	ground almonds, toasted	125 ml
1	large onion, finely chopped	1
¼ cup	finely chopped fresh parsley	50 ml
1 tbsp	finely chopped fresh tarragon, or 1 tsp (5 ml) dried	15 ml
2 tsp	salt	10 ml
1 tsp	freshly ground black pepper	5 ml
½ tsp	ground nutmeg	2 ml
2 tbsp	sweet butter	25 ml

1. In a food processor or meat grinder, grind chicken.
2. In a large bowl, combine chicken, eggs, cream, breadcrumbs, almonds, onions, parsley, tarragon, salt, pepper and nutmeg; mix thoroughly.
3. For ease in handling, refrigerate chicken mixture 30 minutes before making burgers. Divide mixture into 8 portions and shape into burgers.
4. In a skillet, heat butter, add burgers, and cook, turning once, about 10 minutes, until firm and no longer pink.

Makes 8 patties.

Variation: Chicken Loaf

1. Preheat oven to 350°F (180°C).
2. Spread chicken mixture in a buttered 9x5-inch (23x12-cm) loaf pan. Place pan in larger pan and pour hot water into larger pan to a depth of 1-inch (2.5-cm).
3. Bake in oven for 35 minutes, until tester inserted in center comes out clean.
4. Serve hot, or cold with Summer Fruit Chili Sauce

Makes 1 loaf.

Beef

Beef is one of the great meats of the world. Since we cannot deal here with everything from Beef Bourgignon to Beef Wellington, I have tried to select a variety of beef recipes that stress the unusual and, in one case, the elevated: the fillet roast of beef with pepper sauce.

The brisket recipe is a great main course dish for taking to the country or cottage for weekends away. The cabbage rolls are fit to serve to kings, but their true appeal is filling in as a delicious surprise for a ski weekend party or an in-town impromptu buffet.

Fillet Roast of Beef with Pepper Sauce

The special combination of herbs and spices in this recipe can be used on lamb, veal, and pork roasts and chops. You might want to make a double batch, so that you can put one in a covered jar or shaker for later use. Keep in a dry, cool spot.

4½ lbs	beef fillet	2 kg
2 tbsp	dried oregano	25 ml
1 tbsp	dried thyme	15 ml
1 tbsp	celery seed	15 ml
1 tbsp	dried marjoram	15 ml
1 tbsp	garlic powder	15 ml
1 tbsp	coarse salt	15 ml
1 tbsp	cracked green or black peppercorns	15 ml

1. In a bowl or jar, combine oregano, thyme, celery seed, marjoram, garlic powder, salt and peppercorns. Rub seasoning mix on all sides of fillet to coat completely. (Store any remaining mixture in a tightly covered container in a cool, dry cupboard for up to 6 months.)
2. Place beef on a plate; cover lightly with waxed paper. Allow to stand in refrigerator for 1 to 2 hours.
3. Preheat oven to 425°F (220°C).
4. Place fillet on rack of shallow roasting pan and roast in oven for 10 minutes.
5. Reduce heat to 325°F (160°C) and roast for another 30 minutes, until rare, or 40 minutes, until medium rare.
6. Remove to a warm platter. Let stand 10 minutes before slicing.
   Serve with Pepper Sauce.

Makes 10 to 12 servings.

Pepper Sauce

It's nice to see your daughter following in your footsteps when it comes to a career. I could never have gotten this recipe from Jacques, one of the owners of Le Bistro, but my daughter did with her persistence. It's a beautiful shiny sauce with galaxies of green, pink and black peppercorns floating in it. Looks great, tastes better. It can also be served with steaks, hamburgers and lamb chops.

1 tbsp	sweet butter	15 ml
3	shallots, finely chopped	3
2 tbsp	brandy	25 ml
1 tsp	Dijon mustard	5 ml
½ tsp	black peppercorns, lightly crushed	2 ml
½ tsp each	drained, whole green and pink peppercorns	2 ml each
½ cup	heavy or whipping cream	125 ml
	salt	

1. In a small skillet, heat butter. Add shallots and sauté 4 minutes, until softened.
2. Add brandy and flame. Stir in mustard, peppercorns and cream. Bring to a boil, reduce heat, and simmer, stirring, 4 to 5 minutes, until thickened.
3. Taste and season with salt.

Makes 4 to 6 servings.

A simple but good Californian Cabernet Sauvignon makes a fine match.

Hint – For a child's garden birthday party, prepare individual packages of treats and prizes, using unusual inexpensive toys and curios found in Chinatown. Wrap them in bright Chinese paper and suspend them from the trees in the yard at heights that the children can reach themselves. Hang colorful Chinese streamers and lanterns everywhere.

Rare Beef Tenderloin in Oyster Sauce

A wonderful way to serve beef tenderloin. This is the only stir-fry for which I use both a frying pan and a wok. That allows me to give the beef just the few moments it needs to turn brown and delicious on the outside, while remaining blue and juicy on the inside. That's the way we like it at my house.

1 lb	beef tenderloin, cut in thin slices	500 g
¼ cup	oyster sauce	50 ml
¼ cup	cold water	50 ml
2 tbsp	red wine	25 ml
1 tbsp	soy sauce	15 ml
1 tsp	Worcestershire sauce	5 ml
½ tsp	granulated sugar	2 ml
½ tsp	cornstarch	2 ml
¼ tsp	freshly ground black pepper	1 ml
1	pkg (½ oz/14.2 g) dried mushrooms	1
3 tbsp	vegetable oil	45 ml
4	green onions, thinly sliced	4
2	cloves garlic, finely chopped	2
1	can (10 oz/284 g) water chestnuts, cut in half	1
½ lb	snowpeas (2 cups/500 ml)	250 g
1	medium carrot, thinly sliced	1

1. In a medium bowl, combine oyster sauce, water, wine, soy sauce, Worcestershire sauce, sugar, cornstarch and pepper; mix until smooth. Add beef, cover and marinate 1 hour or overnight in refrigerator.
2. In a bowl, soak mushrooms in warm water to cover for 1 hour. Drain and thinly slice.
3. In a wok or skillet, heat 2 tbsp (25 ml) oil. Add onions and garlic; stir-fry about 2 minutes, until softened.
4. Add water chestnuts, snowpeas, mushroom slices and carrot. Stir-fry about 5 minutes, until carrot is tender-crisp.

X 617-848-2908

Rte. 6A at 28, Box 666, Orleans, Massachusetts 02653 • (508) 255-1330

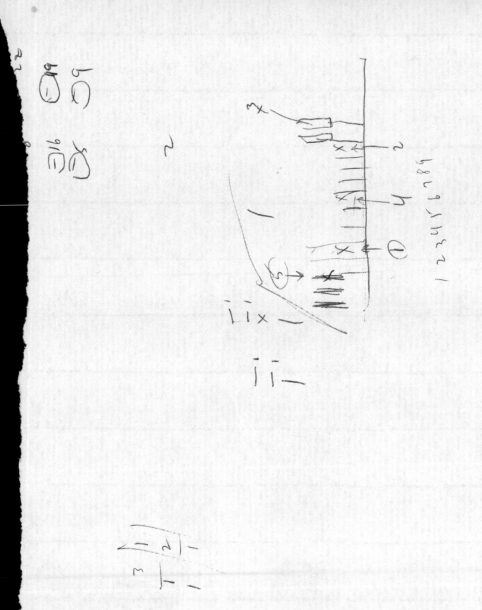

5. With slotted spoon, remove beef from marinade, reserving marinade. Drain beef on paper towel.
6. In a separate skillet, heat remaining oil and add beef; stir-fry 1 to 2 minutes, until rare. Do not overcook.
7. Stir reserved marinade into vegetable mixture. Cook, stirring, about 2 minutes, until sauce is thickened.
8. Add beef to vegetable mixture; toss to combine. Serve immediately.

Makes 4 servings.

An opportunity to bring out your best red Bordeaux or Californian Cabernet Sauvignon. A Côte Rotie or Hermitage from the Rhône are excellent candidates.

Hint – Preparations for the Guests to Wok – Invite them to wok over. Even if they can't, it brings up the subject and you can tell them what you are planning. Before your guests arrive, spread a few pieces of bright red cotton on your living room furniture. If you have a Chinese objet d'art, feature it. Use those little umbrella toothpicks for drinks that have fruit in them. Burn a joss stick just before the guests arrive to approximate an Oriental atmosphere. Serve a selection of hors d'oeuvres or finger foods. When you invite your guests to pick up their drinks and join you in the kitchen, have one last simple treat waiting for them while they watch you perform your magic.

Oriental Beef Shishkabobs

I marinate these tidbits before I go out, knowing they will take only moments to prepare when my guests arrive. Serve with cooked rice vermicelli, chopped mint, shredded lettuce and Dipping Sauce.

2 lb	beef sirloin steak	1 kg
⅓ cup	vegetable oil	75 ml
1 tbsp	sesame oil	15 ml
1 tbsp	granulated sugar	15 ml
1 tbsp	soy sauce	15 ml
1 tbsp	toasted sesame seeds	15 ml
1	clove garlic, finely chopped	1
1 tsp	salt	5 ml
½ tsp	freshly ground black pepper	2 ml
¼ tsp	five-spice powder	1 ml
	toasted sesame seeds	

1. Cut beef into 2x1x¼-inch (5x2.5x.5-cm) slices. Place in a glass bowl.
2. Combine vegetable oil, sesame oil, sugar, soy sauce, sesame seeds, garlic, salt, pepper and five-spice powder. Pour over meat; cover and marinate for 3 to 4 hours in refrigerator.
3. Thread meat onto wooden or metal skewers, 6 inches (15 cm) long. (Soak wooden skewers in a pan of warm water, 1 hour before using.) Barbecue, grill, or broil, turning once, about 6 minutes or until meat is medium rare.
4. Sprinkle with additional sesame seeds. Serve with Dipping Sauce.

Dipping Sauce

½ cup	water	125 ml
¼ cup	fish sauce	50 ml
1	small clove garlic	1
½ tsp	granulated sugar	2 ml
¼ tsp	lemon juice	1 ml
dash	hot pepper sauce	dash

In a bowl, combine water, fish sauce, garlic, sugar, lemon juice and hot pepper sauce; mix well.

Makes 6 servings.

Cabbage Rolls

I can't think of a better dish to make, freeze, and hold for those occasions when you want to ask the whole crowd in and you haven't prepared a thing. I often serve a bowl of sour cream on the side, along with skewered mushrooms. The dark raisins and almonds add to the special taste and help produce the deep, dark sauce.

1	large head cabbage (24 medium leaves)	1
	boiling water	
2 lb	lean ground beef	1 kg
1 cup	long grain rice	250 ml
1	egg, well beaten	1
½ cup	water	125 ml
1	large onion, finely chopped	1
1	small clove garlic, finely chopped	1
2 tsp	salt	10 ml
½ tsp	freshly ground black pepper	2 ml
2	large carrots, thinly sliced	2
2	stalks celery, thinly sliced	2
½ cup	raisins	125 ml
12	whole almonds	12
1 cup	lightly packed brown sugar	250 ml
½ cup	lemon juice	125 ml
1	can (28 oz/796 ml) Italian tomatoes	1
1	can (10 oz/284 ml) tomato soup	1
	sour cream	

1. With a sharp knife, remove core of cabbage and discard. In a large saucepan of lightly salted boiling water, place cabbage. Bring to a boil and boil 5 minutes. Remove leaves, one at a time, being careful not to break them. Drain leaves on paper towel.
2. Preheat oven to 350°F (180°C).

3. In a large bowl, combine beef, rice, egg, water, onion, garlic, salt and pepper; mix well. Place heaping tablespoons of filling in middle of each cabbage leaf, fold edge over, turn in sides and roll up tightly.
4. In a shallow baking or roasting pan, layer carrots and celery. Arrange cabbage rolls over this "bed" of vegetables. Spread raisins, almonds and brown sugar over rolls. Pour on lemon juice, tomatoes and tomato soup. Cover and bake in oven for 2 hours.
5. Remove cover and bake 1 hour longer, until cabbage rolls are tender. Serve with sour cream.

Makes 24 cabbage rolls.

Brisket in Ginger Ale

This is how my Mom taught me to make brisket many years ago; it is still the best way. Since my guests have always exclaimed over the glazed carrots, I have allowed two for each person. If you have some brisket left over the next day, you are in for a treat, either hot with gravy or cold with horseradish sauce.

4 to 5 lbs	beef brisket	2 to 2.5 kg
2	cloves garlic, finely chopped	2
1 tsp	paprika	5 ml
1 tsp	salt	5 ml
½ tsp	freshly ground black pepper	2 ml
¼ cup	prepared mustard	50 ml
1	large onion, finely chopped	1
8	carrots, cut in 2-inch (5-cm) pieces	8
2 tbsp	water	25 ml
1	bottle (24 oz/750 ml) ginger ale	1

1. Preheat oven to 450°F (230°C).
2. Rub brisket with garlic, paprika, salt, pepper and mustard. Place brisket in heavy roasting pan. Sprinkle onion on top of brisket.
3. Bake brisket uncovered in oven for 45 minutes. Remove from oven and drain off all fat.
4. Lower oven temperature to 325°F. Place carrots around brisket. Add water to pan. Baste meat every 20 minutes with ¼ cup (50 ml) of ginger ale. Bake, covered, 3 hours and 25 minutes, until meat is very tender. Remove from oven; pour off liquid in pan and reserve.
5. Remove brisket, cool and wrap; remove carrots to a small container, cover; refrigerate brisket and carrots overnight. Pour remaining pan juices into bowl; place in refrigerator overnight so that fat layer that rises to the top will harden. Lift off fat layer and discard.
6. Preheat oven to 350°F (180°C).
7. Slice brisket and arrange slices in a shallow casserole. Pour reserved pan juices over top. Place carrots around meat. Cover and reheat in oven about 30 minutes, or until heated through.

Makes 8 servings.

German Pot Roast

Again, an unusual ingredient gives this dish its special zing. It's the crushed gingersnaps that do it. Makes a great winter party dish.

4 lb	beef brisket	2 kg
2 tsp	salt	10 ml
4	cloves garlic, finely chopped	4
1	piece (1½-inch/3.5-cm) ginger root, peeled and finely chopped	1
2 cups	red wine vinegar	500 ml
1 cup	water	250 ml
½ cup	dry vermouth	125 ml
⅓ cup	granulated sugar	75 ml
2	onions, finely chopped	2
8	whole cloves	8
2	bay leaves	2
2 tsp	pickling spice	10 ml
1 tsp	whole black peppercorns	5 ml
½ tsp	dry mustard	2 ml
2 tbsp	vegetable oil	25 ml
4	gingersnaps, crushed	4

1. Rub brisket all over with salt. Place brisket in a large bowl and sprinkle garlic and ginger root over top.
2. Combine vinegar, water, vermouth, sugar, onions, cloves, bay leaves, pickling spice, peppercorns, mustard and vegetable oil. Pour marinade over brisket. Cover tightly and refrigerate overnight, turning once.
3. Remove brisket from marinade and reserve 2 cups (500 ml) of marinade. Pat meat with paper towels. In a Dutch oven, heat oil; add brisket and cook, turning once or twice, for about 10 minutes, until brown.
4. Preheat oven to 350°F (180°C). Pour reserved marinade over brisket; cover and bake in oven for 2 to 3 hours, or until meat is tender.

5. Let stand 10 minutes to firm. Remove meat to board and slice. Cover and refrigerate until required. Place pan juices in refrigerator until fat layer hardens.
6. Preheat oven to 300°F (150°C).
7. Arrange brisket slices in 8½x12½-inch (21x31-cm) shallow casserole. Remove fat from pan juices and strain juices into a saucepan. Add crushed gingersnaps. Bring to a boil, reduce heat, and simmer 2 minutes, until thickened. Pour over brisket slices.
8. Reheat in oven about 15 minutes, until hot. Serve immediately.

Makes 8 servings.

This dish needs a sturdy red. Serve an Italian Barolo or French Cornas to balance the flavors.

French Country Meatloaf

I serve this loaf with Dijon mustard and a cold salad. All meat loaves cry out for sauces and condiments, particularly when cold. Try some of the recipes in the Condiments section, like Dilled Carrot Sticks or Colleen's Chili Sauce. This is a large loaf and wonderful served cold.

2 lb	lean ground beef	1 kg
1 lb	ground veal	500 g
1 lb	ground pork	500 g
1	large onion, coarsely chopped	1
1 cup	chopped fresh parsley	250 ml
8	green onions, finely chopped	8
¼ cup	chopped fresh basil leaves or	50 ml
	1 tbsp (15 ml) dried	
2 tsp	Dijon mustard	10 ml
2 tsp	salt	10 ml
1 tsp	freshly ground black pepper	5 ml
½ tsp	hot pepper sauce	2 ml
3	eggs, well beaten	3
¾ cup	fresh breadcrumbs	175 ml
½ cup	light cream	125 ml
12	slices bacon	12

1. Preheat oven to 350°F (160°C).
2. In a large bowl, combine beef, veal, pork, onion, parsley, green onions, basil, mustard, salt, pepper and hot pepper sauce.
3. Combine eggs, breadcrumbs and cream; stir into mixture.
4. Lay six bacon slices side by side in a 9x13-inch (23x33-cm) baking pan. Place meat mixture on top of bacon. With hands shape into a loaf. Lay remaining bacon slices on top of loaf. Bake in oven, basting frequently with pan juices, 1½ to 2 hours, until meat is no longer pink.

5. Cool for 30 minutes.
6. Slice and serve.

Makes 12 servings.

My favorite wines with meatloaf have always been the full-bodied earthy wines of the Rhône. On a cold winter evening, nothing else comes close.

Hint – Meatloaf Pans – There are all kinds of fancy pans sold for making loaves, but my advice is to make it in a rectangular baking pan rather than a loaf pan. Just shape it and let it bake. All you lose is a little fat, which you would have to skim off anyway, and lifting the loaf onto a serving plate is much easier when you can get a grip on it.

Lamb

Succulent cuts of lamb are available year-round, but to me, lamb is spring. It is synonymous with great bowls of daffodils and tulips on the table, and with fresh herbs just budding. I find myself humming a little descant of "Parsley, mint, rosemary, and lamb" to the tune of "Scarborough Fair."

Beyond lamb roasts, I have given you a number of recipes for Indian curries, which is another role this meat is perfectly suited for. Try them all any time of year, but especially in the spring, when the world drips with wet lilac and honey.

Spicy Lamb Chops in a Tomato Rosemary Marinade

Somewhere, someone tasted a tomato and said, "Needs rosemary!" So here it is. The classic Tomato Rosemary Marinade for lamb chop barbecues and grills.

12	loin lamb chops (¾-inch/2-cm thick)	12
½ cup	tomato paste	125 ml
½ cup	vegetable oil	125 ml
2 tbsp	soy sauce	25 ml
2 tbsp	red wine vinegar	25 ml
4	cloves garlic, finely chopped	4
1 tbsp	dried rosemary leaves	15 ml
1 tsp	salt	5 ml
½ tsp	coarsely ground black pepper	2 ml

1. Arrange lamb chops in a shallow baking dish.
2. Combine tomato paste, oil, soy sauce, vinegar, garlic, rosemary, salt and pepper. Pour over lamb chops and marinate, covered, overnight in refrigerator.
3. Broil or grill 5 minutes on each side, or until cooked to desired doneness.

Makes 6 servings.

The traditional partners for lamb are still the best: a very good bottle of Bordeaux or a Cabernet Sauvignon equivalent from California or Australia. When you're feeling decidedly untraditional, have some fun experimenting with an excellent quality Rioja.

Indian Lamb Chops in a Snappy Yogurt Marinade

The marinade makes these lamb chops. Let them soak in it until your guests are ready to have you barbecue.

12	loin lamb chops (¾-inch/2-cm thick)	12
	salt and freshly ground black pepper	
1 cup	yogurt	250 ml
1 tbsp	crushed coriander seeds	15 ml
2 tsp	ground cumin	10 ml
1 tsp	garam masala	5 ml
1	red onion, coarsely chopped	1
2	cloves garlic, finely chopped	2
1	lime, grated rind and juice	1
1	slice (½-inch/1-cm) ginger root, peeled and chopped	
¼ tsp	hot pepper sauce	1 ml
	coarsely ground black pepper	

1. Arrange lamb chops in a shallow baking dish and season with salt and pepper. Combine yogurt, coriander, cumin, garam masala, onion, lime rind and juice, ginger root and hot pepper sauce. Pour over lamb and allow to marinate, covered in refrigerator, overnight.

2. Broil or grill chops 5 minutes on each side or until cooked to desired doneness. Top with coarsely ground black pepper.

Makes 6 servings.

Hint – Add 2 tsp coffee to darken colorless gravy without changing the taste.

Lamb Calcutta

The shreds of coconut and the chunks of apple make this a very sweet and gentle curried lamb. Serve with your favorite chutney and my Sweet Rice.

2 lb	lean boneless lamb, cut in 1-inch (2.5-cm) cubes	1 kg
¼ cup	olive oil	50 ml
2	large apples, peeled, cored and coarsely chopped	2
2	large onions, coarsely chopped	2
1	clove garlic, finely chopped	1
2 tbsp	all-purpose flour	25 ml
1 tbsp	curry powder	15 ml
½ tsp	salt	2 ml
½ tsp	dried marjoram	2 ml
½ tsp	dried thyme	2 ml
1½ cups	beef stock	375 ml
½ cup	dry red wine	125 ml
1	lemon, grated rind and juice	1
½ cup	raisins	125 ml
¼ tsp	ground cloves	1 ml
¼ cup	shredded coconut	50 ml
2 tbsp	sour cream	25 ml

1. In a large skillet, heat 2 tbsp (25 ml) oil; add lamb cubes, half at a time. Cook, turning, about 10 minutes, until lightly browned. Remove to a warm dish and keep warm. Repeat with remaining lamb.
2. In the same skillet, heat remaining oil. Add apples, onions and garlic. Sauté about 5 minutes, until softened. Stir in flour, curry powder, salt, marjoram and thyme. Cook, stirring, for 3 minutes.
3. Gradually stir in stock, wine, lemon rind and juice, raisins, cloves and browned lamb cubes. Bring to a boil, reduce heat, cover, and simmer 20 to 30 minutes.
4. Stir in coconut. Cover and simmer 15 minutes longer.
5. Just before serving, blend in sour cream.

Makes 6 servings.

Lamb Tajine

Don't be surprised if a neighbor drops by to investigate the aroma wafting from your kitchen. Use a deep, glazed earthenware dish to slow-cook this marvelous combination of lamb, artichokes, prunes and spices. (The name comes from the North African cooking method.) On a cold winter night, I serve this on a bed of Rice and Vermicelli. This dish tastes even better the next day, so make it in advance.

2 lb	lean boneless lamb, cut in 1-inch (2.5-cm) cubes	1 kg
2 tbsp	olive oil	25 ml
4	carrots, diced	4
2	onions, diced	2
1 tsp	ground cumin	5 ml
½ tsp	ginger	2 ml
1	clove garlic, finely chopped	1
6	large tomatoes, peeled and chopped	6
2 tbsp	lemon juice	25 ml
1 cup	prunes, pitted and halved	250 ml
1 cup	cooked artichoke bottoms	250 ml

1. In a large, heavy-bottomed pot, heat olive oil; add lamb cubes. Cook, turning, about 7 minutes, until browned.
2. Add carrots, onions, cumin, ginger and garlic. Cook, stirring about 5 minutes, until softened.
3. Stir in tomatoes and lemon juice; reduce heat and simmer for 20 minutes.
4. Stir in prunes and artichokes. Cover and simmer 10 more minutes.

Makes 6 servings.

Swedish Lamb Roast

There are all kinds of surprises in this very pretty dish, not the least of which is a cup of coffee with cream and sugar. The candied carrots are another bonus: you can adjust the number of carrots to the number of guests you have invited. I should add a note here about how to serve roasts. There is nothing quite so awkward as an inexperienced person trying to carve at table. I am not bad, but I still won't do it. I always let the roast cool down, carve in the kitchen and then warm everything up at the last moment.

1	leg of lamb (4 to 5 lb/2 to 2.5 kg)	1
½ tsp	salt	2 ml
¼ tsp	freshly ground black pepper	1 ml
1	medium onion, thinly sliced	1
8	medium carrots, thickly sliced	8
1 cup	beef stock	250 ml
1 cup	very strong coffee	250 ml
½ cup	light cream	125 ml
1 tbsp	sugar	15 ml

1. Preheat oven to 425°F (220°C).
2. Sprinkle lamb with salt and pepper. Insert roast meat thermometer in thickest part of roast. Place in roasting pan; sprinkle sliced onion around lamb. Roast in oven for 30 minutes.
3. Reduce oven temperature to 350°F (180°C). Add carrots and stock to pan. Roast 30 minutes longer.
4. Combine coffee, cream and sugar; baste lamb and roast 20 minutes longer, or until meat thermometer registers 150°F (65°C) or medium rare.
5. Remove roast to warm serving platter; let stand 10 minutes to make carving easier. Surround with carrots. Serve warm pan sauce in sauce boat.

Makes 6 to 8 servings.

Lamb Basted

I couldn't resist the pun. You can use a boned shoulder or a leg of lamb for this. If you use the leg, I suggest you get the butcher to bone it. I like to start this the day before because I can let the roast cool and skim off all the fat.

1	boned shoulder or leg of lamb (4 to 5 lb/2 to 2.5 kg)	1
2	cloves garlic, halved	2
1 tsp	salt	5 ml
1 tsp	freshly ground black pepper	5 ml
½ tsp	chili powder	2 ml
½ tsp	dry mustard	2 ml
¼ tsp	ground ginger	1 ml
1 tsp	lemon juice	5 ml
1 cup	tomato sauce	250 ml
½ cup	dry red wine	125 ml
	beef stock	

1. Preheat oven to 500°F (260°C).
2. With the point of a knife, cut four slits in surface of lamb and insert pieces of garlic in slits. Combine salt, pepper, chili powder, mustard and ginger. Sprinkle over surface of lamb. Place roast on a rack in a roasting pan. Sprinkle with lemon juice. Insert roast meat thermometer in thickest part of roast. Roast in oven for 20 minutes.
3. Reduce oven temperature to 300°F (150°C). Combine tomato sauce and wine; brush over roast. Return lamb to oven and roast, basting frequently with tomato mixture, for 2 to 2½ hours until meat thermometer registers 150°F (65°C) or medium rare.
4. Pour any liquid in bottom of pan into a measuring cup. Skim off fat. Add enough beef stock to make 2 cups (500 ml). Taste and season with salt and pepper if desired. Heat and serve as "jus" with lamb.

Makes 8 servings.

Barbecued Butterfly Lamb

I serve this with brown rice and sautéed red onions. I add a summer salad of blanched green beans and broccoli, raw zucchini, sliced or diced tomatoes, raw onion slices, and fresh mushrooms, all tossed with my Tomato Vinaigrette. One tip: make sure the knife you use for slicing and crisscrossing is super sharp.

1	butterflied leg of lamb	1
	(4 to 6 lbs/2 to 3 kg)	
2	large cloves garlic, coarsely chopped	2
½ cup	dry red wine	125 ml
¼ cup	olive oil	50 ml
¼ cup	lemon juice	50 ml
¼ cup	Dijon mustard	50 ml
¼ cup	chopped fresh mint leaves	50 ml
1 tbsp	dried rosemary leaves	15 ml
1 tbsp	dried oregano	15 ml
¼ tsp	freshly ground black pepper	1 ml

1. Place lamb in a large glass bowl.
2. In a bowl combine garlic, wine, oil, lemon juice, mustard, mint, rosemary, oregano and pepper; mix well. Pour over lamb. Cover and marinate in refrigerator for several hours or overnight. Turn lamb over in marinade several times so it is well coated.
3. Remove lamb from marinade, reserving marinade.
4. Before barbecuing, with a sharp knife score fat with crisscross lines to prevent meat from curling. Place lamb on barbecue grill 4 to 5 inches (10 to 12.5 cm) above hot coals. Barbecue lamb for 40 to 45 minutes, turning every 10 minutes and basting frequently with reserved marinade, until lamb is cooked to the desired doneness.
5. Allow roast to stand 10 minutes to set juices. With a very sharp knife, slice thinly and serve.

Makes 8 to 10 servings.

Lamb Burgers or Lamb Loaf

The burgers have to marinate for 4 hours. The loaf goes straight to the oven.

2 lb	ground lamb	1 kg
½ cup	dry breadcrumbs	125 ml
1	large onion, finely chopped	1
1 tsp	chopped fresh cilantro	5 ml
1 tsp	ground cumin	5 ml
½ tsp	ground turmeric	2 ml
½ tsp	crushed chili pepper	2 ml
½ tsp	salt	2 ml
¼ tsp	freshly ground black pepper	1 ml
1	egg, lightly beaten	1
½ cup	yogurt	125 ml
1 tbsp	lime juice	15 ml

Marinade

2 cups	yogurt	500 ml
2	cloves garlic, finely chopped	2
1½ tsp	white pepper	7 ml
1 tsp	chopped fresh mint	5 ml

1. In a bowl, combine lamb, breadcrumbs, onion, cilantro, cumin, turmeric, chili pepper, salt and pepper.
2. Combine egg, yogurt and lime juice. Stir into lamb mixture; mix thoroughly.
3. Divide into eight portions; with hands shape each portion into a burger. Place burgers in a glass baking dish.
4. Combine yogurt, garlic, pepper and mint. Pour half over burgers. Reserve remainder of marinade.
5. Cover and marinate burgers for 4 hours in refrigerator, turning once.
6. Remove burgers from marinade. Sauté, broil, or grill, turning once, about 10 minutes, until browned. Serve immediately with remaining marinade.

Makes 8 servings.

Variation: Lamb Loaf

1. Preheat oven to 350°F (180°C).
2. Prepare Lamb Burger mixture. With hands shape lamb mixture into loaf, 9x6x2-inch (23x15x5-cm). Place in center of baking pan. Bake in oven for 40 minutes, until firm and brown.
3. Serve loaf hot or cold with marinade as a sauce on the side, if desired.

Makes 1 loaf.

❀ *Braid a wreath of cedar or pine rope around the base of a silver three-candle candelabra. Decorate with small gold balls, thin gold ribbon, and walnuts.*

Pork

Anonymous Quote – *"Can a creature that finds truffles be all bad?"*

Notes

Tiffany's Barbecued Ribs

You can bake these "barbecued" ribs till they're done; or remove when almost finished and zap on the grill. Either way, there won't be any left—guaranteed. Worthy partners here range from a medium- or full-bodied red such as Gogondas or St. Joseph to an Australian Shiraz or California Zinfandel.

2 lbs	back ribs	1 kg

Sauce

1	can tomato paste (5½ oz/156 ml)	1
2 cups	water	500 ml
1 cup	ketchup	250 ml
⅓ cup	applesauce	75 ml
¼ cup	tomato juice	50 ml
1	stalk celery, chopped	1
1	carrot, chopped	1
½	orange, chopped with peel	½
1 tbsp	brown sugar	15 ml
1 tbsp	honey	15 ml
1 tbsp	red wine vinegar	15 ml
2 tsp	pickling spice	10 ml
1 tsp	freshly ground black pepper	5 ml
1	bay leaf	1
¼ tsp	crushed dried chili peppers	1 m

1. In a large saucepan, combine all the sauce ingredients and bring to a boil. Reduce heat and simmer for about 1 hour.
2. Put ribs into a 9x13-inch (23x32-cm) baking dish and cover with sauce. Cover with tin foil and refrigerate for 4 hours.
3. Preheat oven to 325°F (160°C).
4. Bake in oven for 1 hour and 15 minutes. Uncover and bake another 45 minutes, basting as necessary. Preheat barbecue to high, take ribs out of sauce and barbecue ribs a final 15 minutes or leave in oven for 15 minutes. Serve with the sauce.

Makes 4 servings.

Chinese Barbequed Wings and Ribs with Orange

After umpteen visits to Chinatowns in New York, San Francisco and Toronto, I was inspired to write this recipe. The secret is consommé, which makes this old-fashioned finger food good and sticky (get out your finger bowls). Serve with mounds of rice, crispy green salad and pots of jasmine tea.

1½ lbs	chicken wings, tips removed	750 g
1½ lbs	pork side ribs, cut in 2-inch (5-cm) pieces	750 g
¼ cup	honey	50 ml
2½ tbsp	slivered orange rind	30 ml
2 tbsp	molasses	25 ml
2 tbsp	soy sauce	25 ml
5	cloves garlic, finely chopped	5
1 tbsp	hoisin sauce	15 ml
1	can beef consommé (10 oz/284 ml)	1

1. In a small bowl, combine honey, orange rind, molasses, soy sauce, garlic, hoisin and consommé; stir well.
2. In a shallow baking dish, arrange wings and ribs. Pour sauce over, cover and marinate 1 hour in refrigerator or overnight.
3. Preheat oven to 375°F (190°C).
4. Bake uncovered 60 minutes until meat is tender and glazed and sauce is sticky.

Makes 10 to 12 servings.

Ginger Pork Cubes

This is best served hot from the skillet on toothpicks.

2 lb	boneless pork, cut in 1-inch (2.5-cm) cubes	1 kg
¼ cup	vegetable oil	50 ml
1 cup	finely chopped onion	250 ml
1	large clove garlic, finely chopped	1
½ cup	soy sauce	125 ml
1 tbsp	white vinegar	25 ml
¼ cup	chopped preserved ginger	50 ml

1. In a small skillet for table-top service, heat oil. Add pork and cook cubes, turning several times for about 15 minutes, until brown.
2. Add onion and garlic; cook 5 minutes, until onion is softened.
3. Stir in soy sauce, vinegar and ginger. Cover and simmer for 10 minutes.
4. Skewer cubes with toothpicks and serve from skillet.

Makes 3 to 4 dozen.

Peanut Pork Satay

The wonderful surprise in this elegant satay is that the cooked pork is rolled in chopped peanuts just before you serve it. The fun comes in the crunch. If using as a main course, offer rice, bowls of chopped green onions and chutneys. If using as an hors d'oeuvre, hand around with drinks and napkins.

2 lb	boneless lean pork, cut into 1-inch (2.5-cm) cubes	1 kg
¼ cup	fruit chutney	50 ml
¼ cup	soy sauce	50 ml
2 tbsp	peanut butter	25 ml
1 tbsp	grated fresh ginger root	15 ml
2	cloves garlic	2
1	onion, quartered	1
	juice of 1 lime	
1 cup	finely chopped salted peanuts	250 ml

1. Place pork cubes in glass bowl or heavy plastic bag.
2. In a food processor or blender, combine chutney, soy sauce, peanut butter, ginger root, garlic, onion and lime juice. Process until smooth. Pour over pork cubes. Toss to coat with sauce. Cover and marinate overnight in refrigerator.
3. Thread pork cubes on 12 skewers.* Grill over medium coals on barbecue, or broil under broiler about 4 inches (10 cm) from heat for 20 to 25 minutes, or until meat is no longer pink.
4. Roll skewers of meat in chopped peanuts and serve.

Makes 6 main course servings or 12 appetizers.

* If wooden skewers are used, soak them in a pan of cold water for about 1 hour before threading meat.

Canadian Bacon with Raisin Glaze

A whole piece of Canadian bacon, which looks like a small boneless loin of pork and is sometimes known as back bacon, makes a great roast for a casual supper, particularly when it is slathered with the raisin glaze and then served with Russian mustard, fresh-baked muffins and apple butter. I sometimes substitute a boneless pork loin—fresh or smoked—for a deliciously different menu.

4 lb	piece Canadian bacon	2 kg
	Raisin Glaze	

1. Preheat oven to 325°F (160°C).
2. With a sharp knife, cut bacon to within ½-inch (1-cm) of bottom into ½-inch (1-cm) slices, but do not cut through. Place on a rack in a shallow roasting pan. Pour water ½-inch (1-cm) deep into pan to prevent drying. Bake in oven for 1¼ hours.
3. Prepare Raisin Glaze. Brush over bacon and between slices.
4. Return to oven for 30 minutes and brush occasionally with glaze, until brown and shiny.
5. Place on a serving platter. At serving time cut between slices and serve. Pour any remaining glaze into a sauce dish.

Makes 10 to 12 servings.

Raisin Glaze

½ cup	raisins	125 ml
½ cup	boiling water	125 ml
2 tbsp	melted sweet butter	25 ml
1 tbsp	molasses	15 ml
1 tbsp	Worcestershire sauce	15 ml
1 tbsp	Russian mustard	15 ml
2 tsp	grated fresh ginger root	10 ml
¼ tsp	ground cloves	1 ml
pinch	nutmeg	pinch

1. In a blender or food processor, combine raisins and water; process 30 seconds, or until puréed.
2. In a bowl, combine raisin purée, butter molasses, Worcestershire sauce, mustard, ginger root, cloves and nutmeg. Mix well.
3. Brush over Canadian Bacon (back bacon) roast, pork loin or ham steaks.

Makes 1½ cups (375 ml).

Tourtière or French Canadian Meat Pie

This is the traditional dish served after Midnight Mass on Christmas Eve. Recipes for it are generations old, and no two are exactly the same. This one was pried loose by my daughter from the mother of her best friend. It is a hearty, nourishing pie and can be made either as a single large pie or as individual pies. Be sure to serve homemade Chili Sauce with this.

3 lb	ground pork	1.5 kg
¼ lb	salt pork, diced	125 g
1	small onion, coarsely chopped	1
1	clove garlic, finely chopped	1
2 cups	beef stock	500 ml
2 tbsp	celery leaves, finely chopped	25 ml
2 tbsp	chopped fresh parsley	25 ml
1	small bay leaf	1
⅛ tsp	nutmeg	0.5 mg
⅛ tsp	dried chervil	0.5 mg
pinch	ground cloves	pinch
pinch	cayenne pepper	pinch
2	slices dry French bread, crumbed after crusts removed	2
	Lemon Tang Pastry for two double-crust 9-inch (23-cm pies)	

1. In a large skillet, fry salt pork about 7 minutes, until lightly browned.
2. Add onion and garlic; continue cooking for 3 minutes, until onion is softened.
3. Add ground pork, stock, celery leaves, parsley, bay leaf, nutmeg, chervil, cloves and cayenne. Bring to a boil, reduce heat, and simmer, stirring occasionally, for 35 to 40 minutes, until pork is no longer pink.
4. Stir in breadcrumbs. Set aside to cool.
5. Preheat oven to 425°F (220°C).

6. Roll out pastry for 2 double-crust 9-inch (23-cm) pies. Fit pastry into pie plates and trim edges.

7. Spoon pork mixture into pie shells, spreading it well into the sides of the pastry. Cover with pastry tops. Trim, seal and flute edges. Cut steam vents.

8. Bake in oven for 15 minutes.

9. Reduce heat to 350°F (180°C) and continue to bake 25 to 30 minutes longer, until crust is golden.

10. Serve hot or freeze and reheat at serving time.

Makes 8 servings.

This French-Canadian dish goes best with a Portuguese Bairrada Garrafeira.

Veal

Veal is young, milk- or corn-fed beef, but while beef will add flavor, veal absorbs whatever you choose to flavor it with, hence its delicacy and adaptability.

Sweetbreads au Porto

This recipe has won over people who have avoided sweetbread up to tasting time. It is a favorite of mine. I serve this with a light Saffron Rice. Serve a mature red Burgundy or Bordeaux. If you prefer white, select a Rhine Riesling or a Silvaner Spatlese.

2 lb	veal sweetbreads	1 kg
1 tbsp	lemon juice	15 ml
½ cup	sweet butter	125 ml
2	onions, finely chopped	2
1 cup	thinly sliced mushrooms	250 ml
pinch	each of thyme, salt and freshly ground black pepper	pinch
¼ cup	all-purpose flour	50 ml
1 cup	beef stock	250 ml
½ cup	Port	125 ml
	all-purpose flour, salt and freshly ground black pepper	

1. In a bowl of ice water, soak the sweetbreads for 30 minutes. Drain and place in large saucepan. Pour boiling water over to cover. Add lemon juice, bring to a boil, reduce heat, cover and simmer 10 minutes, until tender.
2. Drain and cool immediately in ice-cold water. Remove all connective tissue and membrane. Slice into ½-inch (1-cm) slices. Set aside.
3. In a medium saucepan, melt ¼ cup (50 ml) butter. Add onions and sauté until softened. Add mushrooms, thyme, salt and pepper; sauté until mushrooms are lightly browned.
4. Sprinkle flour over mixture and stir until all is absorbed. Slowly add stock, stirring constantly over medium heat until smooth. Add Port and bring to a boil; reduce heat, cover and simmer 10 minutes.
5. While sauce is simmering, dredge sweetbread slices in flour seasoned with salt and pepper. In a large skillet, melt remaining butter. Add sweetbreads and sauté in batches, if necessary, about 4 minutes, turning until golden brown on both sides.
6. Remove to a warm serving platter; cover to keep warm. Serve sauce with sweetbreads.

Makes 6 servings.

Veal And Mushroom Ragout

This is a versatile little dish that you can make anytime, freeze and take with you to a ski chalet for a weekend gathering. The rich gravy gives you an excuse for whipping up baby dumplings to serve to guests who are cold and ravenous from the slopes. This perfect supper has made me the hit of many a winter party.

3 lb	stewing veal, cut in 1½-inch (3.5-cm) cubes	1.5 kg
¼ cup	all-purpose flour	50 ml
2 tsp	salt	10 ml
1 tsp	dried thyme	5 ml
½ tsp	freshly ground black pepper	2 ml
⅓ cup	sweet butter	75 ml
2 tbsp	vegetable oil	25 ml
2	medium onions, coarsely chopped	2
1	clove garlic, coarsely chopped	1
½ cup	Marsala or sweet sherry	125 ml
½ cup	beef stock	125 ml
1 tbsp	tomato paste	15 ml
¼ cup	light cream	50 ml
20	medium mushrooms, thinly sliced	20
2 cups	green peas	500 ml

1. In a bowl, combine flour, salt, thyme and pepper; coat veal cubes with flour mixture.
2. In a large skillet or Dutch oven, heat 2 tbsp (25 ml) butter and oil. Add veal; cook, stirring, about 10 minutes.
3. Add onions and garlic; cook 5 to 10 minutes, until softened.
4. Stir in Marsala, stock and tomato paste. Cover and cook over low heat 45 minutes, or until veal is tender. Stir in 2 tbsp (25 ml) butter and cream.
5. In a skillet, heat remaining butter; add mushrooms and sauté about 4 minutes.
6. Fold mushrooms and peas into veal mixture. Cook 10 minutes longer, until peas are tender.

Makes 6 servings.

Pasta, Grains, Legumes & Rice

Pasta, Grains, Legumes and Rice

Once considered the poor relations of a first-class menu, these excellent—and healthy—dishes have become honored mainstays of contemporary cuisine.

Pasta

Thai Spicy Noodles
Penne with Caramelized Red Onions
Fettuccine with Tomatoes, Mushrooms and Rosemary
Pasta with Brie
Gorgonzola Pasta with Leeks and Radicchio
Three Cheese Macaroni

Grains and Legumes

Asiago Polenta with Tomato Gin Sauce
Couscous Pilaf with Almonds
Masalchi Lentils

Rice

Spring Paddy Rice
Risoverdi (Green) Rice
Sweet-Scented Rice
Indian Rice
Savory Mushroom Rice
Com Rang (Fried Rice)
Rice Pilaf with Pine Nuts
Jamaican Rice and Peas
Rice and Vermicelli
Lemon Risotto
Risotto Portobello

Pasta

When fresh pasta first appeared, many of us went scurrying to pasta shops to try them all out. Lately, however, I find I much prefer the convenience, diversity of shapes and colors and the guaranteed results of the new packaged varieties.

Thai Spicy Noodles

When I need a hit of Thai Spicy Noodles, the place I go is the BamBoo Restaurant in Toronto, where a creative chef, Wendy Young, developed this dish. The cooking is fast, so it's important to assemble in advance. To adjust the heat from hot to hotter (my version) or hottest, increase or decrease the red pepper flakes.

12 oz	Thai rice noodles	375 g
⅓ cup	fish sauce	50 ml
⅓ cup	lime juice	50 ml
¼ cup	tomato purée	50 ml
⅓ cup	sugar	50 ml
4 tsp	hot red pepper flakes	20 ml
¾ cup	vegetable oil	175 ml
6	cloves garlic, finely chopped	6
1½ lb	boneless chicken breast or thigh, cut in small pieces	750 g
1	large square extra-firm tofu, well drained and patted dry	350 g
12	very large (tiger) shrimp, shelled and deveined	12
4	eggs, lightly beaten	4
¾ cup	ground peanuts	175 ml
4 cups	bean sprouts	1 l
4	scallions, cut in ½-inch (1-cm) pieces	4

Garnish

¼ cup	chopped peanuts	50 ml
6	lemon wedges	6
½	English cucumber, thinly sliced	½
½ cup	chopped cilantro	125 ml

1. Soak rice noodles in cold water for 2 to 3 hours until soft, and drain just before use.
2. In a small bowl, mix together fish sauce, lime juice, tomato purée, sugar and pepper flakes. Set aside.
3. In a large wok over high heat, heat oil, cook garlic 3 minutes until brown. Add chicken, tofu and shrimp, and sauté until lightly browned. Add eggs and continue to stir-fry.
4. Add drained noodles and fish-sauce mixture; continue to stir-fry for about 3 minutes.
5. Add peanuts, bean sprouts and scallions, and continue to stir-fry for another 2 minutes.
6. Garnish with chopped peanuts, lemon wedges, cucumber and cilantro. Serve immediately.

Makes 6 servings.

〰〰〰〰〰〰〰〰〰〰〰〰〰〰〰〰

Hint – Cilantro, also known as coriander or Chinese parsley, is a popular flavoring in Thai soups and stews.

〰〰〰〰〰〰〰〰〰〰〰〰〰〰〰〰

Penne with Caramelized Red Onions

You'll get raves with this creation. I use red onions because they get so nice and gooey. Together with the Feta cheese and crunch of the hazelnuts, this dish always prompts the question, "What is in this? I love it!" Prepare the onions the night before. In fact, make extra. The caramelized results are great to toss into omelets, as a side for a fillet roast, on pizza or focaccia.

¼ cup	butter	50 ml
¼ cup	olive oil	50 ml
6	large red onions, thinly sliced	6
½ tsp	salt	2 ml
1 cup	dry white wine	250 ml
½ lb	spinach, chopped	250 g
½ lb	arugula, chopped	250 g
1 lb	penne	500 g
1 cup	crumbled Feta cheese	250 ml
1 cup	hazelnuts, toasted and chopped	250 ml
¼ tsp	freshly ground black pepper	1 ml
	freshly grated Parmesan cheese	

1. In a large pot of salted boiling water, cook pasta 8 to 10 minutes, until al dente. Drain.
2. In a very large skillet over low heat, heat butter and oil. Add onions; cook 20 minutes, stirring occasionally.
3. Add salt and wine and cook 15 minutes more, stirring occasionally, until onions are soft and caramelized.
4. Stir in spinach and arugula and cook 5 minutes. Stir in Feta and hazelnuts.
5. Toss pasta with red onion mixture. Garnish with Parmesan cheese. Serve immediately.

Makes 4 servings.

Fettuccine with Mushrooms, Tomatoes and Rosemary

The mushrooms give this dish a nice woodsy flavor the rosemary makes it even more interesting. Moist but not saucy, it's a wonderful low-cal winter pasta, and an ideal first-course dish before a grilled-fish blast.

10 oz	fresh oyster mushrooms, stems removed, thickly sliced	300 g
	juice of ½ lemon	
3 tbsp	sweet butter	50 ml
1 tbsp	vegetable oil	15 ml
1	onion, finely chopped	1
1	clove garlic, finely chopped	1
½ tsp	salt	2 ml
¼ tsp	freshly ground black pepper	1 ml
¼ cup	sherry	50 ml
½ cup	chicken stock	125 ml
2	sprigs fresh rosemary, chopped	2
2	large, ripe tomatoes, peeled, seeded and chopped	2
1 lb	fresh fettuccine	500 g
1 cup	freshly grated Parmesan	250 ml
6	small sprigs rosemary	6

1. In a small bowl, toss mushrooms with lemon juice. Set aside.
2. In a large skillet, heat butter and oil over medium-high heat until butter foams. Stir in onion and sauté 3 minutes until soft. Add garlic and cook 30 seconds longer. Stir in mushrooms and cook until soft.
3. Add salt, pepper, sherry, stock, rosemary and tomatoes and cook one minute longer. Set aside.
4. In a large pot of salted boiling water, cook pasta 10 minutes until al dente. Drain.
5. Toss pasta with sauce and half of the grated cheese. Add more pepper if necessary. Divide on six heated plates and place sprig of rosemary in center of each. Pass remaining cheese and pepper at table.

Makes 6 servings.

Pasta with Brie

Smoothed and gentled by the melted Brie, this dish makes a pleasing change from Alfredo cream sauce. In fact, there's no cream in it. Serve with a vigorous twist of the peppermill.

1 lb	tricolor fusilli	500 g
1 cup	olive oil	250 ml
3	cloves garlic, finely chopped	3
3	tomatoes, peeled, seeded, julienned	3
1 cup	chopped, fresh basil	250 ml
1 lb	Brie, chopped with rind	500 g

1. In a pot of salted boiling water, cook fusilli about 10 minutes, until al dente. Drain.
2. In a large skillet, heat ½ cup (125 ml) of the oil, add garlic and sauté until golden. Add tomatoes and basil and cook 2 minutes.
3. Add Brie, pasta and remaining ½ cup (125 ml) oil, toss thoroughly. Serve just as Brie begins to melt.

Makes 6 servings.

Gorgonzola Pasta with Leeks and Radicchio

This is my updated version of old-fashioned macaroni and cheese—always perfect for a crowd of hungry friends. Assemble the night before and pop into the oven as soon as your guests start arriving in the late afternoon. Just add a salad of bitter greens, crusty bread and wine for a simple, delicious homemade meal.

1 lb	fusilli	500 g
⅓ cup	sweet butter	75 ml
6 oz	Shitake mushrooms, sliced	175 g
3	leeks, white only, chopped	3
2½ cups	light cream	625 ml
½ lb	grated Parmesan	250 g
½ lb	shredded Bel Paese	250 g
½ lb	crumbled Gorgonzola	250 g
¼ tsp	salt	1 ml
¼ tsp	pepper	1 ml
1	head small radicchio, shredded	1
6	leaves fresh sage, chopped	6

1. Preheat oven to 400°F (200°C).
2. In a large pot of salted boiling water, cook pasta about 5 minutes. Drain and set aside.
3. In a large skillet, melt butter; add mushrooms and leeks; sauté about 5 minutes until leeks are soft but not brown. Remove from heat and place in a large bowl. Add cream, cheeses, salt, pepper, radicchio and sage. Mix until combined.
5. Turn into a prepared 9x13-inch (23x32-cm) baking dish and bake covered with foil for 20 minutes. Uncover and cook 15 minutes more until heated through and golden.

Makes 8 servings.

Three Cheese Macaroni

Italian cooks often combine more than one or two of their marvelous cheeses to make a pasta dish in which you'll never miss the meat. This should be served hot from the oven while the cheese is still bubbling. It makes a truly satisfying vegetarian dinner when you add simple Tomato Provençale (baked tomatoes with garlic and breadcrumbs), as Colleen's son Christian will attest.

1 lb	macaroni	500 g
3 tbsp	sweet butter	40 ml
1 cup	grated Parmesan cheese	250 ml
1 cup	grated Swiss cheese	250 ml
1 cup	grated Mozzarella cheese	250 ml
1 cup	light cream	250 ml
1 tsp	salt	5 ml
¼ tsp	white pepper	1 ml

1. In a large pot of salted boiling water, cook macaroni about 12 minutes, until al dente. Drain.
2. Preheat oven to 400°F (200°C).
3. In a casserole, toss macaroni with butter. Stir in cheeses, cream, salt and pepper. Bake in oven for 20 minutes, until top is golden brown.

Makes 4 to 6 servings.

Grains & Legumes

I'm far from being a vegetarian, so when I choose a grain dish it's because I really love it. These are some of my all-time winners.

Asiago Polenta with Tomato Gin Sauce

A simple, soothing dish with a gentle sauce to nourish your soul. Since the polenta is baked in the oven instead of fried, your body will thank you too.

2 cups	grated Asiago cheese	500 ml
½ cup	grated Romano cheese	125 ml
2 tbsp	chopped fresh basil	25 ml
1 tbsp	olive oil	15 ml
1	shallot, finely chopped	1
2	cloves garlic, finely chopped	2
4 cups	chicken stock	1 l
1 cup	cornmeal	250 ml
1 tsp	salt	5 ml

Sauce

2 tbsp	olive oil	25 ml
1	onion, chopped	1
2	cloves garlic, finely chopped	2
4	tomatoes, peeled, seeded and chopped	4
1 tsp	salt	5 ml
1 tsp	sugar	5 ml
¼ tsp	freshly ground black pepper	1 ml
1 tbsp	gin	15 ml
2 tbsp	chopped fresh basil	25 ml

Garnish

½ cup	grated Romano cheese	125 ml
8	fresh basil leaves	8

1. In a bowl, stir together Asiago, Romano and basil. Set aside.
2. In a saucepan, heat olive oil. Add shallot and garlic. Sauté 10 minutes until soft. Add stock and bring to a boil.

3. Gradually whisk in cornmeal and salt, reduce heat and continue cooking, whisking until thickened and mixture comes away from sides of the pot.

4. Pour ⅓ of the polenta mixture into a prepared 8x8-inch (20x20-cm) pan. Sprinkle with half of the cheese mixture. Repeat layers, ending with the polenta mixture, to make five layers. Cool, cover and refrigerate until firm, 1 hour.

5. Preheat oven to 350°F (180°C). Uncover the polenta and bake for 40 minutes until golden.

6. In a skillet, heat oil and slowly cook the onion until soft. Add garlic, tomatoes, salt, sugar and pepper and cook 10 minutes more.

7. Add gin and basil and transfer sauce to a food processor or blender. Process 1 minute or until smooth.

8. Cut polenta into 8 squares and serve on top of sauce. Garnish with additional basil and Romano.

Makes 8 servings.

Couscous Pilaf with Almonds

A distinctive starter course to a loin of pork. Roasting the seeds is the secret to the great flavors in this dish. Generous amounts of thinly sliced red onions and red pepper add not only taste and texture, but radiant color.

1 tsp	coriander seeds	5 ml
1 tsp	cumin seeds	5 ml
2 tbsp	olive oil	30 ml
1	onion, thinly sliced	1
1	clove garlic, finely chopped	1
1	fennel bulb, trimmed and thinly sliced	1
1	red pepper, thinly sliced	1
1½ cups	chicken stock	375 ml
1 tsp	sweet butter	5 ml
½ cup	raisins	125 ml
1 cup	couscous	250 ml
½ cup	slivered almonds, toasted	125 ml

1. In a large skillet over high heat, roast coriander and cumin seeds about 2 minutes, or until they begin to pop.
2. Reduce heat and add olive oil, onions, garlic, fennel and red pepper. Cook stirring, about 10 minutes, or until softened. Keep warm.
3. In a saucepan, bring stock, butter and raisins to a boil. Remove from heat and stir in couscous. Cover and let sit for 5 minutes.
4. In a serving dish, stir together vegetables and couscous.
Garnish with almonds.

Makes 6 servings.

Masalchi Lentils

Masalchi means "spice blender," which is exactly what makes this subtle, aromatic dish so appealing. It's ideal served on turmeric rice for a vegetarian dinner.

2 cups	dried lentils	500 ml
8 cups	water	2 l
2 tbsp	olive oil	25 ml
4	medium onions, sliced	4
1	clove garlic, finely chopped	1
1 tsp	ground cumin	5 ml
1 tsp	ground coriander	5 ml
1 tsp	ground ginger	5 ml
1 tsp	cinnamon	5 ml
1 tsp	turmeric	5 ml
2	cardamom seeds	2
3	cloves	3
2	carrots, thinly sliced	2
6	tomatoes, peeled, seeded and chopped	6
½ tsp	salt	2 ml

1. Rinse lentils and place in a large, heavy-bottomed pot. Cover with water and bring to a boil. Reduce heat and simmer for 30 to 40 minutes until lentils are tender. Drain and set aside.
2. In a skillet, heat oil, add onions and garlic, and sauté 3 minutes until onions are softened. Stir in spices and cook 1 minute.
3. Stir in carrots, tomatoes, salt and lentils. Cook 5 minutes until heated through.

Makes 6 servings.

"Rice is good, but lentils are my life." – Hindu proverb

Rice

So many great rice dishes keep surfacing that it's hard to believe Western society ever ran on plain old meat and potatoes.

Spring Paddy Rice

This is called Spring Rice because of the green of the young sweet peas. An excellent side dish to serve with roasts—especially veal.

2 tbsp	olive oil	25 ml
2 tbsp	sweet butter	25 ml
1	medium onion, chopped	1
1½ cups	long grain rice	375 ml
3 cups	hot chicken stock	750 ml
1 tsp	salt	5 ml
½ tsp	white pepper	2 ml
3 cups	peas	750 ml
¼ cup	grated Parmesan cheese	50 ml

1. In a large skillet, heat oil and 1 tbsp (15 ml) butter. Add onion; sauté 5 minutes, until softened.
2. Add rice; cook 3 minutes longer, until translucent.
3. Stir in 2 cups (500 ml) stock, salt and pepper. Bring to a boil, reduce heat, cover and simmer 10 minutes.
4. Add remaining stock and peas; cook, covered 10 minutes longer, or until rice is tender and dry. Stir in remaining butter and cheese.

Makes 6 to 8 servings.

Risoverdi (Green Rice)

This is perfect in both color and taste to serve with a shrimp curry. For a quick light supper for your friends, add cheese and a green salad.

2 tbsp	olive oil	25 ml
2 tbsp	sweet butter	25 ml
1 cup	minced green onions	250 ml
1 cup	minced parsley	250 ml
1½ cups	finely chopped raw spinach	375 ml
2 cups	long grain rice	500 ml
3 ½ cups	chicken stock	875 ml
1½ tsp	salt	7 ml
¼ tsp	white pepper	1 ml

1. In a large skillet, heat oil and butter. Stir in onions, parsley and spinach. Cover and cook over low heat for 15 minutes.
2. Stir in rice and mix until coated. Add 2 cups (500 ml) stock, salt and pepper. Cover and bring to a boil, reduce heat and simmer for 15 minutes.
3. Add remaining stock and continue to simmer, covered, for 10 minutes more, until rice fluffs with a fork. Serve warm.

Makes 4 to 6 servings.

Hint – *Set up and have tablecloths ironed the day before. Check fireplaces and lay fire days before. Check over silver dishes, glassware and linen you wish to use prior to the party to make sure all is polished or cleaned.*

Sweet-Scented Rice

Serve this rice with curries or spicy hot dishes like Chicken Saag, and the cinnamon, cloves and cardamom will rise up and seduce your guests.

¼ cup	sweet butter	50 ml
1	medium onion, chopped	1
2 cups	long grain rice	500 ml
4 cups	chicken stock	1 l
4	cloves	4
4	cardamom seeds	4
12	peppercorns	12
2	cinnamon sticks (2-inch/5-cm long)	2
½ cup	slivered almonds	125 ml
¼ cup	raisins	50 ml

1. In a large skillet, melt butter. Add onion; sauté 7 minutes, until golden brown.
2. Stir in rice and coat well with butter. Add stock and bring mixture to a boil.
3. Transfer to a buttered 8-cup (2-l) casserole with a lid.
4. Preheat oven to 320°F (160°C).
5. In a small piece of cheesecloth, tie together cloves, cardamom seeds, peppercorns and cinnamon sticks. Place in rice and cover.
6. Bake in oven for 25 minutes, until rice is tender.
7. Remove cheesecloth bag of spices. Before serving, stir in almonds and raisins.

Makes 6 to 8 servings.

Indian Rice

I don't know how I happened to call this Indian Rice. I just know it has had its name and its place in my esteem for years. It is the combination of brandy-soaked raisins and pine nuts that endear it to me, as well as the warm, yellowy color it gets from the rich chicken stock.

2 oz	brandy, port or sherry	60 ml
½ cup	raisins	125 ml
3 tbsp	clarified butter	45 ml
1	medium onion, finely chopped	1
1	clove garlic, finely chopped	1
2 cups	long grain rice	500 ml
½ tsp	curry powder	2 ml
4 cups	rich chicken stock	1 l
½ cup	pine nuts	125 ml

1. In a small saucepan, warm brandy. Add raisins, remove from heat and set aside.
2. In a large skillet, heat butter; add onion and garlic. Sauté about 5 minutes, until soft.
3. Stir in rice and curry powder; sauté for 5 minutes, until rice is translucent.
4. Add stock, bring to a boil; reduce heat, cover and simmer for 20 minutes.
5. Bring raisin mixture to a boil, reduce heat and simmer 2 to 3 minutes, until liquid disappears.
6. Add to rice with pine nuts. Cover and continue to simmer about 7 minutes longer, until all liquid has disappeared.

Makes 6 servings.

Variation: Coconut Rice
Use ½ cup (125 ml) flaked, unsweetened coconut in place of raisins.

Savory Mushroom Rice

Check out veal recipes with oodles of gravy and serve this rice with them. It is a natural sopper-upper. It goes just as well with chicken dishes that are rich in sauce. Another great thing about this dish is, you don't have to watch it. Once it goes into the oven, simply set the temperature and timer and concentrate on other things.

2 cups	long grain rice	500 ml
¼ cup	sweet butter	50 ml
2	large onions, finely chopped	2
½ lb	mushrooms, thinly sliced	250 g
2½ cups	rich beef stock	625 ml
1 tsp	salt	5 ml

1. Preheat oven to 350°F (180°C).
2. In a large skillet, heat rice, stirring constantly, until it turns golden. Transfer to an 8-cup (2-l) casserole.
3. In the same skillet, melt butter. Add onions and mushrooms; sauté 5 minutes, until tender. Add to rice. Stir in stock and salt; blend well.
4. Bake in oven for 1¼ hours, adding water if necessary to keep moist, until rice is tender.

Makes 8 to 10 servings.

Com Rang (Fried Rice)

Now this is fried rice! I often serve it as a lunch dish with "hot" cucumber sticks.

1	3-egg omelette	1
¼ cup	vegetable oil	50 ml
2	cloves garlic, finely chopped	2
3	green onions, chopped	3
6 cups	chilled cooked rice	1.5 l
½ lb	cooked ham, shredded	250 g
¼ lb	cooked shrimp, chopped	125 g
1	small carrot, shredded	1
½ cup	cooked peas	125 ml
½ tsp	salt	2 ml
¼ tsp	freshly ground black pepper	1 ml
	soy sauce	

1. Cut omelette into shreds and set aside.
2. In a large skillet, heat oil. Add garlic and green onions and cook 4 minutes, until tender.
3. Stir in rice, ham, shrimp, carrot, peas and omelet. Heat thoroughly.
4. Season with salt and pepper. Serve immediately with soy sauce.

Makes 6 servings.

Rice Pilaf with Pine Nuts

The lovely long grain rice brightened with the pimento, parsley and pine nuts appeals to everyone. It looks festive, tastes like Christmas.

⅓ cup	sweet butter	75 ml
2	cloves garlic, chopped	2
1	medium onion, chopped	1
1¼ cups	long grain rice	300 ml
2½ cups	chicken stock	625 ml
½ tsp	salt	2 ml
¼ tsp	white pepper	1 ml
½ cup	chopped pimento	125 ml
⅓ cup	pine nuts	75 ml
2 tbsp	chopped parsley	25 ml

1. In a medium saucepan, heat butter. Add garlic and onion; sauté over medium heat for 10 minutes, until softened.
2. Add rice and cook 2 minutes longer.
3. Stir in chicken stock, salt and pepper. Bring to a boil, reduce heat, cover and simmer for 25 minutes, until all moisture is absorbed.
4. Remove lid and fluff rice with a fork. Stir in pimento, pine nuts and parsley.

Makes 5 to 6 servings.

Jamaican Rice and Peas

A soothing backup dish to hot Jerk Wings. The coconut milk is the key to its sweetness and exquisite taste.

1½ cups	dried red kidney beans	375 ml
1	clove garlic, crushed	1
6 cups	water	1.5 l
½ tsp	salt	2 ml
2 cups	coconut milk	500 ml
¼ tsp	freshly ground black pepper	1 ml
1	green onion, chopped	1
1 sprig	fresh thyme	1
1	whole Scotch bonnet pepper	1
2 cups	uncooked long grain rice	500 ml
2	slices bacon, chopped	2

1. In a saucepan, combine the kidney beans, garlic, water and salt. Cook, covered, over medium heat for 1½ hours until tender.
2. Add the coconut milk, black pepper, green onion, thyme, Scotch bonnet pepper, rice and bacon. Stir well.
3. Bring to a boil, cover and reduce heat; simmer for 45 minutes, stirring until rice is tender. Remove Scotch bonnet pepper before serving.

Makes 6 servings.

Hint – Coconut milk, available in cans, is not the liquid in the coconut, but the product extruded from its grated pulp.

Rice and Vermicelli

I serve this traditional Middle Eastern recipe with tajine (a North African stew). For a quick dinner, simply add thinly sliced cooked chicken.

1 tbsp	olive oil	15 ml
1 tbsp	butter	15 ml
½ cup	vermicelli, broken into small pieces	125 ml
1 cup	basmati rice	250 ml
1 tsp	cinnamon	5 ml
1 tsp	ground cumin	5 ml
½ cup	currants	125 ml
¼ tsp	salt	1 ml
2 cups	water	500 ml

1. Heat oil and butter in a saucepan. Add vermicelli and rice and sauté about 3 minutes or until vermicelli is browned and rice is translucent.
2. Add cinnamon, cumin, currants and salt. Stir in water. Bring to a boil, reduce heat, cover and simmer 15 to 20 minutes, until tender and liquid is absorbed.

Makes 4 servings.

Hint – Rice originated in the Americas, but is now grown on every continent except Antarctica.

Lemon Risotto

The touch of lemon in this risotto actually makes it taste light enough to serve as a starter to a simple Italian supper of roasted chicken oregano or veal picatta. For a completely different risotto, don't be afraid to add three or four leaves of fresh rosemary or fresh sage in addition to the lemon.

¼ cup	sweet butter	50 ml
1	onion, finely chopped	1
1½ cups	Italian short grain rice	375 ml
½ cup	dry white wine	125 ml
5 cups	simmering chicken stock	1.25 l
2 tbsp	lemon juice	25 ml
½ cup	grated Parmesan cheese	125 ml
1 tsp	grated lemon rind	5 ml
3	chopped fresh rosemary or sage leaves, optional	3

1. In a large skillet, melt butter. Add onion; sauté about 5 minutes, until softened.
2. Stir in rice and mix until coated. Stir in wine. Cook over medium-high heat about 5 minutes, until wine is absorbed.
3. Add 1 cup of the stock to the rice and cook, stirring slowly and constantly, about 6 minutes, until liquid is absorbed.
4. Continue with the rest of the stock, 1 cup at a time, until the rice is tender and creamy. (You may not need all the stock.) With the fourth addition of stock, add lemon juice.
5. Stir in Parmesan, rind and herb, if using. Serve at once.

Makes 4 to 6 first course servings.

Hint – Purposeful Leftovers – Risotto can be transformed into appetizers by shaping them into bite-sized cakes and frying until crispy. Recycle with flair!

Risotto Portobello

Venice and Risotto Portobello go together in my taste memories. This is the definitive version of this traditional Italian dish—which I begged for at a favorite trattoria.

4 tbsp	sweet butter	50 ml
½	onion, finely chopped	½
1½ cups	Italian short grain rice	375 ml
½ cup	dry white wine	125 ml
3 oz	fresh Portobello mushrooms, wiped clean and cut into 1¼-inch pieces	114 ml
1 cup	thinly sliced fresh mushrooms	250 ml
5 cups	simmering chicken stock	1.25 l
⅓ cup	grated Parmesan cheese	75 ml

1. In a large skillet, melt 3 tbsp (15 ml) of the butter. Add onion; sauté about 5 minutes, until softened.
2. Stir in rice and mix until coated. Stir in wine. Cook over medium-high heat about 5 minutes, until wine is absorbed.
3. Add mushrooms to rice mixture and stir well. Add 1 cup (250 ml) of the stock to the rice and cook, stirring slowly and constantly, about 6 minutes, until liquid is absorbed.
4. Continue with the rest of the stock, 1 cup (250 ml) at a time, until the rice is tender and creamy. (You may not need all the stock.)
5. Stir in Parmesan and remaining 1 tbsp (5 ml) of butter. Serve at once.

Makes 4 to 6 first course servings.

Variation: Gorgonzola Risotto

1. Omit mushrooms and final 1 tbsp of butter.
2. Proceed as above. When rice is tender and creamy, stir in Parmesan, 1 tbsp (5 ml) of milk and 4 oz crumbled Gorgonzola cheese.

Potatoes & Vegetables

Potatoes and Vegetables

Remember when the only potatoes we ever saw were the mashed variety? And when we forced down tasteless cubes of vegetables because they were good for us? Hallelujah for the emergence of irresistibly scrumptious —and nutritious—plant food. These recipes will convert even the most incorrigible vitamin-avoider.

Potatoes

Skordalia
Nova Scotia "Stovies"
Jansson's Temptation
Potato, Shiitake and Gruyère Pie
Gratin Savoyard
Cheddar Potatoes
California Roast Potatoes
Baked Mashed Potatoes and Cabbage
Mashed Potato and Onion Soufflé with Burnt Onions and Crackling
Latkes (Crisp Potato Pancakes)

Vegetables

Bombay Fennel
Catalan Spinach
Baked Lettuce
Gratin de Courgettes au Riz
Zucchini with Cherry Tomatoes in Basil Butter
Turnips with Apples
Brussel Sprouts in Maple Syrup Vinaigrette
Ragout of Mushrooms and Leeks with Madeira
Savory Vegetable Buckwheat Pancakes
Baked Mushroom Squares
Skewered Mushrooms with Oregano
Mattar Panir (Peas and Cheese)
Eggplant Bharta
Spicy Greens
Tofu and Vegetables in Black Bean Sauce
Red Onion and Pommery Bread Pudding
Leek and Goat Cheese Tart
Red Cabbage and Red Onions
Thyme Glazed Onions

Potatoes

The venerable spud is as varied and versatile as the apple. Experimentation is clearly in order.

Skordalia

My version of this Greek dish substitutes mashed potatoes for ground almonds, but I do leave a few toasted almonds on top. It's traditionally served with deep-fried calamari. I think it also goes well with grilled harvest vegetables or a rare rack of lamb. Either way, this garlicky treat is not for the meek.

½ lb	red-skinned potatoes	250 g
4	cloves garlic, coarsely chopped	4
1 tsp	salt	5 ml
1	egg yolk, at room temperature	1
⅓ cup	olive oil	75 ml
1 tbsp	lemon juice	15 ml
¼ tsp	salt	1 ml
	freshly ground black pepper	
¼ cup	toasted, slivered almonds	50 ml

1. Preheat oven to 350°F (180°C).
2. On a cookie sheet, bake potatoes 45 minutes until tender. Cool on rack for 15 minutes. Peel and marsh until smooth and fluffy.
3. On a cutting board, sprinkle the garlic with the salt. Using the side of a knife or back of a spoon, mash garlic and salt until puréed.
4. In a small bowl, whisk together egg yolk and garlic. Add to mashed potatoes and beat with electric mixer on medium speed until smooth. Add oil, about 2 tbsp (25 ml) at a time; beat after each addition until well blended. Beat in lemon juice.
5. Season with salt and pepper and sprinkle with toasted almonds.

Makes about 1½ cups (375 ml).

Nova Scotia "Stovies"

An old friend from Nova Scotia passed on this traditional Scottish recipe. Colleen finds it impossible to get it to the table as her family digs into it right off the stove (hence the name, perhaps?). The soft and fragrant onions complement the stock and potatoes—all you need is a serious twist of the pepper mill to finish it off. For a great shore supper, throw some lobster in a pot and shred cabbage for a slaw.

6	medium potatoes, peeled and thinly sliced	6
2	medium onions, peeled and thinly sliced	2
½ tsp	salt	2 ml
¼ tsp	freshly ground black pepper	1 ml
¼ cup	sweet butter*	50 ml
1 cup	chicken stock	250 ml

1. Arrange ⅓ of the onions in bottom of a medium-sized, heavy-bottomed saucepan. Cover with ⅓ of the potatoes, arranged in an overlapping layer. Sprinkle with salt and pepper and dot with ⅓ of the butter. Repeat with remaining ingredients.
2. Pour stock over potato mixture and bring to a boil. Reduce heat, cover and simmer about 45 minutes. Raise heat slightly and cook another 15 minutes, until potatoes are tender and most of the liquid has been absorbed.

Makes 4 servings.

* Bacon fat makes a flavorful substitute for the butter, and lends down-home authenticity.

Hint – If your windshield wiper isn't working, cut a raw potato in half and wipe it over the glass. The rain will run down in a clear sheet, leaving you with a clear field of vision.

Jansson's Temptation

I get out this classic Swedish recipe every New Year's for my open house smorgasbord, along with meatballs, a selection of herring and pickled beet salad. It holds up well at room temperature for a buffet, but if brunch is more your style, serve this dish with eggs, a salad and flatbreads. And don't worry about the ingredients—friends of mine who swear they loathe anchovies love this dish.

7	medium potatoes, peeled and cut into strips 2x¼-inch (5x½-cm)	7
2 tbsp	vegetable oil	25 ml
2½ tbsp	sweet butter	32 ml
2 to 3	large onions, thinly sliced	2 to 3
2	cans (1.75 oz/50 g each) anchovy fillets, drained and rinsed well	2
¼ tsp	white pepper	1 ml
2 tbsp	fine, dry breadcrumbs	25 ml
1 cup	light cream	125 ml
½ cup	milk	125 ml

1. To keep from discoloring, place potatoes in a large bowl filled with water
2. In a large skillet, heat oil with 2 tbsp (25 ml) of the butter. Add onions and cook 10 minutes, stirring frequently until soft but not brown.
3. Preheat oven to 400°F (200°C).
4. Grease a 6-cup (1.5-l) soufflé dish with remaining butter.
5. Drain potatoes and pat dry.
6. Arrange a layer of potatoes on the bottom of prepared dish. Then alternate layers of onions and anchovies, ending with potatoes, adding pepper to each layer.
7. Sprinkle top with breadcrumbs.
8. In a small saucepan, heat cream and milk until warm. Pour over potatoes.
9. Bake 45 minutes or until potatoes are tender and liquid is nearly absorbed.

Makes 6 to 8 servings.

Potato, Shiitake and Gruyère Pie

This moist, rich, earthy dish becomes even more distinctive when served in wedges from a round pie plate as a main course (let it stand for 15 minutes before slicing). For a simple meal, I like it with green salad and a hunk of bread. As a hearty buffet dish, pair it with a strong companion, such as a clove-studded baked ham or a big, rare, standing rib roast.

4	baking potatoes, peeled and thinly sliced	4
2 tbsp	olive oil	25 ml
1½ tsp	salt	7 ml
1 lb	Shiitake mushrooms, wiped clean and sliced	454 g
1	medium onion, thinly sliced	1
3	cloves garlic, finely chopped	3
2 tbsp	chopped fresh parsley	25 ml
1 tsp	fresh thyme	5 ml
½ tsp	freshly ground black pepper	2 ml
3 cups	grated Gruyère cheese	750 ml

1. Preheat oven to 400°F (200°C).
2. Lightly oil a 9-inch (23-cm) pie plate.
3. In a bowl, toss the potatoes with oil and 1 tsp of the salt.
4. In a separate bowl, combine mushrooms, onion, garlic, parsley, thyme, pepper and remaining salt.
5. Arrange ⅓ of the potatoes in an overlapping layer in the pie plate. Cover with half of the mushroom mixture, then ⅓ of the cheese. Repeat layers. Arrange remaining potatoes on top and cover with remaining cheese.
6. Bake in oven 1 hour and 15 minutes or until potatoes are tender and top is golden brown. Serve at once.

Makes 8 servings.

Gratin Savoyard

The golden color of slowly baked potatoes and cheese make this a stunner to serve. I never tire of this dish, and on the few occasions when there's any left over, I know it will reheat perfectly. Serve it with Sunday roasts and special dinners such as Thanksgiving or Christmas. For a vegetarian main course, simply replace the chicken stock with a vegetable stock and serve it with a salad of spinach and mandarin oranges.

2 lbs	potatoes, Yukon Gold or Russet, peeled and thinly sliced	1 kg
⅛ cup	sweet butter	25 ml
2 cups	grated Gruyère cheese	500 ml
1½ tsp	salt	7 ml
½ tsp	freshly ground black pepper	2 ml
1 cup	chicken or vegetable stock	250 ml

1. Preheat oven to 425°F (220°C).
2. Lightly oil an 8-cup (2-l) glass or ceramic baking dish.
3. Arrange ⅓ of the potatoes in an overlapping layer in baking dish.
4. Sprinkle with ⅓ of the cheese, salt and pepper. Dot with ⅓ of the butter. Repeat in two more layers with remaining ingredients. Pour stock over top of potatoes.
5. Bake in middle of oven for 30 minutes. Lower temperature to 350°F (180°C). Bake 10 to 15 minutes longer, until golden brown and very tender.

Makes 6 servings.

Hint – *One pound of cheese yields 4 cups of loosely packed grated cheese.*

Cheddar Potatoes

This recipe is easily reheatable and goes with just about any kind of main course. Serve it with roasts or with one of the heartier salads.

6	medium potatoes, cooked in jackets, peeled and cubed	6
⅓ cup	chopped green onions	75 ml
1 cup	sour cream	250 ml
1½ cups	grated Cheddar cheese	375 ml
1 cup	chicken stock	250 ml
1 cup	light cream	250 ml
½ tsp	salt	2 ml
¼ tsp	freshly ground black pepper	1 ml
¼ cup	sweet butter	50 ml
¾ cup	crushed cornflakes	175 ml

1. Preheat oven to 350°F (180°C).
2. Arrange potato cubes in a 9x13-inch (23x32-cm) baking dish or casserole.
3. In a mixing bowl, combine sour cream, cheese, stock, light cream, salt and pepper. Pour over potatoes.
4. In a small saucepan, melt butter. Stir in cornflakes until covered with butter. Spread on top of potato mixture.
5. Bake in oven for 30 minutes, until heated through and lightly browned.

Makes 6 to 8 servings.

California Roast Potatoes

Crispy, delicious and fun to eat. Make sure everyone gets a helping of roasted garlic; the skin slides right off so they can smear the sweet and juicy insides onto their potatoes. Fresh rosemary is a must with this recipe, which always goes well with roast chicken or lamb.

8	potatoes, cut into chunks	8
16	cloves garlic, unpeeled	16
¼ cup	vegetable oil	50 ml
2 tbsp	fresh rosemary	25 ml
½ tsp	salt	5 ml
¼ tsp	freshly ground black pepper	1 ml

1. Preheat oven to 450°F (230°C).
2. In a large bowl, toss potatoes and garlic with oil, rosemary, salt and pepper until well coated.
3. Spread in a single layer in a roasting pan.
4. Bake 45 to 50 minutes, turning occasionally, until potatoes are crisp and garlic is soft.
5. Serve two cloves of garlic with each portion of crisp potatoes.

Makes 8 servings.

Hint – *When using fresh herbs, use twice the amount of dry herbs called for.*

Baked Mashed Potatoes and Cabbage

Colleen remembers her grandmother making this hearty Irish dish. It makes a fine accompaniment to pot roast, brisket or corned beef. Complete the feast with a great red wine.

6	medium potatoes, peeled and quartered	6
1	head cabbage, diced	1
	(1½ lbs/750 g)	
½ cup	sweet butter, cubed	125 ml
4	green onions, chopped	4
½ cup	milk	125 ml
1 tsp	salt	5 ml
¼ tsp	freshly ground black pepper	1 ml
1½ cups	grated white Cheddar cheese	375 ml

1. In a large saucepan, cover potatoes with water, bring to a boil and cook until tender. Drain and set aside.
2. Bring water to a boil in another saucepan; add cabbage and cook until just tender. Drain and set aside.
3. Preheat oven to 350°F (180°C).
4. Mash potatoes; stir in cabbage, butter, onions, milk, salt and pepper.
5. Place in an 8x8-inch (20-cm) baking dish. Sprinkle with cheese.
6. Bake 30 minutes until heated through and cheese is melted.

Makes 6 to 8 servings.

Mashed Potato and Onion Soufflé with Burnt Onions and Crackling

Let me explain that here I am not using the term "soufflé" in its technical sense. This recipe does not depend on timing or the ability of egg whites to rise and stay put. However, it does have that marvelous soufflé texture and is great to serve with any recipe that has a lot of gravy.

3 cups	mashed potatoes	750 ml
1 tbsp	soft sweet butter	15 ml
3 tbsp	light cream	45 ml
3	eggs, separated	3
1	medium onion, chopped	1
2 tsp	chopped chives	10 ml
1 tsp	chopped fresh parsley	5 ml
1 tsp	salt	5 ml
½ tsp	freshly ground black pepper	2 ml

1. Preheat oven to 350°F (180°C).
2. In a large bowl, beat butter and cream into potatoes by hand. Add yolks, one at a time, beating after each addition. Stir in onion, chives, parsley, salt and pepper.
3. Beat egg white until stiff but not dry. Fold into potato mixture.
4. Spoon into a buttered 6-cup (1.5-l) soufflé dish. Bake in oven for 30 minutes, or until puffy and brown on top.
5. Serve garnished with burnt onions and crackling.

Makes 6 servings.

Burnt Onions and Crackling

A favorite garnish for pâté. Serve liberally on Russian black bread as my grandfather did. He enjoyed eating crackling and sucking sugar until he was 108 years old!

1 cup	raw chicken fat, finely chopped, from 2½ lb (1 kg) chicken	250 ml
4	large yellow onions, coarsely chopped	4
½ tsp	salt	2 ml

1. In a large heavy skillet, heat chicken fat and onions over low heat. Cook, stirring frequently about 1 hour, until fat renders and turns into crackling and onions are crisp and burnt.
2. Strain rendered fat through sieve into a container for further use. Store in refrigerator.
3. Reserve crackling and burnt onions to garnish Mashed Potato and Onion Soufflé.

Makes ½ cup (125 ml).

Latkes (Crisp Potato Pancakes)

These are so delicious I always make lots of them and serve with pots of apple-sauce and thick sour cream. They go like, well, like hotcakes. Latkes also make a great nosh for a cocktail party, but if you use them this way, be sure to make them bite-size.

4	medium potatoes, peeled	4
2 tbsp	finely chopped onion	25 ml
2	eggs, well beaten	2
2 tbsp	all-purpose flour	25 ml
1 tsp	baking powder	5 ml
1 tsp	salt	5 ml
¼ tsp	freshly ground black pepper	1 ml
¼ cup	vegetable oil	50 ml
	sour cream and applesauce	

1. In a large bowl of ice water, chill peeled potatoes for 2 hours. Grate coarsely. Place grated potatoes in a tea towel and press excess moisture from potatoes, until quite dry.
2. In a large bowl, combine potatoes, onion, eggs, flour, baking powder, salt and pepper; mix well.
3. In a large skillet, heat oil. Drop potato mixture, 2 tbsp (25 ml) at a time into hot oil. Cook 5 minutes, over moderate heat, on each side until golden brown.
4. Serve with sour cream and applesauce.

Makes 6 servings.

Vegetables

Don't be afraid to serve the dishes in this section proudly on their own.

Bombay Fennel

A chicken roasted to perfection will complement this delicious golden-hued vegetable dish. It is just as good at room temperature as part of an Indian dinner. Start with Mattar Panir, follow with Bombay Fennel, then Tandoori Shrimp. Whatever your menu, don't forget Indian breads to go with each dish.

2 tbsp	butter	25 ml
2	fennel bulbs, sliced (about 6 cups)	2
1	medium onion, sliced	1
1 tbsp	finely chopped fresh ginger	15 ml
2 tsp	ground coriander	10 ml
1½ tsp	ground cumin	7 ml
½ tsp	cayenne pepper	2 ml
½ tsp	turmeric	2 ml
¼ tsp	salt	1 ml
4	green onions, chopped (green and white parts)	4
2 tsp	vegetable oil	10 ml

1. In a large skillet over low heat, melt butter; add fennel and onions, stirring for 1 minute. Cover and cook slowly about 30 minutes, until tender crisp, stirring occasionally. Set aside.
2. In a small bowl, combine ginger, coriander, cumin, cayenne, turmeric, salt and green onions.
3. In a small skillet, heat oil over low heat; add ginger mixture and cook about 5 minutes until fragrant.
4. Remove and add to fennel, mixing well. Cook an additional 5 minutes. Serve immediately.

Makes 4 to 6 servings.

Catalan Spinach

When I served this to a guest from Spain recently, he was amazed and delighted to find such an authentic dish so far away from home. I first tasted this deliciously soft, sweet vegetable dish in Barcelona. The combination of toasted pine nuts, garlic and sweet raisins make it a sensational quick, one-dish vegetable, which I serve right from the copper skillet I've cooked it in.

¼ cup	olive oil	125 ml
1	clove garlic, finely chopped	1
2 lb	fresh spinach, stemmed	1 kg
¼ cup	toasted pine nuts	50 ml
¼ cup	seedless raisins	50 ml
½ tsp	salt	2 ml
¼ tsp	freshly ground black pepper	1 ml

1. In a medium saucepan, bring lightly salted water to a boil. Add the spinach to the boiling water and blanch for 1 minute. Drain thoroughly; squeeze the spinach dry. Coarsely chop the spinach and transfer to a medium bowl.
2. In a medium skillet, heat oil over low heat; add garlic and cook 5 minutes until soft.
3. Add spinach, pine nuts, raisins, salt and pepper and cook 5 minutes more until flavors are combined. Serve immediately.

Makes 4 servings.

For a wedding at home, swag white, pastel green and pink ribbons over the doorways and mantels, leaving streamers long enough to reach the floor. Do the same for the banisters and railings. At the points of each swag tie large bows of lace ribbon and tuck sprigs of baby's breath into each one. For a finishing touch, scatter masses of white euphorbia in glass ginger jars around the room. Carry the white onto the table by placing three glass bowls with a single gardenia in each at the center of the table.

Baked Lettuce

I serve this as a first course straight from the oven. Use one of your favorite baking dishes to bring it to the table and make sure to serve everyone a wedge of green and a wedge of red lettuce.

1	head Boston lettuce	1
1	head radicchio	1
2 tsp	sweet butter	10 ml
¼ tsp	salt	1 ml
⅛ tsp	freshly ground black pepper	.5 ml

Dressing

½ cup	sour cream	125 ml
4 tsp	milk	20 ml
½ tsp	salt	2 ml
⅛ tsp	ground nutmeg	.5 ml
⅛ tsp	ground cinnamon	.5 ml
⅛ tsp	freshly ground black pepper	.5 ml
¼ cup	toasted pecans, chopped	50 ml

1. Preheat oven to 350°F (180°C).
2. Remove wilted outer leaves from lettuces. Cut into quarters, rinse under cold water and dry well.
3. Butter a shallow baking dish with 1 tsp of the butter and place lettuces cut side up. Season with salt and pepper and dot with remaining butter.
4. Bake for 5 minutes, or until wilted. Keep warm.
5. In a small bowl combine sour cream, milk, salt, nutmeg, cinnamon and pepper. Fold in pecans.
6. To serve, spoon some of the dressing over the warm lettuces, and bring remaining dressing to the table as an accompaniment.

Makes 4 servings.

Gratin de Courgettes au Riz

I like to assemble this classic Provençal dish in the morning and bake it when my guests arrive. The zucchini, wild rice and cheese meld together to make a powerful—and irresistible—impression.

¼ cup	olive oil	50 ml
2	large onions, finely chopped	2
2	cloves garlic, finely chopped	2
2 lbs	small zucchini, cut in ½-inch (1-cm) slices	1 kg
1	bay leaf	1
3 tbsp	cooked wild rice	50 ml
1	egg, lightly beaten	1
½ cup	grated Parmesan cheese	125 ml
1 tsp	salt	5 ml
½ tsp	white pepper	5 ml

1. Preheat oven to 350°F (180°C).
2. In a large skillet heat oil. Add onions and garlic; sauté about 10 minutes until soft but not brown.
3. Add zucchini and bay leaf. Cook over medium heat about 25 minutes, until tender. Set aside and cool.
4. Add cooked rice, egg, ¼ cup of the Parmesan, salt and pepper to the zucchini mixture in skillet.
5. Put in a lightly buttered 8x12-inch (20x30-cm) baking dish.
6. Sprinkle top of casserole with remaining ¼ cup Parmesan. Bake 20 minutes, then raise heat to 400°F (200°C) and bake 8 minutes more, until golden.

Makes 8 servings.

Hint – *One cup raw wild rice yields 3 to 4 cups cooked.*

Zucchini with Cherry Tomatoes in Basil Butter

The most important thing to remember here is that the basil must be fresh and the tomatoes should be barely warmed through. Easy to do in large quantities.

8	medium zucchini, cut into ½-inch (1-cm) slices	8
4 cups	cherry tomatoes, halved	1 l
¼ cup	sweet butter or margarine	50 ml
1 tbsp	lemon juice	15 ml
1 tbsp	chopped fresh basil	15 ml
1½ tsp	salt	7 ml
1 tsp	grated lemon rind	5 ml
⅛ tsp	freshly ground black pepper	.5 ml
2 tbsp	grated Parmesan cheese	25 ml

1. In a pot of salted boiling water, cook zucchini about 4 minutes, until tender crisp. Drain well and add tomatoes.
2. In a small saucepan, heat butter with lemon juice. Pour over vegetables and toss.
3. Season with basil, salt, lemon rind and pepper. Cover and cook 2 to 3 minutes to heat the tomatoes.
4. Sprinkle cheese over top before serving.

Makes 12 servings.

A formal Valentine's dinner party. Swag long bolts of crimson moiré over mantles, mirrors and sideboards throughout the house. Wrap white lace ribbon around the moiré. Place single red roses in crystal bud vases and arrange them everywhere. Make one or two spectacular arrangements of red roses in silver champagne buckets. The odd cherub here and there will complete the atmosphere.

Turnips with Apples

I have converted many a confirmed turnip-hater with this dish—one which my family looks forward to eagerly every Christmas.

2	turnips, cooked and puréed	2
1 cup	applesauce	125 ml
⅓ cup	soft, sweet butter	75 ml
1 tbsp	brown sugar	15 ml
1 tbsp	salt	15 ml
¼ tsp	white pepper	1 ml
2	eggs, beaten	2
2	Granny Smith apples, peeled, cored and thinly sliced	2

1. Preheat oven to 350°F (180°C).
2. In a large bowl, combine turnips, applesauce, butter, sugar, salt, pepper and eggs; mix well.
3. Butter an 8x8-inch (20-cm) baking dish.
4. Pour half the turnip mixture into the dish, top with apple slices and cover with remaining turnip mixture.
5. Bake in oven for ½ hour.

Makes 10 to 12 servings.

Hint – *Three medium-sized apples equals 1 pound.*

Brussel Sprouts in Maple Syrup Vinaigrette

The surprising taste of maple syrup persuades many non-brussel-sprout lovers to reconsider. They can be served hot or cold. I like to spear them on toothpicks for a cocktail party.

1 lb	brussel sprouts, trimmed	500 g
3 tbsp	balsamic vinegar	50 ml

Dressing

½ cup	olive oil	125 ml
2 tbsp	maple syrup	25 ml
1 tbsp	lemon juice	15 ml
1 tsp	dry mustard	5 ml
½ tsp	dried basil	2 ml
½ tsp	salt	2 ml
¼ tsp	freshly ground black pepper	1 ml

1. In a large pot of salted boiling water, cook brussel sprouts about 10 minutes, until tender crisp. Drain well. Place in a bowl and immediately toss with vinegar.
2. Whisk together oil, maple syrup, lemon juice, mustard, basil, salt and pepper.
3. Pour over brussel sprouts and serve immediately or at room temperature.

Makes 4 servings.

Hint – Before measuring out syrup, rub the inside of your spoon or cup with oil. The syrup will slide off easily.

Ragout of Mushrooms and Leeks with Madeira

I like a presentation and this one certainly qualifies. It's a vegetable and starter course in one, ready to serve hot and aromatic when your guests arrive. Serve it on a gorgeous, golden, flat crouton, followed by fillet of beef.

2 tbsp	sweet butter	25 ml
1	leek, white part only, sliced	1
1 lb	white mushrooms, cleaned, stemmed, quartered	500 g
4 oz	Shiitake mushrooms cleaned and coarsely chopped	125 g
1	clove garlic, finely chopped	1
½ cup	Madeira or sherry	125 ml
2	tomatoes, peeled, seeded and chopped	2
½ tsp	dried thyme	2 ml
¼ tsp	salt	1 ml
¼ tsp	freshly ground black pepper	1 ml
1 tsp	cornstarch	5 ml
1 tbsp	water	50 ml

1. In a large skillet over medium heat, melt butter. Add leek, cooking 5 minutes until softened. Add white mushrooms, cooking for 1 minute; add Shiitake mushrooms and garlic, and cook for an additional 1 minute. Add Madeira, tomatoes, thyme, salt and pepper; cook for 3 minutes.
2. In a small bowl, combine cornstarch and water and mix until smooth. Add to mushroom mixture, stirring continually until thickened, 1 to 2 minutes. Serve hot.

Makes 4 servings.

Savory Vegetable Buckwheat Pancakes

Sour cream and soy sauce? Don't knock it till you've tried it with these Oriental starters. Invite your friends into the kitchen while you flip the pancakes so you can serve them right away with pickled shredded cabbage, steamed bok choy and a glass of saki or wine.

2 tsp	sesame oil	10 ml
½	bunch Chinese cabbage, shredded	½
3	carrots, julienned	3
2 tbsp	fresh ginger root, grated	25 ml
3 tbsp	soy sauce	50 ml
2 tbsp	mirin (sweet cooking sake)	25 ml
4	green onions, thinly sliced	4
8 oz	Shiitake mushrooms, thinly sliced	250 g
2 tbsp	fresh cilantro, chopped	25 ml
¾ tsp	hot pepper flakes	4 ml
¾ cup	buckwheat flour	175 ml
¼ cup	all-purpose flour	50 ml
½ tsp	baking soda	2 ml
¼ tsp	salt	1 ml
2	eggs	2
1 cup	buttermilk	250 ml
2 tbsp	butter, melted and cooled	25 ml
2 tbsp	vegetable oil for cooking	25 ml
1 tbsp	sesame seeds, toasted	15 ml

Sauce

1 cup	sour cream	250 ml
	juice of half a lemon	
1	clove garlic, finely chopped	1
2	green onions, thinly sliced	2

1. In a large skillet, heat the sesame oil. Add the cabbage and sauté for 3 minutes until cabbage begins to wilt. Add the carrots, ginger, soy sauce and mirin. Sauté for 5 minutes, until the vegetables are tender.
2. Add the green onions, mushrooms, cilantro and pepper flakes. Cook for 2 to 3 minutes, or until the excess liquid evaporates. Set aside to cool for at least 5 minutes.
3. In a medium-sized bowl, stir together flours, soda, salt. Beat eggs, buttermilk and butter together and stir into flour.
4. In another bowl, mix together sour cream, lemon juice, garlic and green onions. Set aside.
5. Lightly coat a medium-sized heavy skillet with vegetable oil. When very hot, spoon in 1 tbsp (15 ml) of the vegetables and cover with ½ tbsp (7 ml) pancake batter. Cook for about 2½ minutes. Turn over and, pressing down, cook for another 30 seconds. Repeat with remaining batter.
6. Serve immediately with a dab of sauce on each one. Sprinkle with the sesame seeds. Serve hot.

Makes 24 pancakes.

Hint – If a cork is too large to fit into a bottle, leave the cork in boiling water for a minute or two and it will slide in with no problem.

Baked Mushroom Squares

This recipe is versatile and cooperative as only mushrooms can be. Serve them as a side dish with your favorite vegetable stew. I like to serve them with cabbage rolls or try cutting them into larger pieces and serve as a main dish with sour cream and chopped chives.

¼ cup	sweet butter	50 ml
1	medium onion, finely chopped	1
½ cup	milk	125 ml
½ cup	cream	125 ml
1 cup	soft whole wheat breadcrumbs	250 ml
1 lb	mushrooms, chopped fine	500 g
1 tsp	salt	5 ml
¼ tsp	freshly ground black pepper	1 ml
2	eggs, well beaten	2

1. In a small skillet over medium heat, melt butter. Add onions and sauté for 10 minutes, stirring frequently.
2. In a large bowl, combine milk, cream and breadcrumbs. Let stand for 10 minutes.
3. Preheat oven to 350°F (180°C).
4. Combine sautéed onion, breadcrumb mixture, mushrooms, salt, pepper and eggs. Mix well. Pour into a buttered 8-inch (20-cm) square baking dish and bake in oven for 1 hour, until tester inserted in center comes out clean.
5. Cut into squares and serve hot.

Makes 6 servings.

Skewered Mushrooms with Oregano

This is a recipe to prepare for any barbecue party. The oregano makes it a particularly good accompaniment for steaks. The trick is to have the mushrooms at room temperature and then screw the skewer into them. That way they are much less likely to split.

1½ lb	medium mushrooms	750 g
¼ cup	olive oil	50 ml
3	cloves garlic, finely chopped	3
1 tsp	salt	5 ml
¼ tsp	freshly ground black pepper	1 ml
¼ tsp	oregano	1 ml

1. Wash and dry mushrooms. Thread onto wooden skewers with 4 to 5 mushrooms on each one.* Set in a 9x13-inch (23x33-cm) glass baking dish.
2. In a small bowl combine oil, garlic, salt, pepper and oregano. Pour over mushrooms; let stand 1 hour to marinate.
3. Remove skewers from marinade. Grill, broil or barbecue for 8 to 10 minutes, until lightly browned.

Makes 4 servings.

* Be sure to soak skewers in cold water for at least 1 hour prior to using.

Mattar Panir (Peas and Cheese)

I serve this spicy Indian dish with steamed white rice and Mogul Chicken as part of an Indian dinner or buffet. It also makes a terrific light supper with Indian breads and chutneys. Since it reheats perfectly, it can easily be made ahead of time: just add a little water when you reheat. Panir is a cheese readily available at Indian markets.

2	large onions, finely chopped	2
5	cloves garlic, finely chopped	5
3 tbsp	vegetable oil	50 ml
1½ tbsp	finely grated ginger root	22 ml
1	can (14 oz/398 ml) tomatoes	1
1 tsp	salt	5 ml
1 tsp	garam masala	5 ml
½ tsp	ground cumin	2 ml
½ tsp	cayenne pepper	2 ml
¼ tsp	turmeric	1 ml
¼ tsp	ground coriander	1 ml
3 cups	cooked peas	750 ml
½ lb	panir, cut into ½-inch (1-cm) cubes	250 g

1. Heat oil in a large skillet. Add onions and garlic and cook, stirring over medium heat, for 7 to 8 minutes. Add ginger and cook for an additional 2 minutes. Add tomatoes, salt, garam masala, cumin, cayenne, turmeric and coriander and cook 10 minutes more, stirring occasionally.
2. Add peas and cook 5 minutes; gently fold in panir and remove from heat. Cover and let stand 10 minutes.

Makes 8 servings.

Variation: Palak Panir
To make this dish substitute 1½ pounds spinach for the peas.

Eggplant Bharta

If you don't want to serve an entire Indian dinner, this spicy dish is a lovely complement to grilled chicken. However, do include some Indian breads with it. Whether you serve it hot or cold, add a wedge of fresh lime. I like to use the tomatoes, onion and cilantro in this recipe as a garnish (the color of eggplant isn't the greatest but the taste is superb). If there's any left over, I heap it onto a big slice of dark walnut bread with a thick slice of tomato. My husband loves to add it to his scrambled eggs.

2	large eggplants	2
3 tbsp	vegetable oil	50 ml
2	large onions, finely chopped	2
5	cloves garlic, finely chopped	5
1 tsp	ground cumin	5 ml
1 tsp	salt	5 ml
½ tsp	garam masala	2 ml
¼ tsp	cayenne pepper	1 ml
1	tomato, seeded, diced	1
1	small red onion, thinly sliced	1
½	sweet green pepper and diced	½
8	sprigs fresh cilantro	8

1. Preheat oven to 375°F (190°C).
2. Prick eggplants with sharp knife in several places.
3. Place on baking sheet and bake 50 minutes, or until skin is blackened. Cool slightly.
4. Peel off skin, reserving pulp.
5. In a large, deep skillet, heat oil over medium heat. Add onions and garlic and cook 5 to 7 minutes or until lightly browned.
6. Stir in cumin, salt, garam masala and cayenne. Cook, stirring, 1 minute.
7. Add eggplant, mashing pulp with wooden spoon and stirring into sauce. Reduce heat to medium-low, cover and cook, stirring often, 15 to 20 minutes, or until mixture is smooth and rich and oil begins to separate from solids.
8. Garnish with tomato, onion, green pepper and cilantro.

Makes 8 servings.

Spicy Greens

Ditch the boring green beans for this lively new recipe. Great under Grilled Curried Mahi Mahi or next to your crispy roast chicken.

4 tbsp	olive oil	50 ml
1 lb	kale, thinly shredded	500 g
1 lb	spinach, thinly shredded	500 g
¼ cup	cider vinegar	50 ml
1 tsp	crushed dried chili peppers	5 ml
1 tsp	sugar	5 ml
½ tsp	salt	5 ml

1. In a large skillet, heat 2 tbsp (25 ml) of the oil over high heat until shimmering. Add half the greens, stirring quickly for 30 to 45 seconds, or until just wilted. Transfer to bowl. Repeat with remaining oil and greens.
2. Add vinegar, chili flakes and sugar to skillet, bringing to a boil. Add to greens with salt and toss. Serve immediately.

Makes 4 servings.

Tofu and Vegetables in Black Bean Sauce

This is the recipe I serve my vegetarian friends, but I have to admit that I love it too. The ginger and black bean sauce give the tofu and vegetables a real kick. The only other course you need is a bowl of steamed rice to sop up the delicious sauce. Make sure to buy extra firm tofu for this recipe.

1 cup	chicken or vegetable stock	250 ml
¼ cup	tamari sauce	50 ml
1	clove garlic, finely chopped	1
2 tbsp	black bean sauce with garlic	25 ml
1½ tbsp	honey	22 ml
1 tbsp	grated fresh ginger root	15 ml
1 tbsp	cider vinegar	15 ml
1 lb	firm tofu,	500 g
	cut into 1-inch (2.5-cm) cubes	
2 cups	broccoli florets	500 ml
2 cups	thinly sliced mushrooms	500 ml
1 cup	carrots, thinly sliced	250 ml
1 cup	celery, thinly sliced	250 ml
1 cup	onions, thinly sliced	250 ml
1 cup	bok choy, shredded	250 ml
2 tbsp	water	25 ml
1 tbsp	cornstarch	15 ml
1 tbsp	sesame oil	15 ml
4	drops hot pepper sauce (optional)	4

1. In a large skillet or wok over medium heat, combine stock, tamari sauce, garlic, black bean sauce, honey, ginger and vinegar. Bring to a boil.
2. Add tofu and all vegetables; reduce heat and simmer about 5 minutes or until vegetables are tender crisp.

3. In a small bowl, combine water and cornstarch and stir in 2 tbsp (25 ml) hot liquid from wok; mix until smooth. Stir into vegetables; cook, stirring, about 2 minutes, until thickened and glazed.
4. Add sesame oil and hot pepper sauce. Serve at once.

Makes 8 servings.

~~~~~~

Hint – Use a zester to grab ginger.

~~~~~~

Red Onion and Pommery Bread Pudding

This is an impressive alternative to Yorkshire pudding with a standing rib roast. It's a favorite at our house in the depths of winter, when we enjoy it with a glass of red wine and a salad. Don't be afraid to throw in whatever breads you have on hand and to experiment with spicy mustards.

1 tbsp	sweet butter	15 ml
1	red onion, sliced	1
1	clove garlic, finely chopped	1
2	slices country white bread	2
2	slices pumpernickel bread	2
2 tsp	pommery or grain mustard	10 ml
2	green onions, chopped	2
4	eggs	4
⅔ cup	heavy or whipping cream	150 ml
⅔ cup	milk	150 ml
½ tsp	salt	2 ml
½ tsp	freshly ground black pepper	2 ml
pinch	nutmeg	pinch*

1. Preheat oven to 325°F (160°C).
2. Lightly oil 7-inch (15-cm) round glass or ceramic baking dish.
3. In a medium-sized skillet, melt butter. Add onion and garlic; sauté 5 minutes, until softened. Place onion mixture in a large bowl.
4. Spread breads with mustard and cut into 1-inch (2.5-cm) cubes. Add bread and green onions to onion mixture. Toss thoroughly to mix well. Place mixture into casserole dish.
5. In a bowl whisk eggs until they are just frothy. In a saucepan combine cream, milk, salt, pepper and nutmeg; heat but do not boil. Whisking constantly, slowly pour cream mixture into eggs.

6. Pour custard over bread mixture in casserole dish. Bake in oven 30 minutes, until set.
7. Remove to a wire rack to cool for 10 minutes before serving. Serve warm.

Makes 6 servings.

* This recipe can easily be doubled. Bake in a 9- or 10-inch (23- to 25-cm) round casserole for 45 minutes.

Leek and Goat Cheese Tart

This is a favorite of mine when there's a gang coming over for a brunch buffet. Toasted breads, piled high in earthenware and baskets, go well with the soft, smooth texture of the tart. I also offer my guests endive and radicchio salad, a fudgy dessert and, of course, pots of freshly brewed coffee. As a starter to a more formal meal, serve as individual tartlets. For a quick and easy soufflé, dispense with the crust altogether.

2 tbsp	sweet butter	25 ml
3	leeks, white part only, washed and chopped	3
½ tsp	curry powder	2 ml
3 oz	soft goat cheese, in chunks	75 g
3	eggs	3
1	egg yolk	1
¾ cup	light cream	175 ml
½ cup	heavy or whipping cream	125 ml
1 cup	milk	250 ml
½ tsp	salt	2 ml
¼ tsp	white pepper	1 ml
pinch	cayenne	pinch
1	9-inch (23-cm) pie crust	1

1. Preheat oven to 425°F (220°C).
2. In a large skillet over medium-low heat, sweat the leeks for about 10 minutes until they are translucent.
3. Add curry powder and cook for another 2 to 3 minutes.
4. Remove the pan from heat and stir in goat cheese until it melts. Set aside.
5. In a bowl, whisk together eggs, yolk, creams, milk, salt, pepper and cayenne. Stir in the leek mixture, mixing thoroughly.
6. Pour into the pie crust and bake for 12 minutes. Reduce heat to 325°F (160°C) and bake another 25 minutes, until just firm.
7. Remove from oven and let cool 15 to 20 minutes before serving.

Makes 6 servings.

Red Cabbage and Red Onions

Just shave your cabbage, peel the apples, insert your onions and away it goes. Leave it on low simmer for as long as you like, or switch it off and reheat later. It is also good cold.

1	head red cabbage (1½ lb/750 g), finely shredded	1
¼ cup	red wine vinegar	50 ml
½ tsp	salt	2 ml
2 tbsp	sweet butter	25 ml
2	red onions, thinly sliced	2
2	apples, thinly sliced	2
½ cup	chicken stock	125 ml
2 tbsp	brown sugar	25 ml
2 tsp	caraway seed	10 ml
½ tsp	freshly ground black pepper	2 ml

1. In a large bowl, combine cabbage, vinegar and salt. Let stand 5 minutes.
2. Heat butter in a large skillet. Add cabbage, turning 2 to 3 times. Stir in onions, apples, stock, sugar, caraway and pepper.
3. Cook, covered, over low heat for 1 hour, until cabbage is tender. Serve warm.

Makes 6 servings.

Thyme Glazed Onions

Baked in their skins and then deglazed with balsamic vinegar, these onions add luscious personality to smoked meats. I use a cast-iron skillet, first in the oven, then on top of the stove for deglazing.

4	red or yellow medium onions, unpeeled	4
4 tsp	olive oil	20 ml
¼ cup	balsamic vinegar	50 ml
1 tbsp	coarsely chopped fresh thyme	15 ml

1. Preheat oven to 375°F (190°C).
2. Coat unpeeled onions with olive oil.
3. Place onions in a medium-sized cast-iron skillet.
4. Bake in oven 1 hour or until soft. Remove onions from skillet. Cut in half lengthwise; arrange cut side up on a serving platter.
5. Deglaze skillet with vinegar, scraping up the juices. Reduce until syrupy, about 5 minutes.
6. Pour over onions and serve at room temperature.

Makes 4 servings.

Hint – Put a little bread into your mouth when you're cutting onions. It helps to stop your eyes from watering.

Breads

Breads

I don't know why it is but even the most self-disciplined dieters will allow themselves a slice or two of good home-made bread (buttered, of course) when they won't touch other goodies on the tea table.

Breads

Pecan Bread
Oatmeal Bread
Jalapeño Cornbread
Quick Onion Beer Bread
Irish Soda Bread

Pecan Bread

When this bread is made with pecans and onions, it is wonderful to serve with salads and soups and lots of fresh butter. In its sweet version, minus the onions, it is good for formal dinners. I like to pass plates of it with the dessert cheese tray.

1 tsp	granulated sugar	5 ml
½ cup	lukewarm milk	125 ml
1	envelope active dry yeast	1
3-3½ cups	all-purpose flour	750-875 ml
1 cup	whole wheat flour	250 ml
2 tsp	salt	10 ml
⅓ cup	water	75 ml
¾ cup	finely chopped onion*	175 ml
¼ cup	soft sweet butter	50 ml
1 cup	coarsely chopped pecans	250 ml
	cornmeal	

1. In a small bowl, dissolve sugar in milk. Sprinkle in yeast. Let stand 10 minutes, then stir well.
2. In a large bowl, combine 1 cup (250 ml) all-purpose flour, all the whole wheat flour and salt. Add yeast mixture and stir 2 minutes, until well-blended.
3. Heat butter in a small skillet and add onions; sauté 5 minutes, until softened. Add onion mixture and pecans to flour mixture.
4. Stir in the remainder of the all-purpose flour to make a dough which leaves the side of the bowl.
5. On a lightly floured surface, knead dough until smooth. Place in a well-greased bowl, turning so that dough is greased all over. Cover and let rise in a warm place for 1 hour, or until doubled.
6. Preheat oven to 425°F (220°C).
7. On a lightly floured surface, punch dough down; knead 2 to 3 minutes.
8. Cut in half and shape each half as an oval loaf, about 10 inches (25 cm) long.

9. Sprinkle baking sheet with cornmeal and place loaves on sheet. Let rise, uncovered, in a warm place for 20 minutes. Slash tops diagonally. Bake in oven for 25 to 30 minutes, until loaves sound hollow when tapped on top.

Makes 2 loaves.

* If serving with dessert cheese, substitute ¾ cup (175 ml) currants for the onions.

Oatmeal Bread

Because this recipe makes two loaves, I make the first one plain to serve with soups, and the second one with currants and cinnamon to go with cheeses.

2 tbsp plus 2 tsp	granulated sugar	35 ml
½ cup	lukewarm water	125 ml
2	envelopes active dry yeast	2
3 cups	rolled oats	750 ml
2½ cups	boiling water	625 ml
½ cup	molasses	125 ml
1 tbsp	salt	15 ml
¼ cup	shortening	50 ml
½ cup	cold water	125 ml
6 cups	all-purpose flour	1.5 l
2 tbsp	sweet butter	25 ml

1. In a cup combine 2 tsp (10 ml) sugar and lukewarm water; stir to dissolve. Sprinkle yeast over and let stand 10 minutes; stir well.
2. In a large bowl, combine rolled oats, boiling water, molasses, remaining sugar, salt, shortening and stir to blend. Add cold water to oatmeal mixture and stir until lukewarm.
3. Stir in yeast mixture. Add half of the flour and beat with a wooden spoon until well-blended. Add enough of remaining flour, mixing first with spoon then with hands, to make a firm but not stiff dough.
4. Turn out onto a floured board and knead about 8 minutes, until elastic.
5. Put in a greased bowl, cover with a damp cloth, and let rise in a warm place about 1 hour and 15 minutes, until double in bulk.
6. Punch down and let rise again, about 45 minutes to an hour, until double. Punch down.

7. Grease two 9x5-inch (23x13-cm) loaf pans. Divide dough into two equal parts and shape each into a loaf. Place in prepared pans. Brush tops with melted butter and let rise in a warm place about 1 hour, until double.

8. Preheat oven to 425°F (220°C). Bake for 15 minutes, then reduce temperature to 375°F (190°C) and continue to bake 45 minutes, or until loaves sound hollow when tapped on top. Cool on racks.

Makes 2 loaves.

Variation: Oatmeal Fruit Loaf

Before shaping portion of dough into loaves, roll each portion to form a 9-inch (23-cm) wide rectangle. For each loaf combine 2 tbsp (25 ml) brown sugar, ½ cup (125 ml) raisins or currants, and 1 tsp (1 ml) cinnamon. Sprinkle over surface of rectangle, roll up and tuck in ends, and place in prepared pan. Continue as recipe directs.

Hint – Prevent raisins from sinking to the bottom of a cake by dusting them lightly with flour before adding to the mix.

Jalapeño Cornbread

Serve with spicy chili or top with lots of rare roast beef slices and your favorite relish.

1 cup	yellow cornmeal	250 ml
½ cup	all-purpose flour	125 ml
1 tsp	baking powder	5 ml
½ tsp	baking soda	2 ml
½ tsp	salt	2 ml
3	eggs	3
¾ cup	milk	175 ml
¼ cup	vegetable oil	50 ml
1 cup	corn niblets	250 ml
1 cup	shredded sharp Cheddar cheese	250 ml
¼ cup	finely chopped jalapeño peppers	50 ml

1. Preheat oven to 400°F (200°C).
2. Lightly grease a 9x5-inch (23x12-cm) loaf pan.
3. Combine cornmeal, flour, baking powder, baking soda and salt.
4. In a large bowl lightly beat eggs; stir in milk and oil. Add corn, cheese and peppers; mix well.
5. Stir dry ingredients into liquid until evenly mixed. Do not beat. Pour batter into prepared loaf pan.
6. Bake in oven for 35 to 40 minutes, until toothpick inserted in center comes out clean. Let cool in pan 10 minutes, then remove to a wire rack.

Makes 1 loaf.

Quick Onion Beer Bread

A quick, full-flavored bread. I serve it fresh from the oven on Christmas morning. It's great toasted with scrambled eggs and the flecks of green onion and fresh dill give it a festive look. For a hot hit, substitute 2 tbsp of jalapeño peppers for the herbs.

3 cups	all-purpose flour	750 ml
1 tbsp	baking powder	15 ml
1 tbsp	granulated sugar	15 ml
¾ tsp	salt	4 ml
1 cup	grated white Cheddar cheese	250 ml
¼ cup	green onions, finely chopped	50 ml
2 tbsp	coarsely chopped fresh dill or basil	25 ml
1	bottle beer (12 oz/355 ml)	1

Topping

1	small onion, thinly sliced into rings	1
¼ cup	grated white Cheddar cheese	50 ml
1 tbsp	sesame seeds	15 ml

1. Preheat oven to 350°F (180°C)
2. Grease a 9x5-inch (23x12-cm) loaf pan.
3. In a large bowl, combine flour, baking powder, sugar and salt. Stir in cheese, onions and dill. Pour in beer, blending until thoroughly mixed.
4. Spoon into loaf pan and arrange onion rings over top; sprinkle with cheese and sesame seeds.
5. Bake in oven for 50 to 55 minutes, until a wooden toothpick inserted into the center comes out clean.
6. Let stand 5 minutes in pan. Remove from pan and serve.

Makes 1 loaf.

Irish Soda Bread

This is so quick and easy to make you'll find yourself whipping it up just for the raves you'll get. I love it for the exquisite flavor of green onions and rosemary. Serve it hot from the oven with a pot of sweet butter and homemade soup. It's also a winner toasted with scrambled eggs or topped with cream cheese and lox.

4 cups	all purpose flour	1 l
1 tbsp	baking powder	15 ml
1 tsp	baking soda	5 ml
1 tsp	salt	5 ml
5	whole green onions, sliced thinly	5
1 tbsp	fresh rosemary	15 ml
1	egg	1
2 tbsp	vegetable oil	25 ml
1½ cups	buttermilk	375 ml

1. Preheat oven to 350°F (180°C).
2. In a large mixing bowl, combine flour, baking powder, baking soda, salt, green onions and rosemary.
3. With mixer on low, add egg and oil. Gradually add buttermilk and mix until blended.
4. Turn out onto a floured board and knead about 3 minutes, until smooth.
5. Shape the dough into 2 loaves approximately 3x6-inches (8x15-cm) and place far apart on an ungreased, floured baking sheet.
6. Bake for 40 minutes, until tester comes out clean.

Makes 2 loaves.

Hint – Baking Powder – Buy in small amounts and make sure you date the container. Once it's a year old, throw it out. There's nothing more disappointing than having a great cake recipe fail because of old baking powder.

Desserts

Desserts

Nothin' says lovin'—from the romantic to the maternal variety—like a sweet treat made from scratch.

Cookies

Almond Wedges
Lemon Curved Cookies
Palm Leaves
Molasses Crinkles
Spice Cookies with Ginger Icing
Gingerbread Cookies
Lace Wafers
Crisp Brandy Cones
Pecan Puffs
Chocolate-Oat No-Fat Chewies

Squares And Tarts

Butter Pecan Turtles
Butter Tarts
Lemon Coconut Squares
Chewy Raspberry Squares
Fudgy Brownies with Mocha Frosting
Lime Tart Brulée

Cakes And Crumbles

4 C's Cranberry Loaf
Pear and Cranberry Crisp
Apple Crumble
Triple-Berry Crumb Cake
Hummingbird Cake
Date Pecan Cake
French Orange Butter Cake
Dreamy Coffeecake
Gingerbread Cake
Mocha Mousse Cake
Chocolate Fondant Cake
Killer Chocolate Cake with Chocolate Frosting
Chocolate Cheesecake

Puddings And Other Sweets

Lemon Custard Pudding
Hot Fruit Compotes
Rum and Raisin Bread Pudding
Lemon Soufflé
Summer Berries in Lemon Mousse
Orange Creme Caramel
Tiramisu
Cinnamon Rice Pudding
Rich Praline Mousse

Cookies, Squares & Tarts

Iced, rolled in sugar, sprinkled with candy chips, sandwiched with a creamy filling or drenched in melted chocolate ... cookies in their infinite variety are bound to seduce everybody sooner or later.

Almond Wedges

Fun and quick to make, these are closer to shortbread than cookies—but you won't be disappointed.

2 cups	cake and pastry flour	500 ml
1 tsp	baking powder	5 ml
½ tsp	baking soda	2 ml
½ tsp	salt	2 ml
½ cup	sweet butter, softened	125 ml
½ cup	shortening	125 ml
½ cup	granulated sugar	125 ml
½ cup	lightly packed brown sugar	125 ml
1	egg	1
1 tsp	almond extract	5 ml
1 cup	chopped blanched almonds	250 ml

1. Preheat oven to 325°F (160°C).
2. Lightly oil two 9-inch (23-cm) pie plates.
3. Combine flour, baking powder, soda and salt.
4. In large bowl, cream butter, shortening and sugars until light and fluffy. Add egg and almond extract; beat well. Stir in dry ingredients until well-blended.
5. Press half of dough into each pie plate. Divide chopped almonds evenly and sprinkle over top of dough. Bake in oven 20 to 25 minutes, until golden brown. Let cool 3 minutes. Cut each pan into 12 wedges. Let cool completely.

Makes 24.

Variation

This dough can also be rolled into balls about 1-inch (2.5-cm) in diameter and pressed with a floured fork to flatten them. Bake in 350°F (180°C) oven for 8 to 10 minutes, until golden brown.

Lemon Curved Cookies

Thin, buttery and lemon rich, these are my choice to serve with Chocolate Mousse.

¼ cup	soft sweet butter	50 ml
½ cup	granulated sugar	125 ml
2	egg whites	2
¼ cup	all-purpose flour	50 ml
⅓ cup	blanched almonds, roughly ground in blender	75 ml
¼ tsp	lemon extract	1 ml
	grated rind of 1 lemon	

1. Preheat oven to 425°F (220°C).
2. Line baking sheets with parchment paper or oil lightly.
3. In a bowl, beat butter and sugar until light and fluffy. Add egg whites and beat for a few seconds.
4. Fold in flour, then fold in ground almonds, lemon extract and lemon rind.
5. Drop batter by teaspoonfuls at least 4 inches (10 cm) apart on prepared baking sheets. With the back of a spoon, spread into 3-inch (7-cm) circles.
6. Bake in oven for 3 to 4 minutes, or until lightly browned around edges.
7. With a long spatula, remove cookies immediately and drape them over a rolling pin to form a curved shape. If cookies harden before you can remove them all from the cookie sheet, return them to the oven for a few seconds, and they will soften again. Store in an airtight container.

Makes 2 dozen cookies.

Hint – Lemons will render twice as much juice if you immerse them in hot water first or zap them for 10 seconds in the microwave.

Palm Leaves

I serve these regularly with coffee after a rich dessert.

1½ cups	all-purpose flour	375 ml
1 cup	cold sweet butter	250 ml
½ cup	sour cream	125 ml
2 cups	granulated sugar	500 ml

1. Place flour in a bowl. With a pastry blender or two forks, cut in butter to form coarse crumbs. Stir in sour cream.
2. Knead briefly until mixture sticks together. Form into a ball, wrap in waxed paper and chill in refrigerator for 2 hours.
3. Cut in half. Sprinkle sugar generously on working surface. Roll out half the dough. Sprinkle generously with sugar.
4. Continue to roll to form a 10-inch (25-cm) square, about ⅛-inch (3-mm) thick. Sprinkle top with sugar.
5. Lightly mark a center line in dough. Roll each side over twice to meet in the center. Fold these two thick sides together.
6. Repeat with other ½ of the dough.
7. Wrap each roll in waxed paper and refrigerate 1 hour or freeze ½ hour.
8. Preheat oven to 425°F (220°C).
9. Line two baking sheets with parchment paper.
10. With a sharp knife, cut each roll in ½-inch (1-cm) pieces. Dip both sides of each piece in sugar and place at least 3 inches (7 cm) apart on prepared baking sheets.
11. Bake 6 to 7 minutes, or until sugar is caramelized on underside of cookie.
12. Turn leaves over and bake another 4 to 5 minutes, or until evenly caramelized and golden on both sides. Cool on wire racks.

Makes 40 cookies.

Molasses Crinkles

My family are always begging for these rich dark "Grandma" cookies. We love them for dunking in place of biscotti.

2 cups	all-purpose flour	500 ml
2 tsp	baking soda	10 ml
1 tsp	cinnamon	5 ml
½ tsp	powdered ginger	2 ml
½ tsp	salt	2 ml
1 cup	granulated sugar	250 ml
⅔ cup	corn oil	150 ml
1	egg	1
4 tbsp	molasses	50 ml
1 cup	granulated sugar (for rolling cookies)	250 ml

1. Preheat oven to 350°F (180°C).
2. Combine flour, soda, cinnamon, ginger and salt.
3. In a mixing bowl, whisk together sugar and oil. Add egg and beat until light and fluffy. Beat in molasses. Gradually add sifted dry ingredients until dough just comes together.
4. Shape into small balls. Roll each ball in sugar and place on ungreased cookie sheet at least 1-inch (3-cm) apart.
5. Bake for 15 minutes, until deep brown and cracked on top. Cool 5 minutes, then remove to wire rack.

Makes 55 cookies.

Spice Cookies

Rolling and slicing on the diagonal makes it easy to create this elegant oval cookie. Serve it as a wafer with sorbet, fruit mousse, or make petit sandwiches filled with either ice cream or Ginger Icing. The wise cook will double the recipe and store half in the freezer.

4 cups	all-purpose flour	1 l
2 tsp	ground cinnamon	10 ml
1 tsp	ground nutmeg	5 ml
½ tsp	ground cloves	2 ml
¼ tsp	baking soda	1 ml
1½ cups	sweet butter, softened	375 ml
2 cups	brown sugar	500 ml
1	egg	1

1. Combine flour, cinnamon, nutmeg, cloves and soda.
2. In a mixing bowl, cream together butter and sugar. Add egg, beating well. Add dry ingredients in two additions and mix until blended.
3. Divide dough into thirds. Place one piece on waxed paper and roll into a log 1-inch (3-cm) in diameter. Repeat with other two pieces of dough. Wrap each roll in waxed paper and refrigerate for 2 hours or until firm. Can be frozen at this point. Freezes for up to 1 month.
4. Preheat oven to 350°F (180°C).
5. Line cookie sheets with parchment paper or lightly oil.
6. With a sharp knife, cut each log on a diagonal in ⅛-inch pieces. Place on prepared cookie sheets. Bake in oven for 10 minutes, or until lightly browned. Cool 1 minute, then remove to wire rack.

Makes 6 dozen cookies.

Ginger Icing

Sandwiched between Spice or Gingerbread Cookies or smeared on banana bread, it's all you could ask for.

2¼ cups	confectioner's or icing sugar	550 ml
3 tbsp	chopped, crystallized ginger	50 ml
4 tbsp	cold, sweet butter, cut in cubes	50 ml
3 tbsp	ginger marmalade	50 ml

1. In a food processor, combine sugar and ginger and process 2 minutes, until the ginger is minced.
2. Add butter and marmalade to the ginger mixture and process until thick and well-blended.

Makes 2½ cups (625 ml).

Gingerbread Cookies

This recipe has been a well-kept secret in my family for years—until now, that is. Small, pretty cutouts will look prettier still if you roll out the dough as thinly as possible. Dress them up for special occasions with a dusting of icing sugar. For old-time Christmas tree decorations, simply use a straw to put holes in them before baking. This is a large recipe, so feel free to freeze half the dough to bake later on.

5 cups	all-purpose flour	1.25 l
1 tbsp	ground ginger	15 ml
1½ tsp	baking soda	7 ml
1 tsp	ground cinnamon	5 ml
1 tsp	ground cloves	5 ml
½ tsp	salt	2 ml
1 cup	shortening	250 ml
1 cup	granulated sugar	250 ml
1 cup	molasses	250 ml
1	egg	1
2 tbsp	vinegar	25 ml

Glaze

1	egg, beaten	1
⅓ cup	granulated sugar	75 ml
1½ tsp	ground ginger	7 ml

1. Combine flour, ginger, soda, cinnamon, cloves and salt.
2. In a mixing bowl, cream shortening. Add sugar; beat until light and fluffy. Add molasses, egg and vinegar; beat until combined. Stir in dry ingredients in two stages, just until a soft dough is formed.
3. Divide dough into three portions; wrap and refrigerate about 3 hours.
4. Preheat oven to 375°F (190°C).

5. Line cookie sheets with parchment or lightly oil.
6. In small bowl, mix sugar and ginger for the glaze.
7. On a lightly floured surface, roll dough to about ⅛-inch thickness. Cut into desired shapes with cutters; place on prepared cookie sheets. Brush with beaten egg, sprinkle with ginger-sugar. Bake in oven for 6 to 7 minutes. Cool 1 minute, then remove to wire rack.

Makes about 5 dozen cookies.

Hint – All-purpose flour may be substituted for cake flour; just use 2 tbsp less per cup.

Lace Wafers

Make something rich enough and thin enough and bake it hot enough—and voila, lace! These look so elegant that I line a silver cookie basket with a white linen napkin to serve them in.

¼ cup	shortening	50 ml
¼ cup	corn syrup	50 ml
⅓ cup	firmly packed brown sugar	75 ml
½ cup	all-purpose flour	125 ml
½ cup	finely chopped walnuts or pecans	125 ml

1. Preheat oven to 375°F (190°C).
2. Line baking sheets with parchment paper or oil lightly.
3. In a small saucepan, combine shortening, corn syrup and sugar. Stir constantly over medium heat until mixture starts to boil.
4. Remove from heat and stir in flour and nuts. Drop mixture by the tablespoon at least 3 inches (7 cm) apart onto prepared cookie sheets.
5. Bake in oven for 5 to 6 minutes, or until edges of cookies are lightly browned.
6. Remove from oven and let cool for only 30 seconds. With metal spatula, remove carefully to wire rack to cool. Store in airtight container.

Makes 2 dozen.

An English garden party. Create nosegays of pink heather, paperwhite narcissus and silver roses. Tie each nosegay with an 8-inch piece of antique lace trim, easily found at flea markets and antique fairs. Make one nosegay for each guest to take home. Long after the flowers are gone they will have the lace trim as a reminder of a pleasant afternoon.

Crisp Brandy Cones

This is a deluxe way to serve ice cream or flavored whipped cream. I sometimes add strawberries, raspberries or blueberries to the whipped cream. If you fill the cones with ice cream, pop them in the freezer until you are ready to serve.

½ cup	molasses	125 ml
½ cup	sweet butter	125 ml
1 cup	all-purpose flour	250 ml
½ cup	granulated sugar	125 ml
1 tsp	ground ginger	5 ml
1 tbsp	brandy	15 ml

1. Preheat oven to 300°F (150°C).
2. Line two baking sheets with parchment paper or lightly oil.
3. In a medium saucepan, heat molasses to boiling point. Stir in butter until melted. Gradually add flour, sugar and ginger, stirring constantly. Remove from heat. Stir in brandy.
4. Drop mixture about 2 tbsp (25 ml) at a time, at least 2 inches (5 cm) apart onto prepared baking sheets. Using back of a spoon, spread to a 5-inch (12-cm) circle.
5. Bake in oven for 12 to 15 minutes, or until cookies stop bubbling. Cool slightly.
6. With fingers, roll into cone shapes. If they become too hard to roll, reheat in oven for a few minutes.
7. Cool on wire rack.

Makes 2 dozen cones.

Pecan Puffs

These look gorgeous for your afternoon tea parties and tempt even the dieter.

½ cup	sweet butter	125 ml
¼ cup	granulated sugar	50 ml
1 tbsp	vanilla	15 ml
1 cup	finely chopped pecans	250 ml
1 cup	cake and pastry flour	250 ml
	confectioner's or icing sugar	

1. Preheat oven to 300°F (180°C).
2. Line two cookie sheets with parchment paper or lightly oil.
3. In a bowl, cream butter and sugar until light and fluffy. Stir in vanilla. Add nuts and flour, stir until evenly blended.
4. Roll into small balls, 1-inch (2.5-cm) in diameter, and place on cookie sheets about 2 inches (5 cm) apart. Bake in oven for 30 to 40 minutes, or until lightly golden.
5. Place confectioner's sugar on a small plate. While baked puffs are hot, roll them in sugar.
6. Roll again in sugar when cold.

Makes 2 dozen.

Chocolate-Oat No-Fat Chewies

Substituting crispy rice cereal for high-cal nuts makes this yummy cookie not only fat-free, but a guilt-free chocolate hit—would you believe only 56 calories per cookie?

1 cup	rolled oats	250 ml
⅔ cup	all-purpose flour	150 ml
⅔ cup	granulated sugar	150 ml
½ cup	sifted cocoa	125 ml
1 tsp	baking powder	5 ml
½ tsp	ground black pepper	2 ml
¼ tsp	salt	1 ml
2	egg whites	2
⅓ cup	corn syrup	75 ml
2 tbsp	water	25 ml
1 tsp	vanilla	5 ml
1 cup	crisp rice cereal	250 ml

1. Preheat oven to 350°F (180°C).
2. Use non-stick cookie sheets, or line with parchment paper.
3. Combine oats, flour, sugar, cocoa, baking powder, pepper and salt.
4. In a small bowl, whisk together egg whites, corn syrup, water and vanilla. Stir in dry ingredients until well blended. Stir in rice cereal.
5. Drop dough by tablespoons on prepared cookie sheets. Bake in oven 12 minutes, or until set on outside, but still soft inside. Cool 5 minutes, then remove to wire rack.
6. Store in an airtight container for up to 2 days.

Makes 2 dozen.

Butter Pecan Turtles

Where the name "turtles" came from, I will never know! These are much faster than turtles as they move off the plate and into the mouth.

2 cups	all-purpose flour	500 ml
1¾ cups	firmly packed brown sugar	425 ml
1½ cups	soft sweet butter	375 ml
1 cup	pecan pieces	250 ml
1 cup	chocolate chips	250 ml

1. In a bowl, combine flour and 1 cup (250 ml) brown sugar. With a fork, stir in ½ cup (125 ml) butter until mixture resembles coarse crumbs.
2. Press into bottom of a lightly greased 12x8-inch (30x20-cm) pan. Sprinkle with pecans. Set aside.
3. Preheat oven to 350°F (180°C).
4. In a saucepan, combine 1 cup (250 ml) butter and ¾ cup (175 ml) brown sugar; cook over medium heat, stirring constantly until mixture boils. Continue stirring and boil 1 minute, or until mixture blends; pour over prepared base.
5. Bake for 15 to 20 minutes or until surface is bubbly.
6. Remove from oven and immediately sprinkle chocolate chips evenly over surface.
7. Let stand 1 minute to melt. Spread chocolate with fork.
8. Cool completely until chocolate is set. Cut into 2-inch (5-cm) squares when cool.

Makes 24 squares.

Butter Tarts

These are syrupy, super-delicious and guaranteed to ruin your teeth and your figure.

Pastry

2 cups	all-purpose flour	500 ml
1 tsp	baking powder	5 ml
1 tsp	salt	5 ml
½ cup	sweet butter, at room temperature	125 ml
½ cup	shortening, at room temperature	125 ml
¼ cup	confectioner's or icing sugar	50 ml
1	egg, slightly beaten	1
1 tsp	vanilla	5 ml

1. In a bowl, combine flour, baking powder and salt.
2. In a mixer bowl, cream together butter and shortening; blend in sugar and beat in egg and vanilla.
3. Gradually mix in dry ingredients, 2 tbsp (25 ml) at a time, mixing well after each addition until a dough forms.
4. Wrap and chill dough about 30 minutes, until firm enough to roll.
5. On a floured board or between sheets of waxed paper, roll dough to ⅛-inch (3-mm) thick. With a floured cutter, cut into rounds to fit 18 tart pans. Press into pans.

Filling

½ cup	raisins	125 ml
	hot water	
½ cup	corn syrup	125 ml
¼ cup	firmly packed brown sugar	50 ml
¼ cup	soft sweet butter	50 ml
pinch	salt	pinch
1	egg, slightly beaten	1
½ tsp	vanilla	2 ml

1. Preheat oven to 375°F (190°C).
2. In a small bowl, cover raisins with hot water; let stand 5 minutes.
3. In another bowl, combine corn syrup, brown sugar, butter and salt. Drain raisins and add to butter mixture. Stir until sugar is dissolved and butter melted. Stir in egg and vanilla.
4. Divide mixture among tart shells, filling them ¾ full and making sure the raisins are evenly distributed.
5. Bake in oven for 15 minutes, until pastry is golden and filling lightly browned and bubbling.
6. Let cool in pans for 10 minutes, then remove to cake rack to continue to cool.

Makes 18 tarts.

Lemon Coconut Squares

This is a bar of great appeal, thanks to a buttery oatmeal base, oodles of raisins, and lots of lively lemon.

½ cup	all-purpose flour	125 ml
¼ cup	brown sugar	50 ml
¼ tsp	baking powder	1 ml
pinch	salt	pinch
¾ cup	rolled oats	175 ml
⅓ cup	cold sweet butter	75 ml
2	eggs	2
¾ cup	firmly packed brown sugar	175 ml
	grated rind of ½ lemon	
¾ cup	flaked desiccated coconut	175 ml
¾ cup	raisins	175 ml

1. Preheat oven to 350°F (180°C).
2. In a bowl, combine flour, brown sugar, baking powder, salt and rolled oats. Cut in butter until mixture resembles coarse crumbs.
3. Press into a lightly greased 8-inch (20-cm) square pan and bake in oven for 10 to 15 minutes, or until a light golden brown.
4. Meanwhile in the same bowl, combine eggs, brown sugar, lemon juice and rind. Stir in coconut and raisins.
5. Spread over baked crust and return to oven to 20 to 25 minutes, or until topping is golden.
6. Let cool before cutting into 3-inch (7.5-cm) squares.

Makes 16 squares.

Chewy Raspberry Squares

When I had a gourmet food store, we could never make enough of these super shortbread-based bars with the raspberry topping.

¾ cup	sweet butter	175 ml
¾ cup	granulated sugar	175 ml
2	eggs, separated	2
1½ cups	all-purpose flour	375 ml
½ cup	chopped walnuts	125 ml
1 cup	raspberry jam	250 ml
½ cup	flaked desiccated coconut	125 ml

1. Preheat oven to 350°F (180°C).
2. In a bowl, cream butter and ¼ cup (50 ml) sugar until light and fluffy. Beat in egg yolks. Stir in flour until blended.
3. Spread evenly in lightly greased 8-inch (20-cm) square pan and bake in oven for 15 to 20 minutes, or until golden.
4. While crust is baking, in mixer bowl beat egg whites until foamy.
5. Gradually beat in remaining ½ cup (125 ml) sugar until stiff peaks form and meringue is glossy. Gently fold in walnuts.
6. Spread raspberry jam over crust layer, sprinkle evenly with coconut. Cover with meringue, spreading evenly.
7. Return to oven and bake 25 to 30 minutes, or until lightly golden.
8. Cool completely before cutting into 1x2-inch (2.5x5-cm) bars.

Makes 32 bars.

Fudgy Brownies with Mocha Frosting

All right, so you and your guests will have to do a few extra laps around the block. It's worth it just to sink your teeth into these fudgy brownies. I slather the brownies with Mocha Frosting, then sprinkle nuts over one half of the frosting and coconut over the other, mainly because my family is divided on the merits of the two garnishes.

3	squares unsweetened chocolate (3 oz/84 g)	3
¾ cup	sweet butter	175 ml
1½ cups	granulated sugar	375 ml
¾ cup	all-purpose flour	175 ml
1 tsp	baking powder	5 ml
3	eggs	3
1 tsp	vanilla	5 ml
½ cup	chopped nuts or desiccated coconut (optional)	125 ml
	Mocha Frosting	
	additional chopped nuts	
	and desiccated coconut (optional)	

1. Preheat oven to 350°F (180°C).
2. In the top of a double boiler, over simmering water, melt chocolate and butter. Set aside to cool for about 10 minutes.
3. In a bowl, combine sugar, flour and baking powder. Make a well in the center. Add eggs, vanilla and chocolate mixture. Beat for 1 minute. Fold in nuts or coconut, if desired.
4. Pour into a buttered 8-inch (20-cm) square baking pan. Bake in oven for 20 to 25 minutes, until tester inserted in center comes out clean. Cool. Spread with Mocha Frosting. Sprinkle nuts over half and coconut over the other half, if desired.

Makes 48 squares.

Variation:
Dust with confectioner's or icing sugar instead of frosting.

Mocha Frosting

⅓ cup	soft sweet butter	75 ml
1	egg yolk	1
1½ cups	confectioner's or icing sugar	375 ml
1 tbsp	cocoa	15 ml
2 tbsp	very strong coffee, cooled	25 ml
½ tsp	vanilla	2 ml

1. In a bowl, cream butter and egg yolk until fluffy. Stir in half the sugar.
2. Combine cocoa and coffee. Beat into butter mixture, alternating with remaining sugar.
3. Beat well until smooth and creamy. Stir in vanilla.

Makes 2 cups (500 ml) frosting.

Variation: Orange Frosting

Use 2 tbsp (25 ml) fresh orange juice and the grated rind of one orange in place of the coffee and cocoa.

Lime Tart Brulée

I owe thanks for this formal dinner dessert to a great Toronto baker named Keith Froggett from Scaramouche. For those of us who live in northern climes, the sight of colorful citrus is especially welcome in winter (thank goodness limes are available year-round!). It's also a very pretty dish for a wedding table, garnished with your favorite edible flowers. Bright slices of honeydew and mango are another great complement to the overall subtlety of colors and flavors.

Pastry

1¾ cups	all-purpose flour	425 ml
¾ cup	cake and pastry flour	175 ml
¾ cup	icing sugar	175 ml
1 cup	cold sweet butter, cut in small cubes	250 ml
2	egg yolks	2
¼ cup	heavy or whipping cream	50 ml

Filling

	grated rind of 2 limes	
¾ cup	freshly squeezed lime juice (about 6 limes)	175 ml
1 cup	granulated sugar	250 ml
¾ cup	heavy or whipping cream	175 ml
4	eggs	4

Brulée

3 tbsp	granulated sugar	45 ml

1. Preheat oven to 375°F (190°C).
2. In a food processor, pulse flours and icing sugar for 30 seconds. Add butter and pulse until mixture is crumbly and resembles small peas. In a small bowl whisk together egg yolks and cream. Add wet ingredients to flour mixture. Pulse until dough begins to form.

3. Turn out onto a floured board. Press pastry into a disk 1-inch (2 ½-cm) thick. Wrap and chill dough about 30 minutes, until firm enough to roll.

4. On a lightly floured surface, roll out pastry to about ¼-inch (.5-cm) thick. (Reserve extra dough for another use; it may be frozen.) Line a 10-inch (25-cm) fluted tart pan with removable bottom with pastry (press pastry into pan with fingers if desired). Trim overhang. Using fork, prick bottom of pastry shell. Bake in oven 10 minutes.

5. In a mixing bowl, whisk together lime rind, juice, sugar, cream and eggs.

6. Remove tart pan from oven and place on cookie sheet. Reduce oven temperature to 325°F (160°C). Pour filling mixture into shell. Bake in oven for 25 to 30 minutes, or until filling is just set. Remove from oven and cool on rack.

7. If you have a gas oven,* adjust rack to about 4 inches (10 cm) from broiler. Preheat broiler. Cover edges of pastry with foil to prevent burning. Sprinkle tart evenly with 3 tbsp (45 ml) sugar. Place on rack closest to broiler and watch carefully. Broil until sugar turns golden; remove at once. Allow to cool and set again. Before serving, remove the tart by pushing straight up and away.

Makes 12 servings.

*This method does not work in an electric oven. However, this tart is still delicious without the crunchy caramel top. Pipe a border of whipped cream around the tart and garnish with sugared lime zest.

If you do not have a gas oven, try using a propane torch to brulée your tart. Place tart pan on cookie sheet. Cover edges of pastry with foil. Sprinkle tart with 3 tbsp (45 ml) sugar. Light propane torch and set at medium flame. Hold the torch so that the point of the blue flame just touches the tart's surface. Work in a small area of the tart. Move the flame in a gentle, even motion back and forth over the sugar, just until it begins to turn golden. Continue this over the entire surface of the tart. This is a quick method that gives you lots of control, and will amaze your dinner guests.

 Don't forget your flower garden when you're looking for something to accent your plates. As long as you haven't sprayed them with any chemicals, marigold, gladiolas, violets (though not African), roses and nasturtiums are all decorative and edible.

Cakes

I get a dreamy sense of fulfillment when I set out the ingredients to make a cake. It's because cakes bring a sense of occasion; the birthday cake, the wedding cake, the Christmas cake, the anniversary cake, the graduation cake, the bar mitzvah cake, and so on and so on.

4 C's Cranberry Loaf

Cinnamon, coriander, cardamom and cloves make this cake deliciously unique. Loaded with nuts, fruits and spices, it's a Christmas favorite of mine—a whole lot quicker to assemble than a traditional fruitcake. (I double the recipe so I have an extra loaf to give away as a gift.) Wrapped well, it will stay fresh in the refrigerator for up to 3 months.

1¼ cups	cranberries, fresh or frozen, rinsed and drained	300 ml
⅓ cup	granulated sugar	75 ml
½ tsp	finely grated orange rind	2 ml
¼ cup	soft sweet butter	50 ml
1¼ cups	all purpose flour	300 ml
1 cup	lightly packed brown sugar	250 ml
1 tsp	baking soda	5 ml
1 tsp	ground cinnamon	5 ml
¼ tsp	ground coriander	1 ml
¼ tsp	ground cardamom	1 ml
⅛ tsp	ground cloves	.5 ml
½ tsp	salt	2 ml
1	egg	1
⅓ cup	sour cream	75 ml
½ cup	coarsely chopped pecans	125 ml

1. Preheat oven to 350°F (180°C).
2. In a saucepan, combine ¾ cup (175 ml) of the cranberries, sugar and orange rind. Bring to a boil over medium heat and cook about 5 minutes, until the berries have popped.
3. Remove from heat and add remaining cranberries, coarsely chopped, to cooked mixture. Set aside.
4. Melt butter over low heat until creamy, not liquid, and set aside to cool.

5. In a large bowl, sift together flour, sugar, soda, cinnamon, coriander, cardamom, cloves and salt.
6. In another large bowl, beat egg and stir in sour cream. Fold in dry ingredients until mixed. Stir in melted butter, then cranberry mixture and nuts until blended.
7. Pour into prepared 9x5-inch (23x12-cm) loaf pan. Smooth the top and tap to settle. Bake 1 hour, or until tester comes out clean.

Makes 1 loaf.

At Christmas time, decorate the doorways and mantelpiece with thick garlands of cedar or pine rope. Decorate with real apples, nuts, holly and pomegranates. Dozens of white candles around the rooms add to a feeling of Old World festivity. On a large silver serving platter, build a tower of pineapples, starfruit, pomegranates, Mandarin oranges and assorted nuts. Place sprigs of evergreen and cranberries around the base. Placed on a sideboard, in front of a mirror, this display creates an elegant, luxurious Christmas mood.

Pear and Cranberry Crisp

I pull out this recipe every Christmas. The colors are festive and the moment you serve it warm with ice cream, all thoughts of steamed plum pudding with cold hard sauce are banished forever. For a summer variation, substitute raspberries and apples for the Christmas fruit.

Topping

1½ cups	chopped pecans	375 ml
¾ cup	all-purpose flour	175 ml
½ cup	granulated sugar	125 ml
¼ cup	firmly packed brown sugar	50 ml
1½ tsp	ground cinnamon	7 ml
½ cup	cold sweet butter	125 ml

Filling

1¾ cups	fresh or frozen cranberries, rinsed and drained	425 ml
½ cup	granulated sugar	125 ml
1 tsp	ground cinnamon	5 ml
¼ cup	cranberry juice cocktail	50 ml
2½ tbsp	all-purpose flour	37 ml
4	ripe, firm pears, peeled, cored and cut into ½-inch (1-cm) cubes	4

1. Preheat oven to 350°F (180°C).
2. In a mixing bowl, combine pecans, flour, sugars and cinnamon. Using a pastry blender, cut in butter until mixture is crumbly and resembles small peas. Set aside.
3. In a saucepan, combine cranberries, sugar, cinnamon, cranberry juice and flour. Cook over medium heat, stirring often, about 10 minutes, or until mixture is thickened and cranberries have burst. Stir in pears.
4. Pour the filling into an ungreased 8x12-inch (20x30-cm) baking pan. Sprinkle evenly with the topping. Bake in oven about 30 minutes, until golden brown and bubbling.
5. Serve warm.

Makes 8 to 10 servings.

Apple Crumble

Spartan, Northern Spy or Granny Smiths are best for this.

6 cups	thinly sliced, peeled apples	1.5 l
¾ cup	finely packed brown sugar	175 ml
1 tsp	ground cinnamon	5 ml
¼ tsp	salt	1 ml

Crumble Topping

½ cup	rolled oats	125 ml
½ cup	all-purpose flour	125 ml
¼ cup	100% bran cereal	50 ml
½ cup	firmly packed brown sugar	125 ml
½ cup	cold sweet butter	125 ml
¼ cup	sunflower seeds or chopped almonds	50 ml
	cold heavy or whipping cream, optional	

1. Grease a 9-inch (23-cm) pie plate.
2. In a large bowl, toss together apple slices. Combine brown sugar, cinnamon and salt. Stir into apples.
3. Preheat oven to 375°F (190°C).
4. In a bowl, prepare topping, combining rolled oats, flour, bran cereal and brown sugar. With a pastry blender, cut in butter until mixture is crumbly; stir in sunflower seeds or almonds.
5. Spoon apple mixture into prepared pie plate. Sprinkle evenly with crumble topping.
6. Bake 1 hour or until apples are tender and crumble is golden.
   Serve hot or at room temperature drizzled with cream, if desired.

Makes 6 to 9 servings.

Triple-Berry Crumb Cake

Better leave the knife out beside this cake—you and your friends will be nibbling at the cranberry/blueberry/raspberry crumbs all day. Pre-measure your ingredients and you can assemble this cake very quickly when you're ready to pop it in the oven. (And if there is any left, it will still taste good two days later.)

Crumb Topping

½ cup	all-purpose flour	125 ml
⅓ cup	firmly packed brown sugar	75 ml
1 tsp	cinnamon	5 ml
¼ cup	cold sweet butter	50 ml

Cake

¾ cup	blueberries, fresh or frozen	175 ml
¾ cup	raspberries, fresh or frozen	175 ml
½ cup	cranberries, fresh or frozen	125 ml
2 cups	all-purpose flour	500 ml
1 cup	granulated sugar	250 ml
2½ tsp	baking powder	12 ml
½ tsp	baking soda	2 ml
¾ tsp	salt	3 ml
2	eggs	2
¾ cup	yogurt	175 ml
⅓ cup	sweet butter, melted and cooled	75 ml
1 tsp	grated orange rind	5 ml
1 tsp	vanilla	5 ml

1. Preheat oven to 350°F (180°C).
2. Lightly oil 9-inch (23-cm) round cake pan or spring-form pan.
3. In a bowl, combine flour, sugar and cinnamon. With a pastry blender, cut in butter until mixture is crumbly. Set aside.

4. In a medium bowl, toss berries with 2 tbsp (25 ml) of the flour. Set aside.
5. In a medium bowl, combine remaining flour, sugar, baking powder, soda and salt. Set aside.
6. In large bowl, whisk together eggs, yogurt, butter, rind and vanilla. Stir into dry ingredients until well-blended. Fold in berries.
7. Pour batter into prepared cake pan. Sprinkle evenly with crumb topping.
8. Bake in oven about 1 hour or until cake tester comes out clean. Cool on rack 10 minutes. Turn cake out onto clean tea towel and replace on rack to cool. (A few of the crumbs might remain in tea towel. Replace on top of cake.)

Makes 12 servings.

Hummingbird Cake

A quick and easy one-bowl cake. Loaded with fruits and nuts, it's my tropical version of all-purpose coffee cake.

3 cups	all-purpose flour	750 ml
2 cups	granulated sugar	500 ml
1½ tsp	baking soda	7 ml
1 tsp	cinnamon	5 ml
1 tsp	salt	5 ml
3	eggs	3
½ cup	vegetable oil	125 ml
1	can (8 oz/228 ml) crushed pineapple, undrained	1
1½ tsp	vanilla	7 ml
1½ tsp	grated lemon rind	7 ml
3	mashed bananas	3
1½ cups	chopped macadamia nuts	375 ml

1. Preheat oven to 350°F (180°C).
2. Lightly oil a 10-inch (25-cm) tube pan.
3. Sift together flour, sugar, baking soda, cinnamon, and salt.
4. In a large bowl, combine eggs, oil, pineapple, vanilla and lemon rind; mix well.
5. Add dry ingredients to wet in two additions, mixing well. Fold in bananas and nuts.
6. Pour batter into prepared tube pan. Bake in oven for 1 hour and 15 minutes or until cake tester comes clean. Cool in pan on rack.

Makes 16 servings.

Variation:
Try substituting 1 cup chopped ripe mango for 1 cup of the bananas.

Date Pecan Cake

Few will protest if you serve this cake with butter or cream cheese, but a dusting of icing sugar is all it really needs. Moist and hearty, it travels well, freezes without a problem and adds sweet ballast to any picnic. Or keep it all to yourself—it's a great cake to wake up to.

½ cup	all-purpose flour	125 ml
1 tsp	baking soda	5 ml
1 tsp	ground cinnamon	5 ml
½ tsp	ground cloves	2 ml
½ tsp	salt	2 ml
2 cups	rolled oats	500 ml
1 cup	boiling water	250 ml
2 cups	firmly packed brown sugar	500 ml
¾ cup	sweet butter, softened	175 ml
2	eggs	2
1½ cups	chopped dates	375 ml
1 cup	chopped pecans	250 ml

1. Preheat oven to 350°F (180°C).
2. Lightly oil an 8-inch (20-cm) square cake pan.
3. In a bowl, combine flour, soda, cinnamon, cloves and salt.
4. In a large bowl, combine oats and water; mix well. Let cool slightly.
5. Into moistened oatmeal, beat sugar, butter and eggs until well-blended. Stir in dates and pecans.
6. Add oatmeal mixture to dry ingredients, mixing well.
7. Pour batter into prepared cake pan. Bake in oven 60 minutes, or until tester comes out clean. Cool in pan on rack.

Makes 12 servings.

Hint – Keep cake fresh longer by adding a slice of apple to the cake tin or plate.

French Orange Butter Cake

This is a big cake for a tea time party. The orange sauce is poured over while the cake is still hot and porous and able to absorb most of the goodness.

2 cups	sweet butter	500 ml
1 cup	granulated sugar	250 ml
2 tbsp	grated orange rind	25 ml
½ tsp	vanilla	2 ml
5	eggs	5
3 cups	cake and pastry flour	750 ml
1 tbsp	baking powder	15 ml
¼ tsp	salt	1 ml
¾ cup	milk	175 ml

Sauce

⅔ cup	granulated sugar	150 ml
⅓ cup	orange juice	75 ml
¼ cup	sweet butter	50 ml

1. Preheat oven to 350°F (180°C).
2. In a large bowl, cream together butter and sugar. Stir in orange rind and vanilla. Add eggs, one at a time, beating well after each addition.
3. In a small bowl, sift together flour, baking powder and salt. Stir flour mixture into batter alternating with milk; mix well.
4. Pour into a buttered and floured 10-inch (25-cm) tube pan. Bake in oven for 1 hour, or until golden brown.
5. While cake is in oven, in a small saucepan heat together sugar, orange juice and butter.
6. Remove cake from oven. Pour sauce over cake while still hot. Cool cake on wire rack before removing from pan.

Makes 10 to 12 servings.

Dreamy Coffee Cake

This one reheats beautifully, so you can tuck it in the oven when you put the coffee on and serve it hot for your breakfast parties.

½ cup	sweet butter	125 ml
1 cup	granulated sugar	250 ml
2	eggs	2
2 cups	all-purpose flour	500 ml
1 tsp	baking powder	5 ml
1 tsp	baking soda	5 ml
½ tsp	salt	2 ml
1 cup	sour cream	250 ml
1 tsp	vanilla	5 ml

Filling

½ cup	firmly packed brown sugar	125 ml
1 cup	finely chopped pecans	250 ml
1 tsp	ground cinnamon	5 ml

1. Preheat oven to 350°F (180°C).
2. In a large mixing bowl, cream together butter and sugar for 3 minutes, until light and fluffy. Add eggs, one at a time, beating well after each addition.
3. In a bowl, sift together flour, baking powder, baking soda and salt. Add to creamed mixture alternately with sour cream, beating well. Beat in vanilla.
4. In a bowl, combine brown sugar, pecans and cinnamon.
5. Grease and flour a 9-inch (23-cm) square pan. Spread half the batter in pan.
6. Sprinkle with half the filling mixture. Add remaining batter, smooth top. Sprinkle with remaining filling.
7. Bake in oven for 45 to 50 minutes, or until tester comes out clean.

Makes 9 servings.

Gingerbread Cake

A classic. Serve with Apple Compote, vanilla ice cream or Apricot Walnut Sauce. What more can I say?

2 cups	all-purpose flour	500 ml
2 tsp	baking soda	10 ml
1½ tsp	ground ginger	7 ml
1 tsp	ground cloves	5 ml
1 tsp	ground cinnamon	5 ml
½ tsp	freshly ground black pepper	2 ml
1 cup	sweet butter	250 ml
1 cup	firmly packed brown sugar	250 ml
3	eggs	3
1 cup	dark molasses	250 ml
1 cup	hot strong coffee	250 ml

1. Preheat oven to 375°F (190°C).
2. Butter and flour a 9-inch (23-cm) square pan.
3. Combine flour, soda, ginger, cloves, cinnamon and pepper. Sift together and set aside.
4. In a large bowl, cream butter and sugar; beat 2 minutes until light and fluffy.
5. Add eggs one at a time, beating well after each addition. Add molasses; beat 2 minutes longer until smooth.
6. Add sifted dry ingredients alternately with coffee in three additions to creamed mixture; mix well. (Mixture will be thin.)
7. Pour into prepared pan. Bake for 35 to 40 minutes, or until tester comes out clean. Serve warm.

Makes 8 servings.

Mocha Mousse Cake

This is the dessert for an impressive sweet table. I often pile straight mousse into champagne flutes as an attractive alternative to the cake. Another variation is using crumbled amaretti cookie crumbs. Well-wrapped, this cake will keep in the refrigerator for up to 3 days.

1 cup	cookie crumbs	250 ml
1 tbsp	butter, melted	15 ml
1 lb	bittersweet chocolate, chopped	454 g
½ cup	sweet butter, softened	125 ml
¼ cup	coffee liqueur	50 ml
2 cups	heavy or whipping cream	500 ml

1. Line sides of 9-inch (23-cm) spring-form pan with waxed paper. In small bowl, mix ½ cup (125 ml) of the cookie crumbs with melted butter. Press crumbs into bottom of pan. Set aside.
2. In bowl set over hot, not boiling, water, melt chocolate. Add butter; mix well. Stir in coffee liqueur. Cool to lukewarm.
3. In a large bowl, whip cream. Fold ⅓ of cream into the cooled chocolate mixture. Fold in remaining cream. Pour mixture into prepared pan, smoothing top evenly. Press remaining crumbs on top of cake. Refrigerate at least 4 hours, or overnight, until firm.
4. To serve, unmold spring-form, leaving waxed paper on sides of cake. Use palette knife to loosen cake from bottom of pan; place cake on serving dish. Remove waxed paper.

Makes 10 servings.

Tip:

This cake will slice more easily chilled. Use a thin knife which has been held under hot water, then wiped dry. Repeat for each slice.

Chocolate Fondant Cake

This is the perfect recipe for a chocolate addict.

½ lb	unsweetened chocolate	250 g
1 cup	finely granulated sugar	250 g
½ cup	strong coffee	125 ml
1 cup	sweet butter, cut into 6 pieces	250 g
4	eggs	4
1 tbsp	all-purpose flour	15 ml
	whipped cream	

1. Line a 9-inch (23-cm) layer cake tin with aluminum foil. Hang foil over sides of pan. Butter foil.
2. In a blender or food processor, grind chocolate and sugar until very fine.
3. In a heavy saucepan over low heat, combine chocolate, sugar and coffee; cook 3 to 4 minutes until chocolate has melted. Remove from heat, add butter a piece at a time, until butter is completely melted.
4. In a small bowl, beat eggs 3 to 4 minutes, until lemon-colored. Slowly add flour; mix well.
5. Fold egg mixture into chocolate and blend well.
6. Pour mixture into prepared pan; set pan in a water bath and cook 45 minutes over low heat on top of stove.
7. Meanwhile, preheat oven to 250°F (120°C).
8. Remove pan from water and bake in oven for 30 minutes, or until tester comes out clean. Cool.
9. Cover lightly with cloth and refrigerate 2 to 3 days before serving.
10. Unmold and serve with whipped cream.

Makes 12 servings.

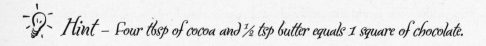

Hint – *Four tbsp of cocoa and ½ tsp butter equals 1 square of chocolate.*

Killer Chocolate Cake with Chocolate Frosting

This is the moist, delicious chocolate cake everyone dreams of.

3	squares (1 oz/28 g each) unsweetened chocolate, chopped	3
1 cup	boiling water	250 ml
2½ cups	sifted cake and pastry flour	625 ml
2½ tsp	baking powder	12 ml
1 tsp	baking soda	5 ml
½ tsp	salt	2 ml
½ cup	sweet butter	125 ml
2½ cups	granulated sugar	625 ml
3	eggs, separated	3
1 tsp	vanilla	5 ml
1 cup	sour cream	250 ml

1. Preheat oven to 350°F (180°C).
2. Lightly butter and flour two 9-inch (23-cm) round layer cake pans.
3. In a small bowl, combine chocolate and water, stirring until chocolate melts. Cool slightly.
4. Sift together flour, baking powder, baking soda and salt.
5. In a large mixing bowl, cream butter. Add 2 cups (500 ml) sugar; continue to cream until light and fluffy. Beat in egg yolks one at a time. Stir in cooled chocolate and vanilla.
6. Add sifted dry ingredients alternately with sour cream. Mix well after each addition.
7. In a bowl, beat egg whites and remaining ½ cup (125 ml) sugar until stiff peaks form. Carefully fold in chocolate mixture.
8. Pour evenly into prepared pans. Bake in oven for 40 to 45 minutes, until tester inserted in center comes out clean. Cool in pan. Remove. Fill and frost with Chocolate Frosting.

Makes 12 servings.

Chocolate Frosting

2	squares (1 oz/28 g each) unsweetened chocolate	2
2 tbsp	sweet butter	25 ml
1	egg yolk	1
1½ cups	confectioner's or icing sugar	375 ml
1 tsp	vanilla	5 ml
¼ cup	milk	50 ml

1. In top of double boiler over simmering water, melt chocolate and butter. Set aside to cool for 10 minutes.
2. Transfer to a large bowl, beat in egg yolk, and continue beating until mixture is thick. Add sugar, vanilla and milk; stir until mixture is creamy.

Makes 1½ cups (375 ml).

Chocolate Cheesecake

A little cream cheese, a little sugar, a touch of chocolate, what's to fear? Maybe that is the rationale your guests will use to justify their second helpings.

Crumb Crust

1	package (8 oz/250 g) chocolate wafers	1
⅓ cup	melted sweet butter	75 ml
2 tbsp	granulated sugar	25 ml

Filling

3	eggs	3
1 cup	granulated sugar	250 ml
3	packages (8 oz/250 g) cream cheese, softened	3
2	packages (6 oz/164 g) semi-sweet chocolate pieces, melted	2
2 tsp	vanilla	10 ml

1. In a blender or food processor or with rolling pin, crush chocolate wafers into fine crumbs.
2. In a bowl, combine wafer crumbs, butter and sugar; mix well. Press evenly over bottom and sides (½-inch/1-cm from top) of 9-inch (23-cm) springform pan.
3. Preheat oven to 325°F (160°C).
4. In a large mixer bowl, beat eggs and sugar about 5 minutes, until light and fluffy.
5. Beat in cream cheese until mixture is smooth. Add melted chocolate and vanilla; beat 3 minutes, until smooth.
6. Turn into crumb crust and bake 1 hour, until cheesecake is firm. Cool on wire rack and refrigerate overnight.

Makes 16 servings.

Puddings and Other Sweets

These are the rich and soothing things you can do with eggs and cream and fruit when you aren't whipping up cakes and pies and cookies.

Lemon Custard Pudding

Sweet and tart and simple. Serve this at the end of a meal that has been spicy and hot.

1 cup	milk	250 ml
1 cup	granulated sugar	250 ml
¼ cup	sweet butter	50 ml
4 tsp	all-purpose flour	20 ml
2	eggs, separated	2
	juice and grated rind of 1 lemon	

1. Preheat oven to 325°F (160°C).
2. In mixing bowl, combine milk, sugar, butter, flour, egg yolks, lemon juice and rind; mix well.
3. Beat egg whites until stiff. Fold lemon mixture into egg whites.
4. Pour into buttered 4-cup (1-l) baking dish or individual custard cups.
5. Place in a larger baking dish. Pour warm water into larger dish halfway up sides of baking dish or cups.
6. Bake in pan of water in oven for 30 minutes or until set.
7. Serve hot, at room temperature or chilled.

Makes 4 to 6 servings.

Place three or four fully open garden roses in a bud vase and put them in the guest bathroom to complete your decorations for the evening.

Hot Fruit Compotes

Delicious, quick and versatile for dessert lovers who don't have a lot of time to prepare. Since you can assemble either the winter or summer compote in minutes, the trick is extravagant presentation: spoon it over ice cream, angel food, pound cake—the possibilities are as limitless as your imagination.

¼ cup	fruit juice, apple or orange	50 ml
2 tbsp	sweet butter	25 ml
2 tbsp	dark brown sugar	25 ml
1½ tsp	vanilla	7 ml
pinch	cinnamon or cardamom	pinch

Summer variation

1	nectarine, pitted and sliced	1
1	large plum, pitted and sliced	1
1	pear, peeled, pitted and sliced	1
½ pint	raspberries	250 ml

Winter variation

2	small bananas, peeled and sliced	2
1	mango, peeled, pitted and sliced	1
3	tangerines, peeled and sectioned	3
1	small pineapple, peeled, cored and diced	1

1. In a sauté pan, combine juice, butter, sugar, vanilla and spice. (For summer variation, use apple juice and cinnamon; for winter variation, use orange juice and cardamom.)
2. Over medium-high heat, cook mixture just until butter is melted and beginning to bubble. Add fruits and cook, stirring gently for 2 to 3 minutes until fruit is softened but not mushy. Berries should be added during the last 15 seconds of cooking.
3. Remove from heat and serve at once.

Makes 4 servings.

Rum and Raisin Bread Pudding

This dessert is based on a wonderful recipe given to me by Helen Willinsky, author of *Jerk: Barbecue from Jamaica*. With its crunchy cinnamon and sugar topping, it makes a stupendous ending to a Jamaican jerk dinner. Or, with the fragrance and comfort level of warm cinnamon toast, it can be served hot from the oven with a big pot of tea on a Sunday afternoon. (It's probably good at room temperature as well—I don't know as I've never had a crumb left!) For an aristocratic presentation, serve it in 3-inch soufflé dishes.

¾ cup	dark rum	175 ml
½ cup	raisins	125 ml
½ cup	sugar	125 ml
¾ tsp	cinnamon	8 ml
¼ tsp	ground nutmeg	1 ml
¼ cup	melted butter	50 ml
1 lb	egg bread	500 g
½ cup	sweetened condensed milk	125 ml
4 cups	whole milk	1 l
5	eggs, well beaten	5

1. Preheat oven to 325°F (160°C).
2. In a saucepan, combine ½ cup (125 ml) of the rum with raisins and bring to a boil. Boil for 3 minutes until raisins are plump.
3. In a bowl, combine rum and raisin mixture, remaining ¼ cup rum, sugar, cinnamon, nutmeg and butter.
4. Break up bread into small cubes and toss in rum and raisin mixture. Put into a prepared 8-inch (20-cm) baking dish.
5. Whisk together condensed milk, whole milk and eggs and pour over bread.
6. Bake in oven 1 hour and 15 minutes or until golden and tester comes out clean. Cover loosely with foil if top becomes too brown. Serve warm.

Makes 8 servings.

Lemon Soufflé

This cool and frothy lemon dessert is a perfect ending to a rich and satisfying dinner. I serve it after the cheese tray; with its collar removed, it looks like a floating cloud. This is perfect for when the table is relatively small, up to eight persons. For larger groups, I serve a tray of lemon soufflés in individual colored glass compotes. By candlelight the effect is quite dazzling.

1 cup	granulated sugar	250 ml
3	envelopes unflavored gelatin	3
6	egg yokes	6
1½ cups	water	375 ml
2 tsp	grated lemon rind	10 ml
¾ cup	lemon juice	175 ml
6	egg whites	6
⅓ cup	granulated sugar	75 ml
2 cups	heavy or whipping cream, whipped	500 ml

1. Cut a piece of waxed paper long enough to fit a little more than once around a 4-cup (1-l) soufflé dish and fold it in half lengthwise. Wrap it around a soufflé dish, extending it 4 inches (10 cm) above the top of the dish. With string, tie it tightly in place.
2. In a medium-sized heavy saucepan, combine ⅔ cup (150 ml) sugar and gelatin.
3. Beat egg yolks slightly, blend in water; stir into gelatin mixture.
4. Cook over medium heat, stirring constantly, until mixture is about to come to a boil and begins to thicken. Do not boil.
5. Remove from heat; cool. Stir in lemon rind and juice.
6. In the refrigerator, chill mixture about 30 minutes, until it mounds slightly when spooned.
7. In a large bowl, beat egg whites until frothy. Gradually beat in remaining sugar and continue beating until stiff and glossy.
8. Fold whites into gelatin mixture, then fold in whipped cream. Pour into prepared soufflé dish.
9. Chill 2 to 3 hours, until firm. Remove collar when ready to serve.

Makes 8 servings.

Summer Berries in Lemon Mousse

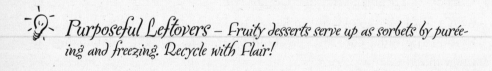

I make this recipe after I've picked wild blueberries, raspberries and strawberries.

4	egg yolks	4
½ cup	granulated sugar	125 ml
6 tbsp	lemon juice	75 ml
2 tsp	grated lemon rind	10 ml
2	egg whites	2
½ cup	heavy or whipping cream	125 ml
1 cup	fresh berries	250 ml

1. In the top of a double boiler before placing it over hot water, beat egg yolks until thick and pale. Beat in sugar, lemon juice and rind.
2. Place over boiling water; cook egg mixture, stirring about 5 minutes until thick. Cool.
3. Beat egg whites until stiff and fold into cooled egg yolk mixture.
4. Whip cream and fold in, along with ¾ cup (175 ml) berries.
5. Spoon into stemmed glasses, garnish with remaining berries, and chill until serving time.
   Note: This dessert is best the day it is prepared.

Makes 5 to 6 servings.

-ᗢ- *Purposeful Leftovers – Fruity desserts serve up as sorbets by purée-ing and freezing. Recycle with Flair!*

Orange Crème Caramel

A delightful variation on the traditional crème caramel. The addition of the orange rind gives it a light and lively zest all its own.

Caramel

½ cup	granulated sugar	125 ml
1 tbsp	water	15 ml

Custard

2 cups	milk	500 ml
2	eggs	2
2	egg yolks	2
¼ cup	granulated sugar	50 ml
1 tbsp	grated orange rind	15 ml
1 tsp	vanilla	5 ml

1. In a small saucepan, combine sugar and water. Place over low heat. Allow sugar to melt, then allow to boil without stirring until the sugar caramelizes and is amber brown. Watch carefully to prevent burning.
2. Pour immediately into a soufflé dish. Turn dish around to coat the bottom and sides evenly with caramel.
3. Scald milk in a saucepan.
4. In a bowl, whisk together eggs, egg yolks, sugar, orange rind and vanilla. Whisk in scalded milk.
5. Preheat oven to 325°F (160°C).
6. Pour custard into prepared soufflé dish, cover with foil and set into larger baking dish. Pour boiling water into larger dish to halfway up sides of soufflé dish. Bake in oven for 40 to 50 minutes, or until just set. Let cool completely.
7. Serve at room temperature or refrigerate until serving time.
8. Turn out of dish onto a serving plate with deep sides just before serving.

Makes 4 to 6 servings.

Tiramisu

Now that this formerly exotic dessert has entered the mainstream, it's important to start with the correct basic recipe. You may rest assured that this is **the** definitive version. The ladyfingers must be the dry, crispy Italian kind, available from Italian markets. Do not buy the softer ladyfingers as they will fall apart when dipped in the hot espresso.

3	egg yolks	3
8 oz	Mascarpone cheese	250 ml
½ cup	granulated sugar	125 ml
¼ cup	cold espresso or strong brewed coffee	50 ml
2 tbsp	Marsala or coffee liqueur	25 ml
2 cups	whipping or heavy cream	500 ml
36	ladyfingers	36
1 cup	hot espresso or strong brewed coffee	250 ml
	powdered cocoa or chocolate shavings	

1. In a bowl, beat yolks for 2 minutes, until light and frothy. Add Mascarpone, sugar, cold espresso and Marsala. Beat until well-blended. Slowly add whipping cream, continuing to beat mixture about 5 minutes, until mixture is stiff.
2. One at a time, dip 20 to 24 ladyfingers halfway into the hot espresso. Stand them up around the edge of a 10-inch (25-cm) wide round glass serving dish. Spread half the Mascarpone mixture in the dish. Dip remaining ladyfingers in espresso and lay them over Mascarpone mixture. Cover with remaining Mascarpone mixture.
3. Refrigerate, covered, for several hours or up to 24 hours. Before serving garnish with a sprinkle of cocoa or chocolate shavings.

Makes 8 servings.

Cinnamon Rice Pudding

This is a hand-me-down recipe from my dear friend Maralyn's mother, Rose. It has been a favorite with my son Milton for years.

½ cup	short grain rice	125 ml
4 cups	milk	1 l
¼ cup	granulated sugar	50 ml
2 tbsp	sweet butter	25 ml
½ tsp	salt	2 ml
½ cup	raisins	125 ml
	cinnamon	
	granulated sugar	

1. In a sauce of salted boiling water, boil rice 10 minutes. Drain.
2. In a large enamel pot, combine partially cooked rice, milk, sugar, butter and salt. Simmer, uncovered, stirring occasionally for about 1 hour or until milk is absorbed. Stir in raisins.
3. Transfer to a glass bowl. Sprinkle with cinnamon and sugar to coat top.
4. Cool and refrigerate until ready to serve.

Makes 4 to 6 servings.

Rich Praline Mousse

Smooth and elegant, this mousse blends rich flavors into a cool and creamy dream dessert.

Praline powder

¾ cup	unblanched almonds	175 ml
1½ cups	granulated sugar	325 ml
½ tsp	cream of tartar	2 ml

Mousse

2	eggs	2
2	egg yolks	2
⅓ cup	granulated sugar	75 ml
¼ cup	light rum	50 ml
1	envelope unflavored gelatin	1
¼ cup	cold water	50 ml
1 tbsp	lemon juice	15 ml
1 cup	heavy or whipping cream	250 ml

1. In a heavy saucepan, combine almonds, sugar and cream of tartar. Heat over medium heat, stirring occasionally, until mixture reaches a deep amber color.
2. Pour into a lightly oiled jelly roll pan. When hard, break up and, in a blender or food processor, grind to a powder.
3. Store in a covered container at room temperature.
4. In a mixer bowl at high speed, beat eggs and egg yolks, about 5 minutes, until thick and yellow-colored.
5. Add sugar gradually and continue to beat until light and fluffy. Fold in rum. Set aside.
6. In a small saucepan, sprinkle gelatin over water and lemon juice and let sit for 5 minutes to soften.
7. Place pan over low heat for about 3 minutes, stirring until gelatin dissolves. Carefully fold the dissolved gelatin into egg mixture until completely blended.

8. Fold in ¼ cup (50 ml) of the praline powder and chill about 20 minutes, until mixture begins to thicken.
9. Whip the cream until stiff; carefully fold into mousse mixture.
10. Spoon into an attractive crystal bowl and chill 3 hours before serving.

Makes 8 servings.

~~~~~~~~~~~~~~~~~~~~~~~~~~~~~~

Hint – *Eggs are easier to separate when cold. But bring to room temperature before beating the whites.*

~~~~~~~~~~~~~~~~~~~~~~~~~~~~~~

Miscellaneous

Miscellaneous

This catch-all section contains the tried and true indefinable favorites handed down from friends, colleagues, great-aunts and next-door neighbors. There are even a few, it must be admitted, that I've outright stolen when the cook was too coy to come clean about the content of some especially fabulous dish.

Savory Sauces and Dressings

Caesar Salad Dressing
Hearty Tomato Dressing
Lime Honey Dressing for Fruit Salad
Favorite Mayonnaise
Rémoulade Sauce
Tartar Sauce
Tomato Coulis

Grab Bag of Favorites

Spiced Popcorn and Nuts
Sugar and Spice Nuts
Bombay Curried Walnuts
Good Morning Special
Lemon Tang Pastry

Condiments

Hot Szechwan Cucumber Sticks
Crunchy Dilled Carrot Sticks
Colleen's Chili Sauce
Pineapple Salsa
Apple Butter
Apple Compote
Roquefort Butter
Glazed Grilled Fruit
Saffron Bananas
Fresh Mint Chutney
Rhubarb-Orange Marmalade
Peach Conserve
Caramel Mocha Sundae Sauce
Apricot Walnut Sauce

Caesar Salad Dressing

Like Caesar's wife, your Caesar salad must be above reproach. It is a classic salad and too much of a departure from the recipe will turn it into something different. I have had Caesars with apples in them, and raisins too, but to me they were no longer Caesar salads. Just the dressing and the torn romaine lettuce—that's the classic.

2	anchovies, mashed	2
1	large clove garlic, finely chopped	1
¼ cup	imported olive oil	50 ml
1 tbsp	white wine vinegar	15 ml
	juice of ½ lemon	
1	egg yolk	1
½ tsp	dry mustard	2 ml
½ tsp	Worcestershire sauce	2 ml
3 drops	hot pepper sauce	3 drops

1. In a jar with a tight-fitting lid, combine anchovies, garlic, oil, vinegar, lemon juice, yolk, mustard, Worcestershire sauce and hot pepper sauce. Cover tightly; shake well.
2. Store in refrigerator for up to 1 week. Shake well before using.

Makes ½ cup (125 ml).

Hearty Tomato Dressing

Don't shy away from this just because it calls for ketchup. When you taste it, you will find that it is a tomatoey, garlicky, totally satisfying vinaigrette. My family and friends ladle more on their salads every time I serve it, especially if the salad has lots of radish, tomato and onion in it.

1 cup	olive oil	250 ml
½ cup	ketchup	125 ml
½ cup	malt vinegar	125 ml
½ cup	granulated sugar	125 ml
1½ tsp	salt	7 ml
1 tsp	grated onion	5 ml
1 tsp	Worcestershire sauce	5 ml
¼ tsp	ground cloves	1 ml
1	clove garlic, minced	1

1. In a blender or food processor, combine oil, ketchup, vinegar, sugar, salt, onion, Worcestershire sauce, cloves and garlic. Process until thick. Or, combine in a bowl and beat with a rotary beater.
2. Pour into a screw-top jar or bottle. Refrigerate for up to 2 weeks. Shake well before using.

Makes 2 cups (500 ml).

Hint – Summertime Stacking Salad – From the bottom up: a slice of red tomato, a thin slice of Buffalo Mozzarella, a slice of yellow tomato, grilled and sliced Portobello mushrooms, another slice of Mozzarella and a slice of red tomato to finish. Garnish with mint, fried onion rings and drizzle with olive oil.

Lime Honey Dressing for Fruit Salad

I serve this dressing in half a Spanish melon and spoon it onto the fruit salad with a white ceramic ladle. A wedge of solid cheese such as Cheddar, and a hot blueberry muffin will round out a quick, light lunch.

1 cup	vegetable oil	250 ml
⅓ cup	lime juice	75 ml
⅓ cup	honey	75 ml
½ tsp	paprika	2 ml
½ tsp	salt	2 ml
½ tsp	prepared mustard	2 ml
	grated rind of 1 lime	
	dash hot pepper sauce	

1. In a blender or food processor, combine oil, lime juice, honey, paprika, salt, mustard, lime rind and hot pepper sauce. Blend until smooth.
2. Pour into a screw-top jar or bottle. Refrigerate until needed. Serve on melons or a mixture of fresh fruit.

Makes 1½ cups.

Favorite Mayonnaise

This is light and delicious and can be augmented with Dijon mustard or any of your favorite herbs.

3	egg yolks	3
1 tbsp	lemon juice	15 ml
½ tsp	salt	2 ml
⅛ tsp	white pepper	0.5 ml
pinch	dry mustard	pinch
pinch	cayenne pepper	pinch
1¼ cups	olive oil	300 ml

1. In a blender or food processor, combine yolks, lemon juice, salt, white pepper, dry mustard and cayenne; blend until smooth, about 1 minute.
2. With machine running, gradually pour in oil in a thin steady stream. Blend about 3 minutes, until thick.

Makes 2 cups (500 ml).

Rémoulade Sauce

Capers, sweet pickle, Dijon mustard, all whipped into the creamy mayonnaise, make this pretty close to the ultimate in elegant, luxurious sauces. It lifts such party specialties as fried fish fingers, shrimps, scallops and cold lobster to new heights of delight.

1 cup	mayonnaise	250 ml
1	green onion, finely chopped	1
1 tbsp	sweet pickle relish	15 ml
1 tbsp	drained capers, finely chopped	15 ml
1 tbsp	chopped fresh chervil, or 1 tsp (5 ml) dried	15 ml
1 tbsp	chopped fresh parsley, or t tsp (5 ml) dried	15 ml
1 tsp	Dijon mustard	5 ml

1. In a bowl, combine mayonnaise, onion, relish, capers, chervil, parsley and mustard; mix well.
2. Spoon into a small dish. Store, covered, in refrigerator.

Makes 1¼ cups (300 ml).

Tartar Sauce

This is a classic sauce for cold poached fish and other cold dishes like beets or rare roast beef slices. Easy to make so resist buying the commercial variety.

1 cup	mayonnaise	250 ml
¼ cup	finely chopped onion	50 ml
2 tbsp	sweet relish	25 ml
1 tbsp	chopped pimento	15 ml
1 tbsp	lemon juice	15 ml
1 tsp	Dijon mustard with basil	5 ml
½ tsp	salt	2 ml
¼ tsp	freshly ground black pepper	1 ml

1. In a bowl, combine mayonnaise, onion, sweet relish, pimento, lemon juice, mustard, salt and pepper; stir well.
2. Store in the refrigerator in a plastic or glass-covered container.

Makes 1½ cups (375 ml).

Tomato Coulis

This is the perfect condiment for grilled vegetables or warmed Camembert cheese.

2 tbsp	sweet butter	25 ml
2 tbsp	olive oil	25 ml
1	carrot, finely chopped	1
1	medium onion, finely chopped	1
1	clove garlic, finely chopped	1
2 lb	tomatoes, peeled and finely chopped	1 kg
1 cup	rich beef stock	250 ml
½ tsp	dried thyme	2 ml
½ tsp	dried basil	2 ml
½ tsp	brown sugar	2 ml
½ tsp	salt	2 ml
pinch	white pepper	pinch
1	bay leaf	1

1. Preheat oven to 350°F (180°C).
2. In a large skillet, combine butter and oil; heat until butter melts.
3. Add carrot, onion and garlic. Sauté 5 minutes, until onion is soft.
4. Stir in tomatoes and stock; bring to a boil.
5. Stir in thyme, basil, sugar, salt, pepper and bay leaf. Transfer to a casserole.
6. Bake for 1 hour and 30 minutes, until thick.
7. Cool. Remove and discard bay leaf.
8. Transfer sauce to container of blender or food processor; process 1 to 2 minutes until smooth
9. Store in refrigerator for up to 1 week.

Makes 1½ cups (625 ml).

Spiced Popcorn and Nuts

This will "sell out" for your movie night. If you make extra, you can put it in a jar, tie a ribbon around it, and give it to a hostess as a gift.

½ cup	popping corn	125 ml
2 tbsp	vegetable oil	25 ml
2 tbsp	sweet butter	25 ml
½ cup	peanuts, salted or unsalted	125 ml
½ cup	pecans	125 ml
2 tsp	ground cumin	10 ml
1 tsp	garlic powder	5 ml
½ tsp	chili powder	2 ml
½ tsp	white pepper	2 ml
½ tsp	salt	2 ml

1. In a hot air popper or in a large pot with a tight-fitting lid, pop corn.
2. In a large saucepan, heat oil and butter. Add peanuts, pecans, cumin, garlic powder, chili powder, white pepper and salt. Sauté over medium heat 1 to 2 minutes, until aromatic and lightly-colored. Be careful not to burn.
3. Add popped corn and toss until well-coated with seasonings.
4. Store in tightly-covered container. Keeps 2 to 3 weeks.

Makes 8 cups (2 l).

Hint – Throw an informal evening with your VCR and a new movie or two. You could bring back the double feature! Naturally you'll want to have dishes of treats for the "lobby." The suggestions here are a little more sophisticated and tasty than just plain buttered popcorn.

Sugar and Spice Nuts

The orange rind gives these nuts an extra zip.

1½ cups	pecan halves	325 ml
1 cup	unblanched whole almonds	250 ml
1 cup	walnut halves	250 ml
1 cup	whole filberts	250 ml
1	egg white	1
1½ tbsp	water	20 ml
⅔ cup	granulated sugar	150 ml
1 tsp	salt	5 ml
1 tsp	ground cinnamon	5 ml
1 tsp	ground coriander	5 ml
1 tsp	ground ginger	5 ml
1 tsp	ground nutmeg	5 ml
1 tsp	ground cloves	5 ml
	grated rind of 1 orange	

1. Preheat oven to 275°F (150°C).
2. In a large bowl, combine pecans, almonds, walnuts and filberts.
3. In a mixer bowl, beat egg white and water 2 minutes, until foamy. Add sugar, salt, cinnamon, coriander, ginger, nutmeg, cloves and orange rind. Fold egg mixture into nuts.
4. Arrange on a large baking sheet and bake, turning occasionally, for 45 minutes, until brown and crisp. Cool.
5. Store in a tightly covered container at room temperature for up to 3 weeks.

Makes 6 cups (1.5 l).

Bombay Curried Walnuts

An exotic Eastern flavor that you'll never get at the local cinema. This is the only recipe that Colleen's son Christian took with him when he went away to school in England.

¼ cup	sweet butter	50 ml
2 tbsp	curry powder	25 ml
2 tbsp	Worcestershire sauce	25 ml
2 tsp	salt	10 ml
4 cups	walnut halves	1 l
½ cup	dried cranberries or cherries	125 ml

1. Preheat oven to 300°F (150°C).
2. In a skillet over medium heat, combine butter, curry powder, Worcestershire sauce and salt. Add nuts, stirring to cover with seasonings.
3. Transfer to a baking pan and bake in oven for 10 to 15 minutes, until nuts are golden brown. Remove from oven and toss with cranberries.
4. Cool and store in airtight container for up to 3 weeks.

Makes 4 cups (1 l).

Good Morning Special

If you'd rather prepare your eggs ahead of time, try this recipe. It can be made the night or day before and placed in the refrigerator to pop in the oven when friends appear.

6	slices French bread, crusts removed	6
2 tbsp	sweet butter, melted	25 ml
16	medium mushrooms, thinly sliced (1½ cups/375 ml)	16
1 cup	grated Cheddar cheese	250 ml
1 cup	grated Colby cheese	250 ml
6	slices bacon, cooked and crumbed	6
4	green onions, chopped	4
4	eggs	4
2 cups	milk	500 ml
2 tsp	Dijon mustard	10 ml
½ tsp	salt	2 ml
¼ tsp	freshly ground black pepper	1 ml
¼ tsp	paprika	1 ml
⅛ tsp	cayenne pepper	0.5 ml

1. Cut bread into cubes to measure 2 cups (500 ml). In bottom of 8-inch (20-cm) square baking dish, arrange bread cubes. Drizzle butter over cubes.
2. Scatter mushroom slices, cheeses, bacon and green onions over bread cubes.
3. In a bowl, beat eggs, milk, mustard, salt, pepper, paprika and cayenne until frothy. Pour over mixture in pan, cover and refrigerate overnight.
4. Preheat oven to 325°F (160°C). Bake for 1 hour, until just firm and lightly browned.

Makes 6 servings.

Lemon Tang Pastry (No Fail)

No matter how perfect a mother you have, it doesn't necessarily follow that she bequeathed to you the perfect pie pastry recipe. However, I will give you the best!

5 cups	all-purpose flour	1.25 l
2 tsp	granulated sugar	10 ml
2 tsp	salt	10 ml
½ tsp	baking soda	2 ml
1 lb	cold lard	500 g
1	egg	1
1 tbsp	lemon juice	15 ml
	cold water	

1. In a large bowl, combine flour, sugar, salt and baking soda. Mix well. With a pastry blender or two knives, cut in lard until mixture is crumbly and resembles small peas.
2. In a measuring cup, combine egg and lemon juice; beat well. Add water to egg mixture to measure 1 cup (250 ml).
3. Pour over flour mixture. Stir until a ball of dough starts to form.
4. Turn out onto floured board, divide into 6 portions, shape into balls and wrap in plastic wrap. Press down to smooth and push out any air bubbles.
5. Use immediately or wrap and store for later use.
6. Can be refrigerated for 2 to 3 weeks or frozen for up to 6 months.

Makes pastry for 3 double-crust 9-inch (23-cm) pies (one ball to a crust).

Hot Szechwan Cucumber Sticks

A crunchy hot side salad for a Chinese meal.

1	English cucumber	1
½ cup	white vinegar	125 ml
½ cup	granulated sugar	125 ml
¼ cup	chili oil	50 ml
dash	hot pepper sauce	dash
¼ tsp	shredded fresh ginger root	1 ml

1. Cut cucumber into 2-inch (5-cm) sticks. Place in a bowl, cover with lightly salted ice water. Let stand ½ hour. Drain and rinse.
2. In a bowl, combine vinegar, sugar, chili oil, hot pepper sauce and ginger root. Pour over cucumber sticks; marinate in the refrigerator for ½ hour only.
3. Remove from marinade and serve.

Makes 6 servings.

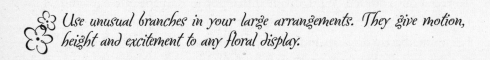

Use unusual branches in your large arrangements. They give motion, height and excitement to any floral display.

Crunchy Dilled Carrot Sticks

Serve instead of pickles.

2 lb	carrots, scraped and cut into 4-inch (10-cm) sticks	1 kg
½ cup	chopped fresh dill	125 ml
2	cloves garlic, peeled and halved	2
2 cups	white vinegar	500 ml
2 cups	water	500 ml
¼ cup	granulated sugar	50 ml
2 tbsp	salt	25 ml
½ tsp	cayenne pepper	2 ml

1. In a saucepan of boiling water, cook carrots, covered, for 5 minutes, until just tender-crisp.
2. Drain and rinse under cold water until chilled. Pack into hot sterilized jars. Into each jar, place half a garlic clove and 1 tbsp (15 ml) dill.
3. In a saucepan, combine vinegar, water, sugar, salt and cayenne. Bring to a boil.
4. Pour into jars, leaving ¼-inch (5-mm) head space. Seal with sterilized lids.
5. Store in refrigerator 3 to 4 days before serving. Keeps for 2 to 3 weeks.

Makes 6 jars (8 oz/250 ml).

Colleen's Chili Sauce

This is a sweet combination of late summer and early fall vegetables and fruits. Serve it with your favorite roasts and pâtés.

12	ripe tomatoes, peeled and coarsely chopped	12
3	apples, cored, peeled and coarsely chopped	3
2	large onions, coarsely chopped	2
1	small head celery, finely chopped	1
1	small green pepper, finely chopped	1
3 cups	brown sugar, firmly packed	750 ml
1 cup	white vinegar	250 ml
1 tbsp	pickling salt	15 ml
¼ cup	pickling spice tied in cheesecloth	50 ml
⅛ tsp	cayenne pepper	0.5 ml

1. In a large preserving kettle or saucepan, combine tomatoes, apples, onions, celery and green pepper; mix well.
2. Add brown sugar, vinegar, pickling salt, pickling spice bag and cayenne.
3. Bring to a boil, reduce heat and cook slowly for 1 to 1¼ hours, until thickened.
4. Ladle into hot sterilized jars. Seal with self-sealing lids. Label and store in a cool, dry, dark place.

Makes 7 jars (16 oz/500 ml).

Pineapple Salsa

Colleen's husband Dick always demands extra rations of this salsa be made for him to throw in his shredded beef stir-fry. I like it as a side to breakfast sausages and scrambled eggs, or spooned over an open-faced grilled ham and cheese sandwich. It's also scrumptious with grilled chicken and pork tenderloin.

1½ cups	diced fresh pineapple	375 ml
	reserve 2 tbsp (25 ml) juice	
¼ cup	finely chopped red onion	50 ml
¼	yellow pepper, seeded and diced	¼
¼	red pepper, seeded and diced	¼
1	jalapeño pepper, seeded and minced	1
1	medium tomato, peeled, seeded and diced	1
½ cup	chopped fresh mint, loosely packed	125 ml
	juice of 1 lime	
2 tbsp	dark liquid honey	25 ml
½ tsp	salt	2 ml
	freshly ground black pepper, to taste	

1. In a large bowl, combine pineapple, onion, peppers (red, yellow and jalapeño), tomato, mint, lime juice, honey, reserved pineapple juice, salt and pepper. Mix well. Serve.

Makes 2½ cups (625 ml).

Apple Butter

Apple butter is usually thought of in connection with farm kitchens and weekends in the country. But wherever you serve it, this apple butter will leave your friends starry-eyed. Try spooning it over hot baked sweet potatoes, or mounding it on freshly baked gingerbread.

15	large Macintosh apples	15
½ cup	water	125 ml
4 cups	firmly packed dark brown sugar	1 l
½ cup	white vinegar	125 ml
½ cup	dark corn syrup	125 ml
1 tbsp	ground cinnamon	15 ml

1. Cut apples into quarters; remove cores, but do not peel.
2. In a large saucepan, combine apples and water. Bring to a boil, reduce heat, cover, and cook, stirring occasionally, about 15 minutes or until apples are tender.
3. Put through a Mouli or press through a sieve to strain out skin. Makes about 8 cups (2 l) applesauce.
4. Place applesauce in a large saucepan. Stir in brown sugar, vinegar, corn syrup and cinnamon. Bring to a boil, reduce heat, and simmer, stirring frequently, for about 3 hours or until thickened.
5. Ladle into hot sterilized jars and seal tightly with lids. Label and store in a cool, dry, dark place.

Makes 3 jars (8 oz/250 ml).

Hint – *Flavored butters, mint sauce, chutneys. These are the very special taste makers that can make a curry magic or a hamburger sophisticated.*

Apple Compote

Serve with Gingerbread Cake or over ice cream.

5	apples, peeled and cut into ½-inch (1-cm) wide wedges	5
¾ cup	granulated sugar	175 ml
½ cup	water	125 ml
	juice and rind of 1 lemon	
2 tbsp	apple jelly	25 ml
2 tbsp	sherry	25 ml

1. In a large skillet, combine apple wedges, sugar, lemon juice and rind. Bring mixture to a boil. Reduce heat, and simmer 15 minutes, until fruit is tender.
2. Stir in jelly and sherry. Bring mixture to a boil. Continue cooking about 5 minutes, until thick.

Makes 4 servings.

Roquefort Butter

This little butter combines a number of tastes that complement the unique accent of this gorgeous French cheese. Delicious on rounds of toast, grilled vegetables, or spread on barbecued burgers to lift them to the realm of Cordon Bleu.

½ cup	soft sweet butter	125 ml
¼ cup	crumbled Roquefort or blue cheese	50 ml
¼ cup	snipped chives	50 ml
1 tbsp	fresh lemon juice	15 ml
¼ tsp	Worcestershire sauce	1 ml
1 tsp	Cognac	5 ml

1. In a small bowl with a wooden spoon or an electric mixer at medium speed, beat butter until light and fluffy. Gradually beat in cheese, chives, lemon juice, Worcestershire sauce and Cognac.

2. Transfer to a small crock or bowl. Serve immediately or cover and store in refrigerator for up to 1 week.

3. Before serving, let stand at room temperature about 10 minutes until slightly softened.

Makes ¾ cups (175 ml).

Glazed Grilled Fruit

You'll notice that the three fruits used here are of a quick-cooking nature. Use the fruit halves as containers for your favorite chutneys, or enjoy them as an accompaniment to grilled meats.

8	peaches, nectarines, or large apricots	8
¼ cup	melted sweet butter	50 ml
2 tbsp	honey	25 ml
2 tbsp	lemon juice	25 ml
1 tbsp	brandy	15 ml

1. Wash fruit but do not peel. Cut in half and remove pits.
2. In a bowl, combine butter, honey, lemon juice and brandy.
3. Place fruit halves, cut side down, on oiled barbecue rack about 6 inches (15 cm) above medium hot coals. Brush with glaze. Grill 3 minutes.
4. Turn, brush glaze on cut side. Grill 3 minutes longer, until lightly browned and glazed.
5. Transfer to a heated plate, cut side up.

Makes 8 servings.

Saffron Bananas

The bland bananas, sour cream and/or yogurt, and golden saffron are just what a hot curry demands.

½ tsp	saffron threads, or ⅛ tsp (0.5 ml) saffron powder	2 ml
2 cups	sour cream or yogurt or mixture of both	500 ml
2	bananas, sliced	2

1. In a bowl, combine saffron and sour cream. Add bananas, stirring to cover with cream.
2. Refrigerate 2 hours before serving.

Makes 4 servings.

Fresh Mint Chutney

This is a quick chutney to serve along with Chicken Saag or Lamb Curry or any other Indian-type dish. It's bright green with just a dash of heat.

1 cup	mint leaves, washed and stemmed	250 ml
¼ cup	rice vinegar	125 ml
1	medium onion, chopped	1
½	jalapeño pepper, seeded, stemmed and chopped	½
	salt, to taste	

1. In food processor, combine mint leaves, vinegar, onion, pepper and salt. Process with on/off motion 1 to 2 minutes, until finely chopped and mixed. Season with salt to taste.
2. Transfer to covered container. Chill well for about 30 minutes before using. Store in refrigerator.

Makes 1 cup (250 ml).

Rhubarb-Orange Marmalade

Remember the bitter mouth-puckering taste of homemade marmalade when you were a kid? Well, here it is again.

	rind and juice of 3 oranges	
4 cups	chopped rhubarb	1 l
1 cup	water	250 ml
½ cup	chopped raisins	125 ml
3 cups	sugar	750 ml

1. Cut rind into thin strips about ¾-inch (2-cm) long. In a heavy saucepan, combine rind, orange juice, rhubarb, water and raisins. Bring to a boil; cook about 10 minutes, or until fruit is tender.
2. Stir in sugar; cook over medium heat, stirring occasionally, about 2 hours, until mixture is thick.
3. Ladle into sterilized jars and seal with sterilized lids. Label and store in cool, dry, dark place.

Makes 6 jars (8 oz/250 ml).

Hint – To test Jam Stage – Chill a metal spoon, then dip it into the hot fruit mixture. Raise the spoon up above the saucepan away from the heat. Allow the mixture to cool slightly in the spoon, then tilt it and allow the chilled mixture to drip over the side of the spoon and back into the saucepan. If two drops flow together to form one sheet that falls off the spoon, you have reached the jam stage.

Peach Conserve

This has been a favorite of Sable & Rosenfeld customers for years. The bits of Maraschino cherries complement the gold of the peaches. It is a festive jam to give to friends as gifts.

2	small oranges	2
8	ripe peaches	8
	juice of ½ lemon	
2½ cups	granulated sugar	375 ml
10	Maraschino cherries, finely chopped	10

1. With a sharp knife, cut unpeeled oranges into thin slices, ¼-inch (5-mm) thick. Place in bowl, measure depth, and pour double the amount of water over slices. Let stand overnight at room temperature.
2. Pour oranges and water into a large saucepan. Bring to a boil and cook about 20 minutes, or until almost dry.
3. Blanch, peel and coarsely chop peaches. Sprinkle lemon juice over peaches, add them to saucepan, bring to a boil; stir in sugar. Cook, stirring occasionally, for about 1½ hours, or until mixture sheets from a spoon.
4. Stir in cherries. Allow to boil 1 minute.
5. Ladle into sterilized jars. Seal with self-sealing lids. Label and store in a cool, dry, dark place.

Makes 3 cups (750 ml).

Caramel Mocha Sundae Sauce

I was a dinner guest of Colleen's when she served this over a scoop of French Vanilla ice cream with a side of Apple Brown Betty. And, like everyone else, I couldn't resist using my finger to scoop up the last drop when the spoon had done all it could. I couldn't wait to get home and try it with half-a-cup of toasted walnuts over my favorite sin food, coffee ice cream. Don't be concerned if the whole thing looks like a curdled mess after you've added the milk or coffee. It will end up smooth and satiny—promise!

¾ cup	light corn syrup	175 ml
¼ cup	water	50 ml
1 cup	granulated sugar	250 ml
¼ cup	sweet butter	50 ml
1 cup	evaporated milk	250 ml
¾ cup	strong coffee (espresso)	175 ml
¾ tsp	vanilla extract	4 ml
¼ tsp	salt	1 ml

1. In a large saucepan over medium-high heat, combine corn syrup, water and sugar. Cook, stirring constantly, until boiling. With a spatula, keep scraping sugar crystals from sides of pan.
2. Add butter. Add evaporated milk gradually, stirring constantly.
3. Boil 15 to 20 minutes, stirring constantly until a candy thermometer reaches 234° to 239°F (112° to 115°C) (soft ball stage). Remove pan from heat, stir in coffee, vanilla and salt.
4. Pour caramel mixture into a blender, starting on low and increasing speed until smooth.
5. Pour into a bowl and serve.
   Can be stored in a 24-oz mason jar up to 3 months. Bring to room temperature before serving.

Makes 2½ cups (625 ml).

Apricot Walnut Sauce

Colleen and I love gingerbread hot from the oven, but we've both tired of predictable whipped cream or lemon sauce toppings. We feel this old-fashioned, chock-full-o'-walnuts sundae-style sauce, accompanied by a scoop of French Vanilla ice cream, is the only solution. It's also wonderful drizzled over baked apples before you put them in the oven. Serve these in oversized wine glasses.

1½ cups	apricot jam	375 ml
½ cup	water	125 ml
1 tbsp	granulated sugar	15 ml
1 tsp	grated orange rind	5 ml
4 tsp	dark rum	20 ml
½ cup	chopped walnuts	125 ml

1. In a small saucepan over high heat, combine jam, water, sugar and orange rind. Bring to a boil. Reduce heat and simmer 5 minutes, stirring constantly.
2. Remove from heat. Stir in rum and walnuts. Serve warm over gingerbread.

Makes 2 cups (500 ml).

Hint – Baked Apples – Core the apples and peel the top end. Set in baking dish and fill each with Walnut Apricot Sauce. Moisten the apples with diluted orange juice and place in oven at 325°F (160°C) for 1½ hours, basting occasionally.

Index